MAKE IT HAPPEN

How to get ahead and be happy at work

BLOOMSBURY

A BLOOMSBURY REFERENCE BOOK
Created from the Bloomsbury Business Database
www.ultimatebusinessresource.com

First published in 2005 by
Bloomsbury Publishing
38 Soho Square
London W1D 3HB

British Library Cataloguing in Publication Data
A CIP record for this book is available from the British Library.

ISBN 0–7475–7237–2

Design by Fiona Pike, Pike Design, Winchester
Typeset by RefineCatch Ltd, Bungay, Suffolk
Printed in Italy by Legoprint

All papers used by Bloomsbury Publishing are natural, recyclable products made from wood grown in well-managed forests. The manufacturing processes conform to the environmental regulations of the country of origin.

CONTENTS

Get the Best from Your Career

Get the Best from Others

ACKNOWLEDGMENTS

Special thanks go to: Hilary Bird, Lorenza Clifford, Cobweb Information Ltd, Dena Michelli, Richard Scriven, and Kate Stenner.

Introduction
Dena Michelli

Happiness is a powerful force in the working environment. It helps to tap the energy, enthusiasm, and talent of the people in a business. Being happy at work improves motivation and physiological health, increases creativity and productivity and acts as a vehicle for delighting the customer to improve a company's bottom line.

'A happy workforce is a productive workforce', as the saying goes, and it has been borne out by the recent upsurge in the respectability of the topic of 'happiness'. For example, the first PhD in the Psychology of Happiness has been awarded*, and the NHS has established Happiness Clinics. There has also been an increase in the number of studies on happiness, many conducted by such well-regarded institutions as the London School of Economics.

Although all this attention on happiness clearly can only be a positive thing, it does mask the less palatable truth that in spite of the overall increase in wealth and standard of living in the west, we have never been so miserable. Many people are highly dissatisfied with their life at work and feel that whatever they do, their aspirations will be denied them. Far too many of us see the successes we have worked so hard to build being attributed to others and our efforts lying unrecognised and forgotten. In fact, although the bulk of our time is spent at work, the happiness quotient associated with working sits marginally above commuting and marginally below doing the housework.†

These rather dramatic statistics suggest that merely being happy is a challenge, but being happy *at work* is doubly so. It's not impossible, though, and indeed the personal rewards for understanding one's sources of satisfaction and resolving one's disappointments are equally dramatic, but positively so. All of this is achieved through self-understanding, self-development, and self-determination, where you take responsibility for and control over your own life. Being sure of where your values lie and of the factors that motivate you helps you to create a sense of purpose, a career direction that will satisfy you in the long term. It will help you to identify the knowledge and skills you need to develop to reach your goals and it will also give you a sense of purpose and control over your life.

Unhappy people often feel that they are misperceived, that their contributions are undervalued and that they are subject to others' agendas and priorities. If you feel unable to create your own goals and satisfy your own aspirations, you are likely to fall victim to others' agendas. This passivity is highly stressful, demoralising, and energy-sapping. By contrast, the ability to make active and informed choices on how you live in the world builds confidence, promotes good health, and will pave the way to your

* To Robert Holden, Founder of 'the happiness project' and author of *Happiness NOW!*

† Layard, Richard. 'The Secrets of Happiness. New Statesman'. 3rd March 2003, pp 25–28.

future success and happiness. By planning and actively doing something about your own development, you will find yourself weaving a unique professional fabric that will become your personal 'brand', one to which you feel strongly aligned and that others will value.

'Personal development' is a loose term that has become fashionable in recent years. However, it has suffered from being bandied about somewhat indiscriminately and, as a result, its meaning has been diluted. Organisations have embraced personal development initiatives to release more talent into the business and to build up their succession line so that the future is secure. Many have put in place processes that combine a professional review with a development planning session so that the collective capability of the people in the business is constantly increasing.

But we need to *willing* to be guided by the needs of our employers, too. Progress will only be made through consultation and agreement with those responsible for turning a company's vision into reality; this demands that we enter these development discussions knowing the contribution we wish to make, the tools we need to help us make it, and the means by which we can learn most effectively to transform our aspirations into successes.

Having laid out the case for getting ahead and being happy at work, how do we actually do it? Obviously, if you change nothing, nothing will change. To achieve your goals, you have to focus your energy and make a commitment to follow through. Once you do this, you'll find opportunities to change your habits of behaviour and transform your sense of purpose and effectiveness. Through a series of appropriately focused small steps, you are bound to achieve your goals and enjoy a sense of power and liberation. Taking these steps can also change the way you view the world and make sense of your experiences.

Make It Happen will help you whatever sized organisation you work for and whatever your age and gender. It puts you in charge of your own professional and personal destiny and will enable you to enjoy those rewards so often seen to be enjoyed by others. It will also help you find personal solutions to the points of pressure that cause you unhappiness.

Make It Happen is designed for dipping into whenever you need to and, if you go to the sections that cover the issues that you are facing today or feel that you may face tomorrow, you'll find inspiration and practical help.

Why not take responsibility for your own development? Take the challenge and make it happen for you.

About the editor

Dena Michelli is the author of *Assertiveness in a Week* (Hodder). A human resource consultant specialising in personal and professional development, Dena works in a variety of cultural settings. She bases her practical and positive approach to personal development on the release and best use of natural talent.

Build Self-Confidence

Confidence, for those who are blessed with it, is unremarkable: it's something taken for granted. For those who don't have it, though, it's an extraordinarily difficult quality to develop and sustain.

We all have moments when our confidence blossoms—when we feel good about ourselves, have the knowledge we need to overcome any doubts, and are able to achieve a goal, however large or small. So we know what we're missing when we're feeling low in confidence, and this knowledge alone makes it difficult to regain our equilibrium and sense of self-esteem. Fear is the main emotion that undermines confidence, the 'what if' scenarios that we conjure up in our minds. It's this largely irrational fear that needs to be addressed because, until it is, confidence can never be truly established.

I'm concerned about a member of my team who doesn't have the confidence to make decisions. Even though this person knows the job well, I'm always having to give directions. What should I do?

This person may have lost confidence by having made poor decisions in the past and suffering the consequences for them. Alternatively, the person may have been promoted beyond his or her level of competence. The first thing to do with people like this is to stop telling them what their decisions should be. Every time you make a decision for them, you are only creating greater dependency. Instead, turn this into a learning exercise. Begin to ask them to suggest or recommend their own solution, however small it might be at first. Eventually you'll wean them off their dependence on your expertise. They clearly have the knowledge; now all you need to do is help them regain, or develop, the confidence to act on their own. After you support or show your approval of their suggestions a few times, their confidence will improve and their demands on you will lessen.

I've recently been promoted, and although I had lots of confidence in my former role, I am now beginning to doubt my own abilities—this is such new territory for me. What can I do about this?

It's not uncommon for people to lose their confidence when placed in a new work context, and they're often tempted to go back to their old comfort zone. When a return route isn't open to them, they may try superimposing familiar activities on to their new role. In this case, the problem is more likely to be a lack of knowledge or skills than not being able to perform well. Asking for constructive feedback, coaching, and rewards for small successes will enable you to make the most of your talent and build the confidence you need to succeed.

MAKE IT HAPPEN

Build a confident workforce

Confidence cannot be put on like a coat—it has to be rooted firmly within yourself. If you play-act at having confidence, it comes across as empty or brash. It may help you get through a particular situation, but it won't help you build true strength in the longer term.

Confidence is important in the workplace because it builds trust—trust builds commitment, and commitment builds a quality product or service. It also enables people to use their initiative and make decisions that support organisational goals. For these reasons alone, it's desirable to have a confident workforce, but the additional benefits of improved morale and a happier work atmosphere are the icing on the cake.

The elements that build a confident workforce are:

* people having the knowledge and skills to fulfil their roles
* clear objectives for individuals and teams
* authority in decision-making and accountability for those decisions
* recognition for achieving personal goals
* investment in learning and development
* opportunities to meet new challenges
* celebration of meeting organisational objectives

Boost knowledge and skills

Confidence at work comes from knowing what to do, how to do it, and when to do it. This know-how may be learned in a college or university setting, or it may have been developed on the job. Wherever it comes from, it allows people to work within clear boundaries of competence. They become recognised for their abilities, which reinforces their self-image and builds their confidence. If they're put into a different job where they do not have the same level of familiarity, their confidence may be shaken. So in order to create a confident workforce, care must be taken to make sure everyone has transferable skills.

Set clear role objectives

Confidence often increases with success, and success can only be measured when a goal or objective has been reached. Clear objectives allow people to monitor their progress and adjust their focus in order to achieve what's on their work horizon. Roles without this level of clarity prevent the employee from enjoying success, because there is no 'marker' to show when they've succeeded. After a while in this type of atmosphere, people's enthusiasm and level of energy diminish, along with their confidence. A lack of well-defined objectives causes more personal grief in organisations than almost anything else. It's incredibly disconcerting to find that you're pouring energy into a professional void.

Allow authority and accountability in decision-making

Giving someone authority and then holding them accountable for their decisions is not only healthy for the organisation, but also essential for the individual, if she or he is to feel satisfied with what has been achieved. It's common, however, to find that the two have been separated, and the person is held accountable even when they haven't been given the full authority to get the job done properly. Having accountability with no authority is one of the most stressful situations imaginable.

Recognise the achievement of personal goals

Although some people are internally driven—they don't need external recognition to make them feel as though they've succeeded—almost everyone values some form of public appreciation. This proves the worth of their contribution to the business and increases their visibility, at the same time reinforcing confidence and enhancing their opportunities for promotion and advancement.

Invest in learning and development

Rather than taking it on as part of their duty as an employer, many organisations these days are placing responsibility for learning and development on the individual. However, you wouldn't leave the maintenance of a sophisticated machine to chance, so why leave the responsibility for learning and development with employees? Individuals may not fully understand the goals of the business, and therefore, what kind of development would be most suitable. Learning and development should be jointly planned and agreed upon by the individual and the organisation. Organisational support should be given by way of advice, time for study, or participation in special projects. Internal or external training programmes may be appropriate, especially when there are specific skills or areas of knowledge that need to be developed.

When a business invests in its people, it has a very positive effect on employees' confidence and their ability to add value. Not only should people be given the support to learn and develop, but they should also be challenged to move beyond their comfort zones. This enables them to find new areas of achievement and seek new heights.

Work with individuals

Beyond building confidence in the workforce, there is scope to build confidence on an individual basis too. Although this may not be considered the organisation's responsibility, confident individuals contribute to the general swell of confidence in the workforce. Working with people personally through coaching or mentoring programmes can be effective, and 'buddy' systems or co-coaching arrangements can also strengthen confidence and create a solid foundation from which it can grow.

One of the essential ingredients of confidence is having good communication skills. If someone feels that they can communicate effectively in any situation—conveying thoughts to colleagues, building rapport with difficult clients, getting through to senior management, and so on—their levels of confidence are often high. Confident, effective communication encourages self-respect and respect for others, so it's worth considering how to build communication skills among individual employees, as well as throughout the workforce in general.

Celebrate meeting organisational objectives

Finally, celebrations are very important. A celebration can be as simple as providing a selection of cakes for a high-performing team during a coffee break or as lavish as the business hosting a big party to celebrate the achievement of objectives or exceptional year-end results. Celebrations exist in every aspect of society and not only give life a sense of purpose, but also a feeling of achievement. This essential social activity needs to be embraced by organisations so that everyone feels that they're an indispensable, appreciated part of the business.

WHAT TO AVOID

You can't let go

Many managers feel that allowing their people the freedom to make decisions will disrupt the status quo and result in a loss of control. As a result, they control the decision-making, and alienate their team in the process. Keeping strict control can actually disable the team and undermine the confidence they have in their own abilities. It's important to let go and create an environment where stars can rise and successors can be recognised.

USEFUL LINKS

BusinessTown.com: **www.businesstown.com/people/motivation-team.asp**
More-selfesteem.com: **www.more-selfesteem.com**
Self-confidence.co.uk: **www.self-confidence.co.uk/self/confidence/tips.html**

Manage Your Image: Make an Impact

Image management isn't something many of us think about, yet managing your image well can increase the confidence people place in you and the career opportunities that come to you.

Image management starts with the first impression you make. Perceptions are remarkably difficult to dislodge once they're in place, so it's worth thinking about the kind of impact you wish to create from the outset and working to achieve this, despite any natural reluctance to do so. If you can get this right, it'll be much less complicated to manage your image in the longer term.

I think it's important to be natural. Aren't you setting yourself up for a fall if you try and contrive something that is not 'you'?

Managing your image isn't the same as contriving it. Everything you say and do must feel authentic to you. Image management is about presenting yourself in the best light, not a false light. We all exercise some control over the way we behave in different situations—this is just another situation in which conscious control can bring advantages.

Physically, I don't feel I stand out from the crowd at all. How can I create a good impression?

Creating a good impression isn't size, shape, or attractiveness dependent, thankfully—just think of some of the most successful businessmen, politicians, or celebrities!

A good impression is created through your intention and the way you feel about yourself. Try portraying yourself in different ways in front of a mirror and see what a difference it makes to the way your body responds. Your body language follows your thoughts. Get your thoughts right and you'll have no problem.

I'm feeling particularly daunted by an important presentation I have to give. How can I create a good impression in these circumstances?
First, make sure you understand what people's expectations are and aim to meet these. Check who will be in the audience and anticipate what sorts of questions will be asked of you. Prepare for these, and try to include worst case scenarios. After rehearsing your presentation, make sure you're comfortable in your clothes and that you have confidence in your material. Before the presentation, assume you're successful, behave as if you are, and you'll find that you do brilliantly.

Although I try to manage the impression I create, people seem to misunderstand me all the time. What's going wrong?
You may be misreading the context or misjudging your own behaviour. Stop trying so hard and instead observe people who have a natural aptitude for this skill. You may pick up some clues about what's going wrong for you. Alternatively, you could ask for feedback and advice from people you trust on what you could do more successfully.

MAKE IT HAPPEN

It is said that an impression is created in the first seven seconds of an encounter and that, once created, it's difficult to change it. It's important, then, to learn how to orchestrate these critical few seconds. You may find it helpful to consider the five Cs:

- context
- communication
- credibility
- clothing
- composure/confidence

Context

Firstly, be aware of the context in which you find yourself and try to understand the purpose of the occasion, the motivations of those present, and the circumstances surrounding the situation. Whether you're being interviewed for a job or conducting an important client meeting, it's worth spending time thinking through what your audience's expectations are and how you can meet these. Should you take risks to distinguish yourself from others, or is it a time when you need to demonstrate your compatibility with other people's values?

Communication—verbal and non-verbal

Once you understand the kind of occasion you're facing, you might consider what kind of language would be best to use. Good communicators are able to adjust the tone, tenor, and timing of their speech to maximum effect.

NLP—neurolinguistic programming—has a great deal to say on this subject. It advocates listening to the kinds of words that individuals use; people's words indicate the way they interpret and represent the world. This divides into five different arenas: visual, kinaesthetic, auditory, gustatory, and olfactory, with the first three being the most common. There are those people who 'see' things in their mind's eye and say things like: 'I can see what you're saying', or 'I have a clear vision of what this will look like'. Others make 'sense' of the world through movement, touch and feelings, using the kinaesthetic representational system. They are characterised by using phrases that describe a sense or movement, such as: 'I get a good feeling about this', or 'The change in market dynamics will be a crushing blow to the business'. The auditory representational system is also common. People adopting this approach will say things like, 'I hear what you're saying', or 'It sounds suspicious to me!'

Your approach can be all the more effective if you can match that of your audience, or at least use a mixture of the main three arenas so that there is something there for everyone. Compatible language and body language gives the impression of immediate rapport—enormously helpful in creating an impact.

Remember to ensure that your body language is consistent with what you're saying. If you don't believe in your message, your body will show it somehow, and this mismatch is called *leakage*. You often see it when people are nervous or are saying something they know to be untrue. You'll see their feet shifting, a knee jiggling, or exaggerated gestures to compensate for their discomfort with their own words.

Also, speak clearly and enunciate your words properly so everyone can hear you without having to strain. The speed, tone, and pitch of your voice are all signals that will be picked up by your audience.

Credibility

Don't bluff. Show that you know what you're talking about and use 'war stories' if appropriate to show the depth of your knowledge. Many of us have been trained as children not to blow our own trumpets or boast about our achievements, but you need to find opportunities to demonstrate the extent of your experience and skills. This means making connections with what's being said and using them as openings to illustrate your past experience. Be careful not to overdo it, though; you need to strike a careful balance between demonstrating your capability and being sensitive to how much self-promotion someone can tolerate.

Clothing

Clothes can enhance or destroy a first impression. Too much of a good thing can be a disaster: too bright, too tight, too sexy—extremes will paint a picture of you that will stay in the observer's mind.

Deciding on what to wear largely depends upon the situation. The safest strategy is to reflect the style of those that you'll be meeting, perhaps erring on the side of conservatism. If the context is creative you will have more freedom to be idiosyncratic; but if you are hoping to engage with an organisational culture, it's safer to reflect this in your appearance.

Good grooming is equally vital. Make sure that you're well turned out. Try to avoid dark wet patches under your arms, an unironed shirt or blouse, and food-stained clothes. Clean and tidy is the best bet for most occasions.

Composure/confidence

Composure comes from confidence. When you're sure of what you want and are well prepared, you'll feel confident and therefore seem composed. This will allow you to manage any unexpected turns in the situation without a problem.

Once you've created a good impact, you'll find it relatively easy to maintain. Just as good impressions are hard to displace, so are bad impressions. If you invest in getting it right first time, you won't have to concern yourself with how to change the impression at a later date.

WHAT TO AVOID

You try too hard at first

Image management is a subtle skill. A common mistake is to try too hard, exaggerating your natural characteristics in order to convey confidence. The best way to avoid this is to practise in front of a friend or trusted colleague and ask for feedback on the impression you're creating. Be open to trying something different. If you're embarrassed to try this tack, practise in front of a mirror. You won't get feedback as such, but mirrors never lie!

You leave it to chance

You can unwittingly create a poor image by expecting people to know where your talents or intentions lie without actually telling them. You have to engage actively in creating an image. If you want others to know about something, find a way of weaving it into the conversation. Provide your audience with a hook that they can remember you by. If you 'project' bland, you may be remembered as bland. Or you may not be remembered at all!

You go too far accidentally

Misreading a situation and drawing attention to yourself in a negative way can be difficult to recover from. If this happens, you may find it best to declare your mistake and start again. Few people can rally in situations like this and come up smelling of roses.

You forget that other people have networks

If you forget that impressions travel beyond your immediate audience, you may have to start again with others who have been told about you. Each person you meet has a network. If you create a good impression, word will circulate around this network and you could reap the rewards. If you're indiscreet or misjudge a situation, the 'bad' news will travel just as fast, if not faster. Have it in mind that you aren't just meeting one, or a few people, but in a 'virtual' sense, their close acquaintances too.

USEFUL LINKS

About Human Resources:
http://humanresources.about.com/cs/communication/a/profimage.htm
HRMGuide.co.uk: **www.hrmguide.co.uk/hrm**
iVillage.co.uk: **www.ivillage.co.uk/work/job**

Develop Presence

Presence is an elusive human quality that mysteriously enables someone to command respect, or at least attention. Some people believe you're born with presence, others that it develops as a by-product of success. In fact, it's probably a combination of the two—and almost anyone can certainly nurture and develop it in themselves. It most often seems to result from confidence in what you're doing, when you feel at home with, or passionate about, your role. Presence is most likely to elude us when we're not sure of ourselves and feeling uncomfortable.

I'm not very tall. How can I possibly create presence?

Presence doesn't depend on height. When you think of successful political and business leaders, you'll find that many are small people who have compensated for their lack of stature in other ways. Gandhi, Mother Theresa, Nelson Mandela, and Napoleon are just a few examples. Presence can be created by a state of mind: the old adage, 'think tall and you will be tall' really does work.

I'm came across well in some circumstances, but have problems performing well in the workplace. What do I do?

This isn't an unusual phenomenon. Many people who perform well in one context find that they cannot switch their talent on in a different setting. However, there are useful techniques that will enable you to transfer your talent from one situation to another. One that seems to work very well is 'anchoring'. Briefly, it relies on your ability to capture the feeling when you're doing something really well, and associate it with a gesture, movement, or saying—such as pinching your thumb and forefinger together. This becomes the 'anchor', and when you transfer your anchor into a new setting, all the memories of performing well flood back and allow you to do so at will.

I appear to hold real credibility with the people who report to me, but don't have the same effect on my peers and managers. What can I do?

With your subordinates, you have three things that they don't: knowledge, expertise, and authority. When you're with your peers and managers, they probably have the same or more of these things—or create the illusion that they do. This can be sufficiently intimidating to make you lose your confidence. Try the 'anchor' technique described above to see if you can transfer your confidence into encounters with your peers and managers.

I have been on many presentation skills courses, but I have problems with creating a consistent presence. How can I address this?

Presence very often comes from being in tune with your message. In order to be an effective communicator—both with your body language and speech—you need to be 'at one' with what you're saying. You must have the knowledge to explore the area comfortably with your audience, be at ease with your audio-visual aids, and have a real desire to communicate what you have to say. In addition, you need to feel physically comfortable with who you are and how you appear. Practice is essential, especially if you are often nervous as a public speaker. Giving a presentation on a subject that you feel passionate about is a great place to begin.

MAKE IT HAPPEN

Developing presence is a multifaceted challenge that can be categorised in four different areas. These are:

* physical
* mental/emotional
* mastery
* occasion

Physical

This refers to how you 'manage' your body. People with presence often have good posture, even if they're small. They stand and move well, projecting calm and confidence. Being fit and in good general health are key factors. Exercise, good diet, proper rest, and 'centring' practices like meditation and yoga are important allies. Good-quality clothes that fit well emphasise posture and confidence. They don't need to be expensive or conventional, just carefully chosen to suit the occasion.

Non-verbal behaviour can reinforce the impression you're trying to create. Steady eye contact, a clear voice, and appropriate gestures are powerful channels of non-verbal communication. People with presence also often create the impression of being larger than they actually are, by the clever use of space. If sitting, they may sit with one arm resting on the back of the chair, their body at an angle, and one leg crossed over the other. This position takes up a large amount of space and is very confident and imposing. Look for opportunities to project a 'bigger' persona. Use fuller, sweeping arm movements, rather than just a hand or pointing finger. Exaggerate these gestures in front of a mirror or a friend, so you won't overdo them in public.

The ability to build rapport is invaluable. Good eye contact when engaging with people, even if in an audience, enables you to make valuable human impressions. Paying proper attention to what people say and demonstrating that you've heard their comments is important. So, too, is remembering people, and the context in which you know them. By deliberately using someone's name when you're speaking to them, you can embed it in your mind.

Mental/emotional

The mind is one of the most important tools for creating presence. It can create a tangible impression—on you as well as others—just by 'seeing' something. The art of visualisation is very successful: our thoughts always precede our actions and behaviour so, by making your intention explicit in your mind, you'll already be creating it in reality. Visualise yourself as a person who emanates presence. See your picture in colour; examine it in detail. Note the feelings that arise in you, the sound of an audience applauding, the glow of achievement as you make your exit.

Make positive affirmations, 'I am confident', 'I feel good', 'I have presence'. These will train your brain to believe what you see in your mind's eye. Repeat your positive affirmations regularly so that they become the dominant messages that you transmit about yourself. Make sure they're in the present tense however. If you say 'I will be confident', your brain will believe it to be a *future* scenario, and you may never get there!

Mastery

Know what you know. You've built knowledge and experience over the years and this will enable you to be confident in what you say and do. Ensure that people know your worth in this regard by being open and honest. Share your experiences, tell stories, and engage people at the human level. Be aware, too, of times when others need to have their presence acknowledged. Too often, people on a quest to create presence for themselves stop seeing and listening to others. Try to be inclusive, and 'generosity' will also become part of your presence.

Mastering all these elements will open new doors of opportunity for you: people will gravitate to you, offer you new leadership roles, and spread the good word about your qualities and skills.

Occasion

Projecting presence demands an occasion. This may be any type of occasion, from a gathering of a few people to an audience of many. People with presence are able to create a sense of occasion in even the most ordinary of circumstances, such as walking along the production line, chairing a meeting, or giving a presentation. Think through your dramatic strategy, and practise so that you get the timing and pace right.

Presence is about transmitting a quality that others trust and respond to. It makes them feel as if they're gaining something just from being close to you. If it's to be sustained, having presence carries quite a lot of responsibility. For those who look up to you, you'll be providing guidance and inspiring confidence, reflecting their values, and—perhaps—being their conscience. This is why it's important that you're fully aligned and authentic in your desire for presence.

WHAT TO AVOID

You mistake over-confidence for presence

These two traits are not the same. Over-confidence is about oneself; presence is about others. Over-confident behaviour can come across as self-interested and unempathic, whereas someone with presence is often seen as taking an interest and building relationships. People who demonstrate over-confidence are actually very often lacking in confidence, and are trying to compensate for this.

You think that presence cannot be developed
Having a certain amount of natural presence is a gift. Nevertheless, it's a gift that needs attention and development to mature properly. Look for occasions where you can practise the techniques that will help you project the impression you seek. By building up a series of successes, you'll soon be able to join them together and emanate this quality at will. In time, it may become second nature.

You aren't fully prepared
As discussed above, there are physical, mental, emotional, mastery, and 'occasion' elements involved in presence. It's important to have all of these aligned in the same direction—if you don't, you could ruin all your good work. Imagine looking good, having a clear intention, having the occasion . . . but nothing to say. Or conversely, having a great story or bit of information, but getting the timing all wrong. Each element assists and supports the others, so pay careful attention to all of them.

USEFUL LINKS

iVillage.co.uk: **www.ivillage.co.uk/workcareer/survive**
Mental Health Net: **www.mentalhelp.net/psyhelp/chap14/chap14b.htm**

Manage Perceptions

We all hold differing views of the world, partly because of our different cultural backgrounds, life experiences, and personal values. Naturally this colours our interactions with others. Our behaviour, our skills, style, and approach further affect our relationships. In senior management roles, it's becoming increasingly important to be able to understand and manage the perception others have of us.

This isn't as difficult as you might think. Although it requires a good deal of thought, motivation, and self-awareness, with practice you'll find it easier to communicate with people, to motivate and lead them in a desired direction.

Isn't it rather manipulative to manage perceptions?
Most techniques can be either positive or negative, depending on context. We live in a culture where people and organisations spend enormous sums of money employing others to manage perceptions. It's important to understand that the same skills used by advertising and public relations companies to change perceptions are ones that you can use to influence people around you. At the very least, you should be aware of the

impressions your behaviour creates. At best, you should develop skills that allow you to manage your behaviour in a way that helps you to move forward in your career.

Why is perception management important to my career?
Careers are no longer managed by organisations, but are directed by individuals themselves. You're judged not only on what you do, but on how you do it—so, the evaluation of you by others plays an important role in your career. Those who are able to manage perceptions are likely to find fewer obstacles on their path.

Why do I find it so difficult to change others' perceptions of me?
Changing how others view you requires a consistent flow of new messages. People generally hold on to first impressions, and it's difficult to replace them with something more to your liking. Doing this takes persistent awareness and self-evaluation—both of which take time and energy to develop.

If you wish to change someone's impression of you, you must first understand both that person's existing perception and the one you wish to create. You then need to create a bridge between the two, and find an opportunity to convey a different message. However, you must be honest in the way you portray yourself. If you create an impression that is not essentially *you*, the deception will be easy to spot, simply because living a lie is extraordinarily difficult to sustain.

I don't particularly care what other people think about me, I just want to get on with doing a good job.
Fine, but common wisdom suggests that you should take care of your relationships as you move up the career ladder, because you may encounter the same people later when you're moving back down. People can harbour grudges for years, and you don't want to risk encountering an unforgiving individual in a position of influence. If you find it impossible to change your attitude, you'd better have skills that make you indispensable!

MAKE IT HAPPEN

Understand yourself and how you're perceived

To understand how others view you, you must have an accurate understanding of yourself. Building self-awareness requires courage and commitment.

The first stage is to encourage informal feedback from trusted peers and managers. Remember that people will give subjective views based on their opinion, which may not resonate with you—so you may be surprised at the way you're perceived. Try to remain objective and explore where these views have come from.

You can use more formal tools that enable you to understand yourself, such as psychometrics and personality profiles. The feedback from these is sometimes easier to manage because it's objective and has no third party relationship standing in the way.

Sometimes 360-degree surveys are used to gather the views of different audiences, both inside and outside the business. These tend to focus on behaviour and competence. Be aware of the differences between the two. While both may be learned and modified, changing the way you behave usually involves altering personality traits and perceptions and may be more difficult than acquiring new skills.

When reviewing test results, try not to concentrate just on personal information that is hurtful. Look for patterns in your feedback, and reflect on when and why these may have arisen. Pressure can often allow unintentional behaviour to come to the surface. These may have given rise to impressions that you'd like to change.

Work at your strategy

Before embarking on any perception management strategy, be sure of what your goals are, how you are going to reach them, and how you'll track your success. The key is to not be too ambitious initially: focus on one thing you can change that will create a quick win.

Think of the context in which you're working, and use your feedback to select your initial goals. While there may be indicators and encouragement to change your behaviour, remember that there may also be reactions to those changes. People are accustomed to the 'old' you and may have difficulty adjusting to the 'new' you as well. It's therefore important that you do four things:

* **Communicate** your intentions to people who may be affected. If you have a formal annual performance appraisal, make it a 'learning objective', as this is likely to win more support and forgiveness if things don't work out quite the way you wish. You'll also receive more praise when you're successful.
* **Gain support** from your manager or key members of your team to help keep you focused. A good support group is essential when seeking to change something about yourself—look at the impact of them in groups such as Alcoholics Anonymous and Weight Watchers.
* **Find a coach** to provide ongoing guidance. A coach will be able to offer impartial observations and encourage you to continue, or change, your strategy as you move forward. Coaching takes time and commitment, so you'll need to allow for this in your work plan.
* **Evaluate** your progress at each milestone in your plan, either formally or informally. Frequency is important in gathering informal feedback, but ensure you give people enough time to observe your new behaviour before asking them for it. You might warn those whom you are going to approach for feedback, so they can consciously pay attention to your behaviour. A more formal option is to revisit the 360-degree questionnaire and see whether others have noticed the change.

Don't lose heart if the changes in you aren't immediately recognised by others. It may take months, so consistency and perseverance are key.

A quick guide to perception management

Do	Don't
Increase your own awareness	React emotionally to the feedback you receive
Be aware of the impact you have on others	Get defensive
Interpret the signals that are being transmitted to you by others	Become de-motivated
Be aware of the effect of pressure on you and how this looks to others	Become sycophantic
Be visible at strategic moments	Get too big for your boots and try too hard too quickly
Encourage feedback from those that you value, but at an appropriate pace	Expect too much
Allow others to have their choices	Embroil others in your views of yourself
Give yourself adequate time and make perception management part of your personal development	Pester people for feedback
Be consistent, patient, and forgiving	Be political or manipulative in your behaviour

In a nutshell, perception management is all about creating an impression through conscious activities and awareness of your audience and the impact you have upon them. To succeed, you must define your target audience, align your values with theirs, adjust your communication style, encourage feedback, and be aware of how you adjust and adapt your behaviour.

WHAT TO AVOID

You become impatient

It's easy to get impatient for results and give up too quickly. Behavioural change is not as easy as learning a new skill; it requires dedication, commitment, and consistency. It's only through constant repetition and reinforcement of your new behaviour that people's perceptions will change.

You don't ask for feedback

Some people are embarrassed to ask for feedback and help, particularly when they find themselves in senior roles. This is because much of our behaviour is habitual, and to some extent may even have contributed to previous promotions. However, conduct appropriate to some roles may not be right for others. Promotion into a management position is a good example, when relationships suddenly become much more important than technical skills. In this situation, use a new project or a particular aspect of your new role as a test-bed for the new you.

You go too far

In trying to change your way of behaving, you can get carried away and lose the support of others. While it's important to be enthusiastic, try to understate rather than overstate your intentions. It's always easier to deal with the surprise of your audience, rather than their disappointment.

USEFUL LINKS

About Human Resources:
http://humanresources.about.com/cs/workrelationships/a/workallies.htm

Become More Assertive

Do you find that people get the better of you at work, that you're always the one that draws the short straw and ends up doing things that you'd rather not do? Does this make you resentful or unhappy because you feel helpless and unable to represent yourself strongly enough in the way you communicate?

Assertiveness is an attitude that honours your choices as well as those of the person you're communicating with. It's not about being aggressive and steamrollering your colleague into submission. Rather, it's about seeking and exchanging opinions, developing a full understanding of the situation, and negotiating a win-win situation. Ask yourself:

- **Do you feel 'put upon' or ignored in your exchanges with colleagues?**
- **Are you unable to speak your mind and ask for what you want?**
- **Do you find it difficult to stand up for yourself in a discussion?**
- **Are you inordinately grateful when someone seeks your opinion and takes it into account?**

If you answer 'yes' to most of these questions, you need to become more assertive.

Won't people think me aggressive if I change my communication style to a more assertive one?

There are four types of communication style:

* aggressive—where you win and everyone else loses
* passive—where you lose and everyone else wins
* passive/aggressive—where you lose and do everything you can (without being too obvious) to make others lose too
* assertive—where everyone wins

If you become more assertive, people won't necessarily think that you've become more aggressive because their needs will be met too. All that will happen is that your communication style becomes more effective.

I have had a lifetime of being 'me'. How can I change that now?

If you don't change what you do, you'll never change what you get. All it takes to change is a decision. Once you've made that decision, you'll naturally observe yourself in situations, notice what you do and don't do well, and then you can try out new ways of behaving to see what works for you.

I just don't have the confidence to confront people. Will becoming assertive help me?

This is a bit like the 'chicken and egg'. Once you become assertive, your confidence level will be boosted, yet you need to have sufficient levels of confidence to try it in the first place. Just try the technique out in a safe environment first so that you get used to how it feels, then you can use it more widely.

It's all right for people who have presence, but I'm small so I'm often overlooked. How can I become assertive?

Many of the most successful people, in business and in entertainment, are physically quite small. Adopting an assertive communication style and body language has the effect of making you look more imposing. Assume you have impact, visualise it, feel it, breathe it, be it.

I find it hard to say 'no' to people. How can I change this?

Until you get used to being assertive, you may find this difficult. However, one useful technique is to say, 'I'd like to think about this first. I'll get back to you shortly.' Giving yourself time and space to rehearse your response can be really helpful.

MAKE IT HAPPEN

Choose the right approach

Becoming assertive is all about making choices that meet your needs and the needs of the situation. Sometimes it's appropriate to be passive. If you were facing a snarling dog, you might not want to provoke an attack by looking for a win-win situation! There may be other occasions when aggression is the answer. However, this is still assertive behaviour as *you*, rather than other people or situations, are in control of how you react.

You may find it helpful to investigate some specially tailored training courses so that you can try out some approaches before taking on a colleague or manager in a 'live' situation. This sort of thing takes practice.

Practise projecting a positive image

Use 'winning' language. Rather than saying 'I always come off worst!' say 'I've learned a great deal from doing lots of different things in my career. I'm now ready to move on'. This is the beginning of taking control in your life. Visualise what you wish to become, make the image as real as possible, and feel the sensation of being in control. Perhaps there have been moments in your life when you naturally felt like this, a time when you've excelled. Recapture that moment and 'live' it again. Imagine how it would be if you felt like that in other areas of your life. Determine to make this your goal and recall this powerful image or feeling when you're getting disheartened. It will re-energise you and keep you on track.

Condition others to take you seriously by creating a positive impression

This can be done through non-verbal as well as verbal communication. If someone is talking over you and you're finding it difficult to get a word in edgeways, you can hold up your hand signalling 'stop' as you begin to speak. 'I hear what you're saying but I would like to put forward an alternative viewpoint . . .' Always take responsibility for your communication. Use the 'I' word. 'I would like . . .', 'I don't agree . . .', 'I am uncomfortable with this . . .' Being aware of non-verbal communication signals can also help you build rapport. If you mirror what others are doing when they're communicating with you, it will help you get a sense of where they're coming from and how to respond in the most helpful way.

Use positive body language

Stand tall, breathe deeply, and look people in the eye when you speak to them. Instead of anticipating a negative outcome, expect something positive. Listen actively to the other party and try putting yourself in their shoes so that you have a better chance of seeking the solution that works for you both. Inquire about their thoughts and feelings by using 'open' questions, that allow them to give you a full response rather than just 'yes' or 'no'. Examples include: 'Tell me more about why . . .', 'How do you see this working out? . . .', and so forth.

Assertiveness also helps you learn to deal with people who have different communication styles. If you're dealing with someone behaving in a passive/aggressive manner, you can handle it by exposing what he or she is doing. 'I get the feeling you're not happy about this decision' or 'It appears you have something to say on this; would you like to share your views now?' In this way, they either have to deny their passive/aggressive stance or they have to disclose their motivations. Either way, you're left in the driving seat.

If you're dealing with a passive person, rather than let them be silent, encourage them to contribute so that they can't put the blame for their disquiet on someone else.

The aggressive communicator may need confronting but do it carefully; you don't want things to escalate out of control. One option is to start by saying ' I'd like to think about it first': this gives you time to gather your thoughts and the other person time to calm down. When you're feeling put upon, it's important to remember that you have as much right as anyone to speak up and be heard.

Conflict is notorious for bringing out aggression in people, but it's still possible to be assertive in this context. You may need to show that you're taking them seriously by reflecting their energy. To do this, you could raise your voice to match the volume of theirs, then bring the volume down as you start to explore what would lead to a win-win solution. 'I CAN SEE THAT YOU ARE UPSET and I would feel exactly the same if I were you . . . however . . .' Then you can establish the desired outcome for both of you.

WHAT TO AVOID

You go too far at first

Many people, when trying out assertive behaviour for the first time, find that they 'go too far' and become aggressive. Remember that you're looking for a win-win, not a you win and they lose situation. Take your time. Observe yourself in action. Practise and ask for feedback from trusted friends or colleagues.

You allow others to react negatively to your assertiveness

Your familiar circle of friends will be used to you the way you were, not the way you want to become. They may try and make things difficult for you. With your new assertive behaviour, this won't be possible unless you let them get away with it. If you find you're in this situation, try explaining what you're trying to do and ask for their support. If they aren't prepared to help you, let them go from your circle of friends.

You bite off more than you can chew and get yourself into situations that are difficult to manage

If this happens to you, find a good way of backing down, go away and reflect on what went wrong, rehearse an assertive response, and forgive yourself for not getting it right every time. The more you rehearse, the more assertive responses you'll have in your tool kit when you need them.

USEFUL LINKS

The Oak Tree Counseling: **www.theoaktree.com/assrtquz.htm**
TUFTS University: **www.tufts.edu/hr/tips/assert.html**

Becky Leyland – Building Assertiveness at Work

Becky Leyland is an HR manager in a large multinational company. Dealing assertively with a wide range of people is an integral part of Becky's job, and here she explains how she has built up the necessary skills.

The keys to assertiveness

'Understanding what it means to be assertive is a crucial step in actually being assertive. In short, being assertive is about being decisive and self confident. It's not about getting your own way all the time but it *is* about knowing what your rights are and knowing what others' rights are. To be truly assertive, it's important to find a balance between the two ends of the behaviour spectrum: passivity and aggression. You need to make sure that while you are being supremely self-confident, you don't crush others' confidence and prevent an open and honest exchange of opinions.

'Decisiveness is the easy part, in some respects. The key to successful decision-making starts with being able to make decisions in the first place, and this is all rooted in self-confidence; you have to be able to manage the consequences of your decision, whether they're good or bad. Secondly, decision-making is about being able to weigh up the pros and cons of a variety of different courses of action dispassionately and taking the one you believe delivers the best outcome. Being decisive is much easier when it's based on a sense of realism – there will always be alternative choices that you could have made, and perhaps there was no perfect choice. Remember that it's always better to apologise for a wrong decision than to ask permission to do something in advance – thus espousing the work ethic of empowerment.

'Most of the time, I find it quite easy to be assertive, although occasionally it's possible to look back on conversations and consider what I could have done or said differently with a more confident approach. Being assertive isn't about always having the right answer immediately. In fact, being assertive is often about choosing the right time to make your point, perhaps at a time when you've had chance to reflect and you're able to make your point in a calm and unemotional way.

'At work we have developed a framework of attitudes and behaviours that help to set the context for assertive behaviour. The cornerstone of the framework is respect for others. Mutual respect allows you to express yourself honestly, and to listen and respond to other people when they express their opinions. It's much easier to be assertive in an environment where the employer has stated this is the overriding behaviour code than in one where you find bullying and machismo the cultural norm.'

Dealing with difficult people

'Whatever your work environment and even within the "ideal" office culture, there are always people who are more difficult to deal with than others. In particular, I find it hard to be assertive with people who are disingenuous or insincere. In my experience, you always come across people like this, so identifying them and understanding their pattern of behaviour will help you to work out in advance how you will respond to them when your paths cross again. I've found that the first time you meet this type of person, the conversation tends not to go the way you want it, but reflecting on the exchange of words and role-playing an alternative conversation gives me the confidence (and a mental rehearsal) for the next time.'

Boosting your confidence

'Self-confidence is the key building block for assertiveness. Much of it is developed and learnt during childhood, but there are techniques and tactics that anyone can learn, whatever their age. For example:

* If you have a difficult conversation or meeting ahead of you, be sure of your basic facts. Make some notes and take them with you if you think you'll need to rely on complicated figures and data.
* Prepare well. If you think someone may ask you tricky questions about something, put yourself in his or her shoes and think about what issues may be raised so that you can prepare some potential answers.
* If you don't know the answer to something, don't panic but say that you don't have the data at the present time and that you'll find out and get back to them later. Don't let someone pull your argument apart because they've asked a difficult question.
* Rehearse out loud how you will start the conversation. The more you practise that opening sentence, the more confident it will sound and this will give you help you start the exchange on the right foot.
* Know your rights and know that you don't have to accept somebody speaking to you in a way that undermines your ability or confidence. If you feel that someone is likely to say something hurtful or offensive, think in advance how you will handle that situation. Practise saying something like, "I'm going to have to stop you there. I have to tell you how I'm feeling at this point and I'm not happy to continue this conversation in this way as I find what you're saying very hurtful."
* Read some books that are designed to boost your self-confidence. Many are available and they feature phrases and scenarios that you can work through on your own or with a friend.
* Do some things that make you feel good. Remind yourself about what you're good at and spend time doing those things, such as playing sport, cooking, or going to salsa classes with a friend.
* Don't start sentences with "I'm sorry" when you're not actually apologising for something you've done. This is a key difference between the way men and women communicate, by the way: women say this often as a linking phrase that doesn't actually mean anything, while men view it as a true apology.

Finally, you can always learn from watching others around you. If you have colleagues that you particularly admire and who display great assertiveness skills, watch how they behave and then see if the same tactics will work for you. When they're delivering a difficult message, what do they say and how do they say it? What is their body language telling you?

Start building your assertiveness skills from now on. When someone queue jumps in front of you, take the opportunity to emphasise that you were next in line . . . !

Understand Your Values

During your working life, it's very easy to get so immersed in the day-to-day routine that you forget to think about the larger picture of your life as a whole. You might be very excited to have been offered a new job; you might simply feel grateful that you *have* a job and a regular income; you might be immensely relieved to be one of the survivors after the latest round of redundancies. Any of these situations can take your eye off the really important question: are you in the right job *for you*?

Often this question can be answered simply by whether or not you feel happy and comfortable at work. At other times though, it can be more difficult—you may feel vaguely dissatisfied and restless; looking through your career history, you may have changed jobs a great many times; perhaps you notice that you start a new job with high enthusiasm, only to lose interest or motivation fairly quickly.

All of these scenarios can be the result of a mismatch between your values and your circumstances, so it makes good sense to take a more analytical look at what those values are, and how you can apply them practically to your working life. This actionlist points the way.

What are values, exactly?

Values are about worth: they are the things you hold dear—your guiding principles, standards, beliefs, and things that you prize. Values are the principles and standards you are committed to and live your life by, and you feel unhappy and dissatisfied when they are compromised.

It's worth remembering that values are not set in stone, however. Some of your values may remain the same throughout your life; others may change through maturity, particular experiences, or as a result of circumstances.

Why is it important to understand my values?

In terms of your job, it's essential to understand your values, because it is they that motivate you to work. If you think of your career as a journey, there are three vital elements involved in that journey—interests, abilities, and values. Your interests tell you what direction to pursue; your abilities indicate how long it will take to reach your ultimate goal, and your values dictate whether or not the journey is worth taking in the first place. If, consciously or unconsciously, your values are telling you that a particular direction is not the right one, you're very unlikely to make a success of that journey!

What is the difference between values and ethics?

In this context, values differ from ethics in that there is not necessarily a moral dimension to values. Values, unlike ethics, do not have to be seen by society as 'right' or 'just' or 'responsible' and so on . . . they are simply what is right for *you*. So one of your important values might be 'a short journey to work', for example—which has no moral implications whatever. If we take this thought to its logical extreme, then, even if an organisation prides itself on its ethical standards or working practices, it *still* may not be the right place for you if your own priorities do not happen to be based on moral issues.

MAKE IT HAPPEN

Assess what is important to you

The easiest way to do this is to adopt a structured approach, otherwise your mind tends to skitter about all over the place and things get forgotten or confused. A good method is to create a values 'scorecard', which helps you identify and prioritise what's important to you.

Think carefully about what each of the words or terms below means to you, and then assess how they relate to what you want from work:

Achievement (accomplishing important things)
Aesthetics (attractive workspace)
Affiliation (membership of organisation is a source of pride)
Alignment with boss
Artistic creativity
Autonomy & independence (most work self-determined, and limited direction by others)
Change & variety
Chaos (loosely defined environment; goals and priorities unclear)
Community activity
Commute
Competition
Creativity
Dual careers (place also offers career opportunities for partner)
Employee benefits
Excitement
Fast pace
Friendships
No glass ceiling (work environment offers all groups potential to work at highest levels)
Global focus (potential to live/work abroad)
Help others
Impact society
Influence people
Intellectual status
Knowledge
Legacy (be remembered for specific achievement by those who follow after)
Lifestyle integration (ability to balance family, career and self-fulfilment)
Location
Loyalty (high level of reciprocal loyalty with organisation)
Make decisions
Minimise stress
Moral affiliation (work with people of similar morals, values, and ethics)
Mobility (opportunity to relocate when appropriate)

Moral fulfilment (environment that reflects your own moral standards)
Multicultural affiliation (environment with people from broad range of ages, cultures, etc.)
Power & authority
Precision work
Prestige
Profit & gain
Public contact
Pure challenge (work which requires you to overcome impossible obstacles, difficult problems, etc.)
Recognition
Risk
Security
Self-realisation (potential for you to realise your best talents)
Stability
Supervision (where you are responsible for planning and managing work done by others)
Physical challenge
Time freedom
Travel
Work alone
Work under pressure
Work with others

Once you have pondered the meaning of each, list the words or phrases under the following headings—bearing in mind that you may change your opinion several times as you go through them.

Must haves	High wants	Wants	Don't minds	Don't wants

Check your values against the work you are doing currently

Now think about your list of wants and don't wants against your present job. Are your most important requirements being met? If not, is there anything you can do to change the situation? Who might be able to help you—your boss, line manager, mentor, HR department? Perhaps you could apply for a different role within the organisation to gain you more prestige or a higher salary; perhaps you could work flexi-time to make it easier to fit round family commitments; perhaps you could move nearer to work to cut down on commuting, or spend more time socialising with colleagues to build up friendships. Or maybe a training course would increase your knowledge or give you more intellectual challenge. All of these are just some of the potential options for you, depending on your values.

Many of these values are fairly practical, and even small adjustments in your working conditions could make the difference between them being met or not—with consequent implications for your happiness in your job.

Recognise when you can't change things

Sometimes, however hard you try to alter things, you have to face the fact that the differences between your own values and those of your employer are irreconcilable. In fact, one of the top ten reasons that people cite for leaving their jobs is that their values are at odds with the corporate culture. If this is true in your own case, it is much the most sensible option to start looking for another job that will suit you better—and preferably sooner rather than later, before the mismatch starts to sap your will to live. No matter what the clash is based on, a lack of congruence with the corporate culture will destroy your attitude at work, and it can be difficult to regain your confidence and enthusiasm once things have gone too far.

WHAT TO AVOID

You ignore your inner voice

Many of us are brought up to be good, law-abiding, responsible citizens, and even more of us have an innate fear of rocking the boat. We feel guilty if we cause disruption, and we tend to blame ourselves if we're not happy—'I shouldn't make a fuss', 'I'm being silly', 'I really must learn to apply myself' and so on being common sentiments. However, if you feel restless at work, or are looking for a job and want to make the right decision, it is really important to put yourself and your own priorities first. After all, if you don't make sure that your values are being satisfied, you'll be inspiring in terms of performance—which is hardly in your employer's best interests either!

You place too much importance on little things

Having realised the importance of your own values, you do need to exercise judgment about which are essential to you. Nothing is ever perfect, and you are always going to encounter situations where compromise is required. Say, for example, you think you should have a reserved parking spot at work, but your company operates a first-come first-served policy and everyone parks wherever they can. This is probably not worth going to the wall for (unless perhaps you are physically challenged in some way and have a genuine need to be right outside the office building). This is where prioritising your values into essentials and nice-to-haves is useful, as it helps you decide just how hard you need to push in different situations.

USEFUL LINKS

About Human Resources: **http://humanresources.about.com**

Get Your Message Across

Getting any message across to an audience implies some type of transmission process. Transmission alone isn't always an effective form of communication, though, unless what you send is received in the way that you intend. Messages are often conveyed according to our own agendas and the way we see and experience life impacts on them too. Often we don't take enough account of the context in which the message is spoken or the values, beliefs, and motivations of the recipient. Being aware of and catering for these factors can enable you to tailor your communication in the most effective way and enhance your ability to get your message across.

I have to prepare the ground for a structural change in my department. I know this will cause some upset but I'm sure the business reasons for it are sound. How can I get my message across without alienating my team?

Many people are uncomfortable with change and resist any threat of it. You may not be able to get full support straight away so don't expect too much too soon. Instead, try to make a connection with your team by showing you're aware of how they feel as an entity. For example, you could acknowledge that they've been under too much pressure lately, or that they've been asked to perform tasks that the team was not set up to do. You can then use this mutual touchstone as the basis upon which to explain the pressures and needs of the business and how you propose to accommodate these through structural change; a change that will benefit all parties. Use your political sensitivity and good judgment to decide how much and how far you can go on this occasion; you can always return to the subject and continue the communication at a later date.

I have delivered an important message to my team but they don't act as if they've heard it. What can I do?

Saying something once isn't enough. You need to transmit your message through as many different channels as possible until it's no longer necessary to reinforce your point. If your message is unpopular, you'll have to overcome others' natural inertia to it, and you can only do this by repeating it. You could do this by sending appropriate e-mails or newsletters, or by arranging meetings with the relevant people. If you take this option, remember that what you say and how you say it will be watched closely and discussed afterwards, so be sure that your behaviour mirrors the message you wish to convey. For example, you'll need to maintain eye contact with whoever you're speaking to as this emphasises the sincerity of your message. Remember that some gestures are associated with lying and need to be avoided. They include hiding your mouth with your hand, touching your nose, blinking rapidly, and running a finger along the inside of your collar.

A while ago I was successful in getting my message across and instigating a cost-cutting drive in the business. However, I now need to invest a considerable sum of money in an initiative that, I am sure, will have long-term financial benefits. How can I apparently contradict my own message without losing credibility?

If you suspect that you'll be seen as being inconsistent, the chances are that you will be. In this situation, honesty is the best policy. Address the apparent inconsistency directly and tell others how you'd feel if you saw someone else displaying this type of contradictory behaviour. This is a bold step, but it will make clear that you understand what others may be feeling, and it will disarm potential critics. Having cleared the air, you can then follow up by inviting others to tell you what they think, which allows you in turn to explain your reasoning rationally and pre-empt negative speculation.

MAKE IT HAPPEN

Getting your message across eloquently and elegantly depends on your ability to read a situation accurately and to pick up on the social and political nuances at play in your workplace and among your audience. Some people are able to do this intuitively whilst others need some 'tools' to help them say the right thing at the right time. Tools may include organisational surveys which feed anonymous opinions back to the relevant people and raise issues that are important to employees without fear of repercussion. On the other hand, you may prefer to talk to a particularly politically astute or well-informed colleague to guide your approach.

There are many different situations—ranging from performance appraisals to negotiations to debates—in which the accurate transmission and receipt of a message is vital to progress. In all of these situations, there's a 'space' between the speaker and the listener, and this is filled with personal views, interests, and investments in a particular outcome, all of which can lead to misunderstandings or conflict. Manage this space to your best advantage by considering some of the points listed below.

Set the scene, stating your rationale or aspiration for the message

If you're engaging in a negotiation or meeting, it's a good idea to make clear to your audience why you're talking to them. This helps to address or sideline any alternative agendas or confusion. If you're working on any particular assumptions, make them clear and check that everyone else shares them. This will save a lot of time and crossed wires in the long run as it makes sure that everyone knows where they stand. Clarifying your aim will also help you refocus the meeting if things start to go awry.

Check your assumptions and explore the context properly

Sometimes you may need to make a strong personal connection with your audience before you deliver your message. To do this, you need to be aware of their concerns or expectations. Ask them what they think of the topic in question and find out about their related hopes and fears. Once you understand your audience's interests and motivations, you'll be able to work out the best way of getting your message across. It's often a surprise to find that others don't share our assumptions, so making this initial check will make sure that you don't inadvertently press the wrong buttons.

Meet the recipients where they are

Very often, messages don't get across well because the recipient can't relate to their content or purpose. If there's no point of identification or common interest between speaker and listener, there's equally no ground in which to root the message and as a result, its relevance gets lost. To get around this problem, it's a good idea to begin your speech with a phrase that tries to bridge the gap, such as 'as we're all aware . . .' or 'no doubt you've noticed that . . .'. Effective communicators take their audience's situation as the starting point of their communication and build towards the desired end point or outcome. You may need to do quite a lot of homework, both formally and informally, to be sure that you're properly informed of your audience's circumstances and views.

Use simple and elegant language to reduce ambiguity

People who are experts in a particular field often baffle their audience with technical language or jargon on the assumption that it will have the same resonance with their audience as it does for them. Find out how familiar your audience is with the topic you're speaking on, and then adjust your vocabulary accordingly. Use plenty of examples, anecdotes, analogies, and metaphors if the audience isn't as 'techie' as you. Remember that you can also make your message clearer by using visual aids (such as PowerPoint®, overhead slides, or simple hand-outs). Humour and a touch of drama can sometimes help but it's best to use these sensitively and sparingly.

Repeat key messages using several different channels of communication

Generally, people can take away about three key points from any communication. These three points may be represented in different ways so that all preferred styles of communication can be accommodated. In addition, they may be offered using different channels of communication so that the message is reinforced from many angles. For example, you could follow up a presentation by writing an article for a company newsletter or intranet or by putting up a poster. All of these things will mean that no one can avoid what you're trying to say, even if they don't agree with it!

Listen to others and show respect for their point of view

Getting across your message successfully depends to a large extent on your ability to listen well to other people. We very often assume that we know what others are thinking and what they're about to say. However, these assumptions can 'deafen' us to what's *really* being said, and we end up as poor communicators as a result. Avoid this, then, by listening properly to other people. Don't jump to conclusions or make snap judgments about their position, but instead respect where they're coming from and nurture a real desire to hear and be heard without the 'white noise' of misperception getting in the way.

Address questions or concerns directly

In the same way that we must learn to hear our audience, we also have to help them hear us. Unless they're given an opportunity to have their concerns addressed honestly and constructively, they'll go away feeling negative and may also be ready to damn what you say to others who haven't yet been able to hear you speak. Help your audience by being sure of both your subject and of your objectives in making the communication. Convey the necessary information accurately and remember that you have to seem convinced by it yourself if others are to share your belief. It's a good idea to close the communication 'loop' by asking your audience to summarise what they think you've said. This gives you a valuable opportunity to correct any misunderstandings and to run through your key points one more time. Using language that's familiar to your recipients will enable them to act as another mouthpiece for your message.

Summarise and confirm any resultant actions

There's an old adage about presentations that says 'tell them what you're going to tell them, tell them, then tell them what you've just told them'. Although this may sound like overkill, it's actually a valuable way of conveying messages in a straightforward and powerful way.

In short, use non-complex language to convey up to three points at a time repeatedly. Colour these points with examples, anecdotes, and analogies and be aware of how your message is going down; if people look confused, adjust your style to explain things in plainer terms. If you see that people are straining to hear, speak louder. It's really important at all times to listen, observe, and respect your audience and their point of view, even if the latter is at odds with your own.

WHAT TO AVOID

You over-do it

In our urgency to get our message across, we frequently rush in and speak without thinking things through. This will come across as arrogant and high-handed and immediately set your audience against you. Rushing in like this is often motivated by fear of failure and a compensating thought that if we assert ourselves strongly enough, there'll be no room for disagreement or dissent. Wrong. In fact, if you do feel this fear, the best thing you can do is tread carefully. Show that you respect your audience, that you understand their situation and identify with it personally if you can. This will ease any likely resistance, especially if you ask them for their views and listen carefully to them.

You undermine yourself by accident

We often believe that getting a message across is a content issue. However, it's not so much what you say that counts, but how you say it. Generally, people recognise authenticity and genuineness when they see it and unless you're in tune with your message and your audience, what you say will not be heard or received in the way you wish. To be in tune, you need to use your skills in active listening, body language, and assertiveness as well as believing in what you're saying.

You're not impartial

Having a personal investment in the reception and outcome of your message can cloud your ability to talk about it appropriately and effectively. Think of your message as a bridge that connects you to your audience and your words as the vehicle that travels between the two. This may help you get your personal investment out of the way and help you reach the best outcome for both parties.

You don't allow enough time

Rushing what you're saying often defeats your objective and leaves people feeling bullied and demotivated. When you're planning and timing a speech or presentation, make sure you factor in some time for your audience to ask questions or raise concerns at the end. You need to put people at their ease so that they feel able to address what you've said. Don't be defensive if people ask you questions (remember that they're perfectly entitled to!), but try to use their point to build upon or illustrate another facet of your message.

USEFUL LINKS

1000ventures.com:
www.1000ventures.com/business_guide/crosscuttings/talking_main.html
Mind Tools: **www.mindtools.com/page8.html**

Prepare Presentations

Presentations are useful in many situations, such as pitching for business, putting a case for funding, and addressing staff meetings. Few people like speaking formally to an audience, but there are many real benefits and as you gain experience in giving presentations, you'll probably find that it becomes less of a worry, and even enjoyable. This actionlist will give you some suggestions for preparing the content of your presentation, looking at the objectives that you hope to achieve, pitching it right for your particular audience, and getting your points across in the best way.

What objectives should I set?

The starting point for any presentation is to set clear objectives. Ask yourself why you're giving the talk, and what you want your audience to get out of it. Also consider whether using speech alone is the best way of communicating your message, and whether your presentation would benefit from using visual aids and slides to further illustrate its main points. When you're planning and giving the presentation, keep your objectives in mind at all times—they'll focus your thoughts. Having clear reasons for giving the presentation will ensure that you're not wasting anyone's time, either your audience's or your own.

What do I need to know about the audience?

Before you plan your presentation try as best you can to find out who is going to be in your audience, and what their expectations are. For example, the tone and content of a presentation to the managing director of another firm will be very different to one addressed to potential users of a product. It's important that you know the extent of the audience's knowledge about the topic you'll be discussing. Their familiarity with the subject will determine the level at which you pitch the talk. Try to appeal to what will motivate and interest these people.

MAKE IT HAPPEN

Write your speech

When it comes to presentations, there is no substitute for detailed preparation and planning. While everyone prepares in different ways, all of which develop with experience, here are a few key points to bear in mind while you're preparing.

Start by breaking up the task of preparing your speech into manageable units. Once you know the length of the presentation—say 15 minutes, for example—break the time up into smaller units and allocate sections of your speech to each unit. Then note down all the points you want to make, and order them logically. This will help you develop the framework and emphasis of the presentation.

Keep your presentation short and simple, if you can, as it'll be easier for you to manage and remember. If you need to provide more detail, you can supply a written handout to be given out at the end. A shorter presentation is usually more effective from the audience's point of view, too, as most people dislike long speeches, and will not necessarily remember any more from them.

Avoid packing your talk with facts and figures; you could instead use graphs and charts to illustrate these where they are essential. Aim to identify two or three key points, and concentrate on getting these over in a creative fashion.

Use visual aids and equipment

With any presentation, you'll need to consider whether to use visual aids, such as acetates for an overhead projector (OHP), or a computer presentation package such as PowerPoint®. Remember that visual aids should only be used as signposts during the presentation, to help the audience focus on the main point. It's important not to cram too much information on to one visual aid as you'll probably lose the attention of your audience while they try to read everything on it. Make sure the audience can see the information by using big, bold lettering, and bear in mind that images are often far more effective than words.

At its most basic, a personal computer can be used to develop and produce a series of slides which can be printed onto acetates for use on an overhead projector. A more common usage is to link up the PC with a projector in order to show the information on a large screen.

If you're going to use slides, you should try to standardise them to make them look more professional. Use templates where possible to make sure that they don't blend together, and again, try not to put too much information onto a single slide, or it will become difficult to read. A sensible guideline is to include no more than six points per slide, and to keep the number of words you use for each point to the absolute minimum. Think of what you're writing as the prompts for what you want to say.

The most common presentation packages are Microsoft® PowerPoint® and Corel™ Presentations. Both of these will allow you to develop a presentation using slide templates and give you the option of using charts, graphics, or even photographs to bring your information alive. Packages such as PhotoShop® or Paint Shop Pro® will also allow you to scan in or manipulate photographs, or you could also use some of the available animations for transitions between slides.

You should pay particular attention to the layout and text on the slides and remain consistent throughout. Select a background that contrasts well with the text, and colours that are strong and stand out. It may also be a good idea to include the business's logo on all of the slides. It's important, always, to proofread your slides and acetates. There is nothing more noticeable, or more unprofessional, than a typo or grammatical error projected to ten times its size on a screen!

Practise as many times as you can to make sure that you're very familiar with your speech—allow plenty of time for rehearsal before the event. Once you're confident that your presentation is right, resist the temptation to change it. Remember, *you* may have heard the speech many times, but the audience will be hearing it for the first time. It's also a good idea to practise your speech using the equipment you intend to use; slide projectors and video machines should be tested in advance to make sure you know how to operate them. Make sure you have a contingency plan to cope with any unforeseen mishaps. During your rehearsals, it will also be important to time your speech to ensure it's not too long or too short. Remember that you'll probably need to allow time at the end for a question-and-answer session. Resist the temptation to bring your script into the presentation and instead write the main points on numbered cards, known as cue cards, to provide reminders.

Prepare the venue

Make sure that an appropriately-sized room has been organised for your presentation; take into account the number of people you're expecting, and ensure there is enough seating, lighting, ventilation, and heating. It's a good idea to provide some refreshments for participants such as tea, coffee, and water.

You also need to make sure there will be no interruptions, for example by phone calls, fire drills, or people accidentally entering the room. Whether you're presenting at your own office or elsewhere, you must make sure that any equipment or props you need are available and set up properly before the presentation starts. If you're presenting away from your office, at a conference or a client's premises for example, it's a good idea to visit the site beforehand to make sure it provides the necessary facilities.

WHAT TO AVOID

You don't research your audience

A good knowledge of the audience is absolutely crucial in finding the correct pitch. It's no good blinding your audience with technical jargon if they only have a basic grasp of the subject. Similarly, a very knowledgeable audience will soon switch off if you spend the first few minutes going over the basics.

You go on for too long

If your presentation absolutely has to be longer than 20 minutes, it may be a good idea to insert some breaks so that your audience remains fresh and interested.

You forget to check the room and equipment

This can be disastrous! Imagine, for example, arriving and finding that there is no facility for delivering PowerPoint® presentations, and you have no other method of showing slides. Make sure you're familiar with the environment in which you'll be presenting.

USEFUL LINKS

Mind Tools:
http://www.mindtools.com/CommSkll/PresentationPlanningChecklist.htm
SpeechTips.com: **www.speechtips.com/preparation.html**

Deliver Presentations

A presentation is an ideal environment for you to promote your ideas, your products, or your services. You have a captive audience, are able to provide them with relevant information, and can answer any questions they may have on the spot. For a presentation to be a success you must be able to speak in an articulate, fluent fashion, to hold the attention of the audience, and to leave them wanting to know more.
Some people are natural presenters, while others find it more difficult, but practice and feedback from previous audiences will help you develop your presentation skills. This actionlist will give you some ideas for structuring, preparing, and delivering your presentation.

How should I structure my presentation?

Structure is essential for any presentation. There should be an introduction, a main body, and a conclusion. You can be witty, controversial, or even outrageous if the mood of the presentation allows, but whatever approach you try, your chief aims are to arouse the audience's curiosity, and to get your message across.

What's the best way to introduce my presentation?

The introduction to your presentation needs to attract your audience's interest and attention. A good opening is also important for your own confidence, because if you start well, the rest should follow easily. Plan your opening words carefully for maximum impact: they should be short, sharp, and to the point. Let your audience know how long your presentation will take, as this will prepare people to focus for the period of time you expect to speak. Summarise what you'll be discussing, so that they can work out how much information they'll need to absorb. Explaining the key points in the first few sentences will also help your mind to focus on the task in hand, and refresh your memory on the major points of your presentation. It sometimes helps to get started if you can learn your first few sentences by heart. Let your audience know if you're happy to interact with them throughout the presentation. Alternatively, inform them that you'll be holding a question and answer session at the end.

What should I do in the main body of the presentation?
The main body of the presentation will be dictated by the points that you want to make. Use short, sharp, and simple language to keep your audience's attention, and to ensure that your message is being understood. Include only one idea per sentence and pause after each one so as to make a mental full stop. Use precise language to convey your message, but make sure that your presentation sounds spontaneous—it shouldn't sound like a chapter from a textbook. You need to convey your message clearly, without masking the salient points with waffle. Stick to your original plan for your presentation and don't go off at a tangent on a particular point, and miss the thread of your presentation. Why not try using metaphors and images to illustrate points? This will give impact to what you say, and help your audience to remember what you've said.

How should I conclude my presentation?
You should close by summing up the key points of what you've covered. The closing seconds of your presentation are as crucial as the opening sentence. Consider what action you'd like your audience to take after the presentation is over and attempt to inspire them to do it.

MAKE IT HAPPEN

Think about posture and delivery

There are certain techniques to do with your posture, and the way that you deliver your presentation, that can be used to improve its impact. Maintain eye contact and address your audience directly throughout your presentation. Try to be aware of your stance, posture, and gestures without being too self-conscious. Don't slouch, as you'll look unprofessional. The best way of avoiding this is by always standing when you're doing a presentation. Don't fiddle, for example with a pencil or a piece of paper, try to keep still, and avoid moving around excessively. All these things are distracting for an audience, and will mean that they're missing important points in your presentation.

Remember that your audience has come to learn something. Try to sound authoritative, sincere, and enthusiastic. If you don't sound as if you believe in yourself, this will come across to the audience. Think about the way in which you're speaking. Most people need to articulate their words more clearly when addressing an audience. There is usually no opportunity for the audience to ask you to repeat a word you've missed. Aim to sound the vowels and consonants of words clearly. Be aware, also, of your vocal expression. Try to vary volume, pitch, and speed of delivery to underline your meaning, and to maintain the interest of your audience. Try not to use too many acronyms that are specific to your business or industry as you can't be completely sure that everyone in the audience will know what they mean. If you do need to use them, introduce them and explain them early in your presentation so that everyone can keep up.

Use cue cards, visual aids, and equipment

It's tempting (and, if you're a nervous presenter, comforting) to have the full version of your speech in front of you, but it's best to avoid this and use cue cards instead. These will have a few headings referring to the main subject areas of your speech, and a few key points. In this way you can remember the key points you want to convey, but you have the freedom to talk naturally about them, rather than speaking from an over-rehearsed script, and this will make you seem more spontaneous. You may, however, wish to write the introduction out in full on your first card.

Be careful when using visual aids and equipment in the presentation as these can also be distracting for an audience. Use a pen to point out details on the overhead projector itself, rather than the screen, as this is much clearer. Flipcharts should be written on quickly in long hand, but try not to turn your back on the audience as you write. Commonly available presentation packages often have a facility to enable you to link to specific slides. Additionally, if a specific topic needs further explanation, you could have a built-in series of links so that you can move to some extra slides to explain a particular point. If you intend to use sophisticated technology, then have a technician on hand to help out. It's important to have a contingency plan in case your technology crashes. Make sure you have either a back-up disk, or an alternative presentational medium, or both.

Close your presentation

If you're answering questions at the end of your presentation and you don't know the answer to a question, tell the person you'll find the answer and get back to them later. This will save time, and also prevent you from giving an incorrect answer. If the question is a general discussion point, you could always try throwing the question open to the floor; you may be able to get an interesting discussion going between the members of your audience. If you plan to use handouts to add to your presentation's content, make sure that you give these out at the end. Otherwise the audience will be flicking through your handout instead of listening to you.

WHAT TO AVOID

You lack enthusiasm

If you don't have any interest or excitement in your own speech, then don't expect your audience to be interested or excited. Listening to a single voice for 20 minutes or more can be difficult for an audience, so you must try to inject enthusiasm into what you're saying. You could consider planning some kind of interaction with your audience, too, in the form of activities or discussion.

You speak too quickly

Don't rush your presentation; it's important to take your time. The audience will find it difficult to understand you, or to keep up, if you talk too fast. Make sure you summarise your main points every five minutes or so, or as you reach the end of a section. This will help to clarify the most important issues for your audience, and it's then more likely that they'll remember the central issues long after you've finished your presentation.

You don't check equipment

There is nothing more irritating for an audience, who have all made an effort to turn up on time, than to have to sit around and wait while you struggle to get your laptop to work, or sort your slides out. Make sure everything is exactly in place well before your audience begins to arrive. A technician should be on hand if you're planning to use sophisticated technology.

You don't interact with the audience

Be careful not to look at the floor during your presentation, or to direct your speech at one person. Try and draw your whole audience into the presentation by glancing at everyone's faces, in a relaxed and unhurried way, as you make your points. Keeping in tune with your audience in this way will also help you judge if people are becoming bored. If you do detect this, you could try to change the tempo of your presentation to refocus their attention.

USEFUL LINKS

BusinessTown.com: **www.businesstown.com/presentations/index.asp**
iVillage.co.uk: **www.ivillage.co.uk/workcareer/survive**
SpeechTips.com: **www.speechtips.com/delivering.html**

Overcome Nerves

Being overcome by nerves can be an utterly debilitating experience that sabotages our ability to communicate well and to demonstrate how well we can do our job. The body's nervous reaction to speaking in public, making a presentation to customers or colleagues, or even making an intervention during an internal meeting can, if left unchecked, rob us in just a few seconds of the confidence and experience built up during the course of our career. If you do suffer from nerves in some work situations, take comfort in knowing that you're not alone and that with the help of a few simple techniques, you can overcome the trembling knees, dry mouth, sweaty palms, and a tendency to ramble. It's always tempting to think that a problem will go just go away, but tackling nerves will offer a range of positive results, including being able to be yourself, contributing to events in the way you know you can deep down, and getting the amazing next job you deserve. Overcoming nerves is a great first step on the journey to full confidence.

I have to make a very important presentation and I'm bound to get it wrong. What can I do to avoid disaster?

If you see yourself failing at something, you're more likely to do so. Try to get your imagination under control and instead of seeing yourself getting it all spectacularly wrong, see yourself succeeding extraordinarily. Your body will follow the cues from your mind, so train your mind to be positive and to 'invite' success for yourself. Don't let negative images or words pollute your preparation.

When I get nervous, I speak before I think and say the stupidest things. How can I stop my mouth from running away with me?
Breathe. We're not particularly good at managing our breathing, but it is the key to allowing you the space to observe and hear what's going on. Being sensitive to the needs of others and different situations is an important part of being able to say the right thing at the right time. Give yourself time to take in the information you need and formulate what you're going to say. Don't rush in, breathe calmly, and don't worry about short silences.

I'm an introvert and very shy. What can I do to help myself succeed in public speaking?
Strangely, some of the best performers are introverts and many have severe bouts of nerves before taking the stage and delivering a polished and professional performance. If you're worried, though, one good way of lessening the fear of public speaking is to think of it as having a conversation, rather than giving a talk. It also helps to break the ice by meeting a few people from your audience first; this will help you make a connection with them that you can use and build on while you're on the platform. Be friendly, smile, look people in the eyes, ask questions if appropriate, and take the listening time to breathe, relax, and enjoy the experience if you can.

MAKE IT HAPPEN

Although the effects of a bout of nerves show themselves physically, it's our state of mind that triggers them. Fears that we'll make a fool of ourselves or that we won't achieve our aims commonly drive our nervous reactions, which are often known as the 'fight or flight' response. Thousands of years ago, when we were surviving in a physically hostile world that was populated by human predators or enemies, our fight or flight response enabled us to fuel our strength and overpower a beast or build our speed and outrun a being that was threatening us. In the moment of need, adrenalin would be released, our hearts would pump faster, our blood would be super-oxygenated, and our muscles would be fed to achieve higher levels of performance. This is what enabled human beings to survive and build the (relatively) safe, sophisticated, and cerebral world that we enjoy today. However, in spite of our successful emergence from the primitive world, our bodies still react to fear—whether it be real or imagined—in the same way.

When we're giving a presentation, our fear of failure gives rise to the fight or flight response along with its characteristic bodily reactions, but these now have nowhere to go. We don't take flight and neither do we fight, but instead stand still, tell ourselves not to be so silly, and try to combat the panic. By this stage, there's no point in trying to use our mind to control the effects of fear as our body has taken control and is doing its job perfectly well. This lack of control gives rise to further feelings of anxiety and sends a message to the body to try harder because the threat has not disappeared and there is still work to be done. More adrenalin . . . faster heart beat . . . busy muscles . . . and so it goes on. Trying to break this cycle is the challenge of overcoming nerves and it can be tackled in two ways: through the mind and through the body.

Overcome nerves through the mind

* Try using visualisation as a technique for removing the fear stimulus. Imagine your audience receiving your information enthusiastically, being interested in what you're saying, and applauding when you've finished. Enhance this image with feelings of satisfaction, achievement, and pride. Watch yourself leave the spotlight feeling confident and happy to acknowledge those that come up to you afterwards to congratulate you on your performance.
* Think through your presentation or performance beforehand so that you are both practically and mentally prepared. If you're likely to be asked questions on your presentation, imagine what these might be and prepare some answers. If it helps, write them down, read over them a few times and tick them off your 'checklist' of things to prepare.
* Get as much information as possible. This will help you target your talk appropriately and demonstrate that you understand their needs well and see things from their perspective. Being able to show that you've taken the time to do this will help win them over and put them on your side.

Working through the exercises above will help remove the perceived threat you fear and will fill your mind with positive images. If the threat is removed through visualisation, you're unlikely to experience the severe physiological responses.

Overcome nerves through the body

Some of these well-known relaxation techniques will help prevent your body from triggering the 'fear response'.

* Spend a few minutes to calm your breathing and to take attention away from the impending performance. Breathe deeply into your stomach, hold your breath for a few seconds, and breathe out again. Do this several times in a quiet spot away from the action.
* Relax your body. Sit in a chair and concentrate on each muscle group one by one. Working from your feet to your forehead, contract and relax your muscles. Feel the difference. If you find yourself becoming tense again, go back to the problem area and try again, breathing deeply and steadily as you do so.
* Have some water before your performance to prevent you from drying up and keep another glass beside you so that you can refresh your mouth as you go.

Remember that your body language will reflect your state of mind. If you're nervous, you may brace yourself and try to make yourself appear smaller so that your perceived threat won't see you. You may also want to find something to lean against or hang on to so that you get a feeling of support. Resist the temptation to do any of these, though, as they'll actually give off signals of weakness and draw attention to your nerves. Instead, try the following:

* Practise standing solidly, with your knees locked back, and legs slightly apart. Don't be tempted to entwine your legs around each other like barley sugar—you're more likely to fall.
* If you need to take notes on-stage, use cards rather than floppy bits of A4 paper that will rustle and quiver as your hands shake.
* Open body gestures make you look larger and stronger. Point from the shoulder. Find an opportunity to open your arms in an inclusive gesture. Take up more space on the stage by taking one or two steps from time to time. Look your audience in the eyes and try to find a connection that will build your confidence.
* Project your voice well. Your tone and pitch will convey how much you believe in your message. Talk to the back of the room to achieve the right level of projection. If you have the opportunity and the venue is new to you, ask a friend or colleague to stand at the back as you practise and indicate that they can hear you.
* Dress comfortably and appropriately. Don't take risks with your image until you're sure you can carry it off—this isn't the time to experiment with complicated clothes.

Overcoming nerves isn't an easy task but is one well worth aiming for. Success removes obstacles to your personal and professional development and means you're free to express yourself without hindrance.

WHAT TO AVOID

You put yourself under too much pressure

Putting ourselves under too much pressure to overcome our nerves can be counter-productive. Set reasonable goals, take things one step at a time, and give yourself an opportunity to celebrate each small success and build upon it incrementally. If you challenge yourself in extreme situations, you run the risk of failing in those extremes and it can be very difficult to recover from that. Be gentle with yourself and try to build your confidence steadily and soundly.

You pretend you don't suffer from nerves

When people want to appear confident and competent, they often deny that they suffer from nerves and end up playing a part, rather than being themselves. This is a common mistake which at best makes it seem as if you're suppressing the real 'you', but at worst, can make you seem arrogant. Putting on masks can be helpful in some situations, for example, if the real you is hidden somewhere in the role that you've decided to act out, but removing who you are by 'being someone else' isn't a good way to overcome nerves. Hiding yourself away won't help and in fact sometimes it's just better to acknowledge your perceived short-comings and find yourself a role model, mentor, or coach who can help you find a way through.

You think the problem will go away

Many would-be presenters who are overcome by nerves avoid dealing with it, thinking that they just have to get through their ordeal and somehow arrive at the other side. This is perfectly true, but it can be life-enhancing to face your fears and find a dignified way through. Often when we look our fears in the face, they begin to subside, especially if we practise techniques to master them. Rehearsing is extremely helpful, whether it's in front of friends, family, or even the mirror. If you're able to video yourself rehearsing, so much the better; you'll learn a lot.

USEFUL LINKS

businessknow-how: **www.businessknowhow.com/growth/public-speaking.htm**

Structure and Write Good Reports

The art of writing good business reports doesn't come easily to everyone and as a result, many people consider the task boring and difficult. Inexperienced writers often feel they have to produce great tomes that include everything they know rather than elegant documents that meet their objectives. Unsurprisingly, this can result in over-long documents that are a nightmare to both write and read. Writing reports *can* be a satisfying experience, though. Try to bear in mind that their purpose is to present relevant information that allows good decisions to be made, or to outline the effects of decisions that have already been taken. Good reports are succinct, helpful, and written with the reader and his or her context firmly in mind. They should be structured so that the logic of their arguments can be followed easily. Don't leave out too much information in your pursuit of elegance, however; paring down too much is just as unhelpful as putting too much in.

I have a report to write that covers issues that could become large and unwieldy. How do I control the process and arrive at a neat solution?

Controlling a document's scope can be tricky, but try:

* getting a proper brief from the commissioner of the report. This may be a long conversation, but it sets your parameters.
* thinking about your audience, their perspective, their background knowledge of the topic, and their likely investment in it.
* working out your desired outcome. This will help you organise your information and arguments.
* structuring the report carefully. Make sure it has a beginning, a middle, and an end. Plan the sections and sub-sections carefully and logically.
* finding, organising, and analysing the information that you want to include. Exclude anything you don't really need.

* writing, checking, and double-checking your work. If at all possible, ask someone else to proofread it for you.

I work in a technical area and much of my data is numerical. How can I make this come alive for the reader?
Readers can quickly switch off if confronted by reams of numbers and formulae. Make the data come alive by describing the meaning behind the numbers in words if possible, or by turning it into graphs, charts, or other illustrations.

I've been asked to write a report and if I do it well, it could enhance my reputation and offer me further career opportunities. How can I show myself in the best light?
Producing a highly professional document may help you meet this double agenda, but don't fall into the trap of thinking of the report as your CV—it's a vehicle to show your professional expertise, not an excuse to show off. Keep it simple and use straightforward language. Don't pepper the document with the latest acronyms and jargon—your audience may not be as familiar with them as you. If you *do* need to use this type of language, make sure that you explain the full meaning of an acronym at least once towards the beginning of the report, and you could also include a brief glossary at the back. Language aside, make sure the document follows a logical sequence and leave the reader with some questions or pointers that lead them to recognise your expertise. For example: 'The current debate about [relevant subject] goes beyond the scope of this report, but my conclusions take account of the relevant aspects of these issues'.

MAKE IT HAPPEN

Know your aim

To write a good report, you need to be clear about your audience, what they know already, and what they'll learn from your final document.

You may be writing for a number of different reasons, but each will inform the approach you take. For example, you could be justifying a decision that has already been taken and reviewing its effectiveness. Alternatively, you may be developing a persuasive argument in support of a particular decision that you want taken, or you may be disseminating information in order to provide background knowledge for a debate or a decision in which you have no investment. Each option offers a basic structure that will act as an organising framework.

Visualise your finished document at the outset and get a sense of how you'd like the reader to feel as they read through. This will help you decide what to include, what to leave out, and what tone will work best.

Set the context

Your first task is to draw readers into the material and to remove anything that would detract from them understanding it fully. One way to do this is to create a 'frame' through which readers view the topic and by stating any assumptions made. Often this frame appears in the form of a summary of the purpose, scope, and structure of the report. You may also like to include an outcomes statement to set expectations and guide the reader on how the contents of the report should be considered or applied. For example, you could say: 'It is intended that this report will contribute to the debate on [relevant subject] . . .' or 'This report will set out the rationale for taking a decision on [relevant subject] . . . and conclude with a recommendation on what this decision should be'.

Present the key issues

Reports become difficult to read and understand if the arguments presented are unclear. Rather than criss-cross themes, introduce and address each key issue separately and develop your argument logically. Try not to conflate personal opinions with the facts; be accurate and objective in the way you present your data, findings, or discussion points. Identify the themes that will be developed in the main body report and signpost the sections in which this will be done.

Understand the underlying issues

Now you've identified and explained the key factors, you need to expand on their underlying causes and on the issues that emerge as a consequence of them. Next, explore possible solutions, being careful to mention fully any implications, including costs. (These are often overlooked.) By taking this tack, your logic will pull the readers along and help them come to the same conclusions as you. If your report is designed to favour one option out of many, this is clearly the way you want to go!

Appraise the future

Some people aren't natural decision-makers and feel uncomfortable when weighing up a number of options. Help them along by having a forward-looking section that allows you to explain why one decision is better than another. Sometimes, you can do this most effectively by painting a picture of the future if the 'ideal' decision isn't made. If you do take this approach, however, you must be absolutely sure that your logic is water-tight, as any gaps will give others an excellent opportunity to launch counter-arguments.

Conclude and make your recommendations

A good report alerts the reader about what to expect, informs and argues the case in line with the purpose of the report, and ends with a conclusion or recommendation that draws all the threads together. Powerful conclusions reiterate the points made and assert what needs to be done next.

Think about the executive summary or synopsis

Although the executive summary usually comes at the beginning of any report, it's actually much easier to write it and then slot it into place when you've finished the rest of the document. By this stage, you'll have thought through all your arguments to their logical conclusion, all of which should still be clear in your mind, so it should be a relatively simple task. Remember that it only need be a few paragraphs long and its main aim is to give the reader a brief overview of the report's content and outcome.

Here's a quick checklist covering the main structural points along with some items to consider when reviewing your document.

Report-writing checklist

Context	Have you considered the purpose of the report and clarified its scope and expected outcome? Have you considered the readers and understood their needs, perspective, and motivations for reading the report?
Organisation	Have you made sure that your document is ordered logically and that your arguments are robust? Is there an obvious beginning, middle, and end to your report? Is there a logical thread linking your report together?
Presentation	Have you made sure your document is presented well? This includes the layout, the formatting, and the use of tables, figures, and illustrations. It's true that pictures can say a thousand words but make sure they're relevant and add something to the report. Make sure there is enough white space to make the document inviting to the readers.
Content	Have you covered all the key issues? Have you differentiated between fact and opinion? Have you outlined your assumptions? Are your facts accurate? Are your arguments clear and free from personal or unreasoned bias?
Style	Is your writing clear and concise and is meaning easily conveyed? Often 'less is more' when communicating through the written word. Have you laid out your document effectively and consistently? Have you checked your spellings and grammar?
Conclusions and Recommendations	Are your conclusions a natural outcome of the arguments in your report? Are your recommendations based upon your conclusions and free from prejudice or bias?
Finally . . .	Have you included a succinct summary or synopsis? Does the report look good and is the format of the report stable as you make a final flick through?

WHAT TO AVOID

You include everything you know

Many people assume that they must include *everything* they know about a topic or issue in a report. Remember that 'less is more' and only include information that is essential to the logic and purpose of the report, or that helps build important background to the issue at hand.

You're not objective

It's easy to weave in too much of yourself to a report, especially if you feel strongly about the subject or have a vested interest in it. Try to avoid this is you can, though, as you'll end up creating something that isn't objective or helpful for your audience. Your credibility is on the line if your writing is filled with unsubstantiated facts or emotional assertions, so don't go there. Use good examples to support your points and if you want to refer to other pieces of work (for example, websites, books, or articles), include these prominently so that readers can research further if they'd like to.

You assume others think like you

Report writers often assume that their audience thinks in the same way that they do and that they will therefore reason an argument along the same lines. Don't fall into this trap and remember that others approach things with their own perspective and logic. What you can do, though, is to 'head them off at the pass', if you like, and try to address potential counter-arguments to your own within the body of the report—this will show you have a grasp of others' views. It's a good idea to ask someone else to read through your draft and test your arguments.

USEFUL LINKS

About Writing Business Reports:
http://freelancewrite.about.com/cs/prmarcom/a/busreport.htm
Idaho State University: **http://cob.isu.edu/cis300/reportWriting.htm**

Write Great E-mails

Although e-mail is a widely-used medium, many people do not know how to use it well. As it's an 'instant' way of getting in touch with others, it's easy to overlook the basics of business correspondence such as spelling, grammar, and punctuation in e-mails, but it's important that you maintain high standards however you communicate with others. The style you use for a message will, clearly, depend on the recipient, but take time in judging *what* you're writing and to whom so that your company's image or reputation is always enhanced, never diminished.

I'm rushed off my feet at work, and don't have time to spend ages on writing e-mails. I just tell people what they need to know or ask the questions I need answering. Surely no one will mind?

While nobody could object to a succinct, straightforward e-mail, impolite ones are another thing altogether. However busy you are, it doesn't take much to address and sign off messages properly, or to say 'thank you' if you're asking for help. Obviously you don't need to be formal with people you know very well or work with very closely, but if you're contacting people for the first time or trying to attract new business, it clearly makes sense to be polite.

I have to ask a colleague with a notoriously short attention span a complicated question via e-mail. What's the best way to do this?

Summarise all the key information you need to share with them and then attach a document with background facts and figures. Make sure you have a powerful subject line in your e-mail and then set out an overview of your question, taking care to highlight exactly what you need to know and when. If your question is based on a string of other events or has supporting evidence, list all of this out separately in an attachment, and tell your correspondent what you've done; if they have lots of e-mails to read, they may not even notice you've attached something, so remind them. Once you've sent the e-mail, chase up politely after a few days if you've not heard anything by forwarding the e-mail back to them and asking for their response. If your colleague has an assistant, you could also ask him or her to draw it to their boss's attention if it's really urgent.

MAKE IT HAPPEN

Clearly identify the subject of the e-mail

As e-mail grows in popularity, people in business receive a high volume of messages each day. To deal with this potential flood, they have to prioritise and decide what's important. Make sure, then, that every e-mail you send has a clearly-identified subject.

Most popular e-mail packages include a subject line, so use that to state as concisely as possible what your e-mail is about. Examples include:

* new date for meeting
* price changes on the ABC range
* sales monthly report
* order for Customer XYZ—delivery status
* new managing director appointed

These are brief and to the point but they indicate clearly what the e-mail is about. Even if you're on reasonably friendly terms with the recipient, if you're writing a *business* e-mail, try to avoid using 'Hello' in the subject line. It annoys some people no end and they'll put off reading the message.

Some e-mails cover a subject that changes over a period of time, such as the content of a new brochure or the status of project. To help everyone keep track of the changes and to make sure they read the latest version of information, add a date or version number to the title. For example:

* new brochure copy—draft 4
* project status—July
* revised personnel guidelines—effective December

Be as concise as possible

An e-mail is, first and foremost, a *short* form of communication. It should be brief and to the point and the recipient should be able to understand the main points of your message in the first few lines.

As most e-mails will be read on a small computer screen, it can be difficult and inconvenient to follow long passages of text. If you need to go into more detail, send a document as a separate attachment or tell the recipient to contact you for more information. If you need to go into some detail and sending an attachment *isn't* possible, break your message into small 'chunks' with a heading before each new section. This will make long passages of information easier to read and understand on screen and your correspondents will be able to pick out the most relevant information for them.

Let's say you're thinking of creating a new project and would like your correspondent to be a contributor. To save them trawling through a dense paragraph, you could give a brief overview of the project and then highlight key points:

Your role: To overhaul our annual product catalogue, liaising with teams in-house on content and delivering a final pdf to the printer.
Budget: £800.00 (40 hours at £20.00 per hour)
Deadline: Final pdf delivered no later than 30 September.

Check your spelling and punctuation

An e-mail is a form of business correspondence that has the same status as letters and other printed material. In the hands of a customer, it reflects on the image of the company, so a message riddled with spelling mistakes and bad grammar isn't going to show you in your best light. With this in mind, take a few minutes to check your message for mistakes and sense before you send it. Many popular e-mail programs include spellcheckers to help you do this, but if your system doesn't have one, you could prepare your message in a word processing program, check it, and then copy the final version into your e-mail.

The popularity of text messages and text message speak is beginning to creep over into e-mail. While most people will understand what you mean if you send them a message along the lines of 'C U at 10' or 'mtg off', it's best not to include this type of abbreviation in messages to external clients or contacts. Remember also to use upper and lower case letters in your messages to business contacts. Writing a message completely in lower case gives an impression of something written in haste. Your correspondent might think that you just couldn't be bothered to spend any time on it (and by extension, them).

Lastly, try not to use acronyms too much. They may be understood by your colleagues, but meaningless to other people. If they're essential or completely unavoidable, explain what they mean at the outset of your message so that your correspondent can work out what's going on.

Use an appropriate style

Clearly, there's no single style for e-mail that you can adopt every time you compose one. You could use a friendly, chatty style when you're contacting a colleague or friend, but it's more appropriate to adopt a more formal style when you're contacting someone for the first time or dealing with a customer or an external contact.

For colleagues or regular, familiar contacts, you could open with 'Hi', 'Hello', or just a name ('John' or 'Sarah'). In more formal e-mails, you would use 'Dear Mr/Mrs/Miss/Ms . . .', or 'Dear John/Dear Sarah' if you're on first name terms with the recipient.

At the close of the e-mail, tailor your sign-off to your relationship with the recipient (see table below).

E-mail styles, like all other forms of communication, will differ from country to country. If you have lots of international correspondents, remember that some cultures are naturally more formal than others, so take a lead from the messages your contacts send to you and 'mirror' their tone and style. This will mean that you're less likely to offend anyone inadvertently.

Different ways of signing off

Informal	*More formal*	*Very formal*
Cheers	**Best**	**Yours**
Thanks	**Best wishes**	**Yours ever**
Tnx	**All best**	**Yours sincerely (if you know the name of the recipient)**
Ta	**All best wishes**	**Yours faithfully (if you don't know the recipient's name and have addressed your message to 'Dear Sir or Madam')**
All the best	**Many thanks**	
Later	**Regards**	
See you	**Kind regards** **Best regards**	

Request the action or information you need

Some of your e-mails give information to the recipient while others make a request for action or information. If you need to find something out from somewhere, make sure you've phrased your request clearly so that they know exactly what you want. For example, 'Please could you send me the latest sales report by 22nd November?', or 'Please discuss this with Emma and let me have your views by 2.00 on Thursday. '

If a number of people are involved in a joint process, you may need to give them individual instructions so that everyone understands their wider role. For example: For the team to deliver the new product by July, we need to meet the following targets:

Justin—complete the software by March
Helen—get the test results by May
Seema—request additional funding from the Finance Director by April

Explain how urgent your message is

Make clear whether your e-mail is urgent, important, or routine. With so much e-mail traffic, people need to prioritise their reading and response, so state the level of urgency.

Some e-mail packages allow you to highlight the level of priority, but if you do use this facility, don't abuse it. It's easy to mark every e-mail as urgent or as highly important in the hope that it'll receive attention, but if you do it too often, it'll have a 'crying wolf' effect: people will start to disregard messages that you mark as urgent, even if one of them actually is. Use the facility carefully (and honestly) and you'll get the results you need. To overcome possible reader inertia, you could include an indicator in the e-mail subject line such as 'product review—decision needed by Thursday'. This is informative and gives the recipient a clear instruction.

Don't use too many capital letters to indicate urgency and importance. E-mails like this can prove difficult to read on screen and, again, recipients can become immune to the technique. Also, the use of capital letters in e-mails is regarded by some people as 'virtual shouting' and your correspondents may misread your mood and respond in kind.

Use attachments to provide detail

E-mails that include longer documents, photographs, audio, or video take the form of a message plus an 'attachment'. Attachments allow you to send detailed information to your correspondent, but you should use this facility with caution.

Some attachments can take a great deal of time to transfer and the recipient may have problems downloading them, particularly if they don't have broadband (which allows fast transmission of large amounts of data). Bear this in mind if you have suppliers who have small businesses or who work from home. Attachments that could pose difficulties include:

* video clips
* publications converted to Portable Document Format (PDF)
* presentations
* spreadsheets
* photographs

Before you send attachments, check with your correspondents that their systems can handle these types of files.

Include further contact details

Some e-mail programs allow you to include a 'signature' at the end of your messages. In some cases, this can be a scanned version of your signature, but mostly it's a few lines that allow you to show information that the recipient may not always have easily to hand, such as your job title, postal address, telephone and fax number, and website address. Adding a 'signature' is particularly useful if you're writing to someone for the first time, as it provides some extra context about what you do or who you work for. They can also be used to advertise a new product. You can draw your correspondents' attention to it by mentioning very clearly where they can find out more about it on your website.

WHAT TO AVOID

You let your standards drop

E-mail is an instant medium, so it's easy to create a message quickly without considering the impact on the recipient. Abbreviations, acronyms, minimal punctuation, and unchecked spelling save time in the short term, but poor standards can damage a company's reputation.

Your messages are hard to read

E-mails are normally read on a computer screen, so any information must be concise and clearly laid out. Use upper and lower case letters and a legible typeface for clarity and avoid using capital letters too much. If you have a long message, guide the recipient by using headings for different topics.

USEFUL LINKS

Albion.com: **www.albion.com/netiquette**
CC Consulting: **www.crazycolour.com/os/emailedge_02.shtml**
Lancaster University Information Systems Services:
www.lancs.ac.uk/iss/email/nettiquette.htm

Negotiate with Confidence

We all negotiate a lot more than we think we do, in all areas of our life, and developing negotiation skills is an essential part of moving up the career ladder. Negotiating is the process of trying to find an agreement between two or more parties with differing views on, and expectations of, a certain issue. Good negotiations find a balance between each party's objectives to create a 'win/win' outcome.

Negotiation can be 'competitive' or 'collaborative'. In competitive negotiations, the negotiator wants to 'win' even if this results in the other party 'losing'; this can ultimately end in confrontation. In collaborative negotiations, the aim is to reach an agreement that satisfies both parties, maximising mutual advantage. There is no one right way to negotiate, and you'll develop a style that suits you. Most negotiations will be a mixture of the collaborative and competitive approaches. In situations where you're negotiating the terms of an ongoing relationship (rather than a one-off deal), it's generally more productive to lean towards collaboration rather than competition.

What is competitive negotiation?

This type of negotiation may have an unfriendly atmosphere and each party is clearly out to get the very best deal for themselves—the other party's objectives tend not to come into the equation. If you find yourself involved in a competitive-style negotiation, bear in mind the following:

* **Opening**. If you can, avoid making the opening bid as it gives a great deal of information to the other party. Try not to tell the other party too much and aim to keep control of the meeting's agenda.
* **Concessions**. Conceding in a competitive situation is seen as a sign of weakness, so do this as little as possible. The size of the first concession gives the opposing party an idea of the next best alternative, and tells them exactly how far they push you.
* **Conflict**. If conflict flares up, negotiators need to use assertiveness skills to maintain a prime position, and to defuse the situation.

What is collaborative negotiation?

Many people see negotiation as a battle where the stronger party defeats the weaker party, that is, there is a winner and a loser. In some cases, negotiations can break down altogether, such as in industrial disputes which result in strike action. In this scenario, nobody wins, so there are only losers. It needn't be like this, however. Trying in collaborative negotiation, conflict is minimised and the whole idea is to reach a solution where everyone benefits. This approach tends to produce the best results, mainly because there is much better communication between the parties. In addition, it makes for better long-term relations if it's necessary to work together over a long period.

The opening will involve gathering as much information as possible but also disclosing information so solutions can be developed that are acceptable to both parties. This involves:

* considering a number of alternatives for each issue
* using open questions (which do not have yes/no answers)
* being flexible
* helping the other party to expand their ideas about possible solutions

Both parties will make concessions if necessary, normally aiming to trade things which are cheap for them to give but valuable to the opposing party, in return for things which are valuable to them (but may not be so cheap for the other party).

By listening, summarising, paraphrasing, and disclosing in collaborative negotiations (for example, 'I would like to ask you a question . . .' or 'I feel that I need to tell you that . . .'), conflict will be kept to a minimum, enabling a mutual advantage to be reached.

MAKE IT HAPPEN

Prepare yourself

As with many business situations, good preparation will help to reduce your stress levels. Don't think that preparation time is wasted time; it's anything but. Begin by working out your objectives, and making sure they are specific, achievable, and measurable. It's also important to have a clear idea of what you're expecting from the other party. Be sure that your expectations are realistic and that their results are easy to assess. It's a good idea to write down objectives and to put them into an order of priority. One way to do this is to classify them as 'must achieve', 'intend to achieve', and 'like to achieve'. For example, a new photocopier has been bought for the office. It breaks down after a week and you need to contact the supplier to sort out the problem. The objectives can be defined as:

* **Must achieve**: The use of a photocopier that works.
* **Intend to achieve**: Get the photocopier repaired.
* **Like to achieve**: Get a replacement photocopier.

Ahead of any negotiation, gather as much information as possible about the subject under discussion. The person with the most information usually does better in negotiations. For example, two people have each prepared a very important document. Let's see how this situation can progress.

They both need to have them processed by the one desktop publishing operator in the firm and couriered to the destination for the following morning. However, there is only time to have one job finished before the daily courier collection at 4pm, so the two argue over whose document is the most vital. If they argue too long, neither job will be finished on time and both would 'lose'. The senior member of staff could pull rank, resulting in the junior being the 'loser', with the possible loss of his future co-operation.

If they obtained more information, they would find out that the courier company runs an optional 6pm collection which also guarantees delivery before 11am the next day. A 'win/win' situation could then be achieved.

Discuss and explore

At the beginning of a meeting, each party needs to explore the other's needs and make tentative opening offers. Remember that these need to be realistic or it's unlikely that the discussion will progress to a successful conclusion for everyone. If both parties co-operate, you can make progress; however, if one side adopts a competitive approach and the other does not, problems may arise. You need, then, to analyse the other party's reaction to what's said.

An opening statement is a good way of covering the main issues at stake for each party, and allows the discussion to develop naturally. At this stage, the issues are just being discussed and not yet negotiated. What you're trying to do is develop a relationship with the other person. Ask questions to help you identify their needs and help to keep things moving. As a way of doing this, ask open-ended questions that the person can reply to fully rather than closed questions to which he or she can only answer 'yes' or 'no'. For example, you could begin by saying 'Tell me your thoughts about [the issue under discussion]'.

Make a proposal

Once both parties have had chance to assess the other's position, proposals and suggestions can be made and received. Remember that you need to trade things and not just concede them. The following phrase is valuable:

'If you [give to, or do something for, us], then we'll [give to, or do something for, you]'.

Look for an opportunity to trade things that are cheap for you to give but of value to the other party, in return for things which are valuable to your business. For example, if you are a painter and decorator who needs to rent a reasonably priced flat, you could negotiate with the landlord to paint certain rooms in return for a lower rent. Or say you need to publicise a product and would like to engage someone to do some work for you, but can't quite afford to pay the job rate they had in mind. If you or your business have a website, you could offer to put a click-through link from your website to theirs so that anyone who reads their article can find out more about them and perhaps offer them more work.

Start the bargaining

After discussing each other's requirements and exchanging information, the bargaining can start (as in the first example above). Generally speaking, the more you ask for, the more you get, while you'll concede less if you don't offer as much at the beginning. For example, let's say you've something to sell to another party. You know you have a premium product, but you're not sure quite how blank the other party's cheque is. If you know you'd be happy to sell for £200, you might want to start off by asking for £300, knowing that:

* you'll be able to look as if you're giving ground to the other party
* they think they're getting a bargain
* you may even get a better deal than you'd thought!

If conflict arises when the bargaining starts, explain that the opening position is just that, an opening position and therefore not necessarily the one that will be adopted at the end of the negotiation. Ultimately, an agreement can only be reached when both parties find an acceptable point somewhere between their individual starting positions.

When you make an offer, be very clear about what's on the table. Avoid using words such as 'approximately' or 'about', as an experienced negotiator will spot an opportunity to raise the stakes quite dramatically. Don't make the whole process harder for yourself. For example, if you can only offer £600 for something, say so, or before you know it you'll be being pressed into agreeing to go up to £700.

Similarly, when the other party makes their offer, make sure you find out exactly what it includes. For example, if you're negotiating with a supplier, check whether the cost they are quoting you contains delivery, VAT, and so on or not. Ask for clarification if there's anything you're not sure about and check that the offer matches all the criteria that you noted down during the preparation stages as being on your list of requirements.

Communicate clearly but openly

When you're negotiating with someone face-to-face, use open body language and maintain eye contact. Try to avoid sitting with your arms folded and your legs crossed, for example. Also, try to think through what you're about to say before you say it. Don't use language that will annoy the other person. For example, try to avoid using words like 'quibbling' and 'petty'. Even if you think someone is doing or being either of these things, using these words to them will only make the situation worse. Don't be sarcastic or demean them, their position, or their offer.

Similarly, if you feel that the main discussion is losing its focus and that people are starting to make asides to colleagues, address this by saying 'I sense there's something you're unhappy about. Would you like to discuss it now?'

Listen!

Sometimes when you're nervous about something, you become so focused on what you want to say that you don't pay enough attention to what's being said to you. This can cause all manner of problems, including knee-jerk reactions to problems that aren't really there but which you think you've heard. Active listening is a technique which will improve your general communication skills and will be particularly useful to practise if you have to negotiate a lot. Active listening involves:

* concentrating on what's being said, rather than using the time to think of a retort of your own.
* acknowledging what's being said by your body language. This can include keeping good eye contact and nodding.
* emphasising that you're listening by summarising your understanding of what has been said and checking that this is what the communicator intended to convey.
* empathising with the communicator's situation. Empathy is about being able to put yourself in the other person's shoes and imagine what things are like from their perspective.
* offering interpretations and perceptions to help move the communication forward, then listening for agreement or disagreement. This enables both

parties to start exploring the territory more openly. It's important to listen *for* at this point, which enables you to remain open to new ideas and to think positively about the other's input. Listening *against* results in you closing down to new information and automatically seeking arguments why something won't work.

* questioning and probing brings forth more information and will clear up any misunderstandings about what's being said. If you want to explore someone's thoughts more thoroughly, open questions are helpful. 'Tell me more about . . .?', 'What were your feelings when . . .?', 'What are your thoughts . . .?' These questions encourage the speaker to impart more information than closed questions, that merely elicit a 'yes' or 'no'.
* not being afraid of silence. We often feel compelled to fill silences, even when we don't really have anything to say—yet silence can be helpful in creating the space to gather thoughts and prepare for our next intervention.

Call a break if you need to

Sometimes a short break of 10 or 15 minutes may be a good thing if a negotiation is proving to be more complex or contentious than you'd previously thought. A break will give everyone a chance to cool down or recharge his or her batteries as necessary. It'll also give everyone an opportunity to take a step back from the issue under discussion and return to the table with some ideas if there had previously been an impasse.

Reach agreement

As the discussion continues, listen for verbal indications from the other party such as 'maybe' or 'perhaps'—these could be signs of an agreement being in sight. Also look out for non-verbal signs, like papers being tidied away. Now is the time to summarise what has been discussed and agreed and not to start bargaining again.

Summaries are an essential part of the negotiation process. They offer a way of making sure that everyone is clear on the decisions reached and also give all participants a final chance to raise any questions they may have. As soon as possible after the negotiation, send a letter that sets out the final, agreed decision. A handshake on a deal is fine, but no substitute for a written record. Make sure your letter mentions:

* the terms of the agreement
* the names of those involved
* relevant specifications or quantities
* any prices mentioned plus discounts and so on
* individual responsibilities
* time schedules and any deadlines agreed

Negotiate over the phone or e-mail

Today, most negotiations take place by e-mail or over the phone. To succeed without the 'clues' you get from actually seeing the other person:

* Arrange a time that will allow you to do some preparation beforehand. If someone 'ambushes' you and you're caught off guard, ask if you can ring them back in half an hour or so.
* Have all the necessary paperwork close at hand. For example, if you're discussing the renewal of a contract, make sure you've a copy close by that you can refer to. Also have plenty of paper nearby that you can use to make notes on.
* Make sure that you won't be disturbed. If you have an office, close the door. If you work in an open-plan office, see if you can book a meeting room elsewhere in the building so that you won't be distracted by other people's conversations around you.
* Even though the other party can't see you, use the body language you would use if they were there in person, for example nod if you agree, move your hands as you speak. All of this will filter back in the tone of your voice.
* Take a break and arrange to call the other person back if things are getting heated or you've reached a stalemate.
* Once agreement has been reached, follow up in writing as you would do if you'd conducted a face-to-face negotiation.

WHAT TO AVOID

You open negotiations with an unreasonable offer

Both parties need to see a reasonable chance of getting what they want from the negotiation process. By starting off with an unreasonable offer, you risk killing the process before it starts, or at least increasing the level of mistrust.

You begin negotiations without enough information about what the other party wants

The early discussion and information gathering phases need to be used properly to ensure that both parties aren't 'talking past each other'. Before negotiation begins, you need to have a broad view of the points you might need to concede on, and what you want the other party to concede to you. These can then be 'traded' in accordance with your bottom line.

You let the arguments become personal and vindictive

There is often the temptation for negotiations to become sparring matches between individuals; the risk is that parties could lose sight of the goal of the negotiation if arguments become personal point-scoring exercises.

You lose your temper

Some people are much easier to negotiate with than others and there's a difference between a serious, probing discussion and a bad-tempered slanging match laced with sarcasm. If someone is rude to you while you're negotiating with him or her, don't rise to the bait (even though it can be tempting). Instead, address them politely but assertively, and challenge their behaviour. You could say something like 'I think that comment was inappropriate and unhelpful. Shall we return to the issue?'

You try to rush negotiations in pursuit of a quick agreement

Both parties need to feel comfortable with the pace and direction of negotiations as they develop. This could mean that one or other party might need time to consider certain points or options before moving on to others. You need to respect this need, while at the same time making sure that both parties observe a flexible timeframe for resolution. Endless negotiations will only waste time and money.

USEFUL LINKS

Acas: **www.acas.org.uk**
learndirect: **www.learndirect.co.uk**
Learning and Skills Council: **www.lsc.gov.uk**

Deal with Stress

For many individuals, joining the enterprise culture has entailed a substantial personal cost: stress. The word 'stress' has found as firm a place in our modern lexicon as 'fast food', 'mobiles' and 'CDs'. 'It's a high stress job', people often say, awarding an odd sort of prestige to an occupation. But for people whose ability to cope with day-to-day matters is at crisis point, the concept of stress is not a matter of bravado. For them, stress can be translated into a four-letter word: *pain*.

My boss thrives on pressure and expects me to do the same, but I work more effectively in a less intense environment. How can we work well together?

This is a common problem. If you can find a way to work together, however, your differing styles can actually complement each other. Try to broach this issue with your boss, and put together a plan of action. Having done that, you still may find it easiest to limit your contact with your boss while working on joint projects.

I work well under pressure and have no problem with it, but it's now affecting my relationships with others who don't. What do I do?

Although pressure often gives us the boost we need to get a job done well and on time, it can, however, become so habitual that we fail to recognise its constant presence in our workplace. While people can become very focused in such an environment, they may also begin to neglect other parts of their lives such as their relationships with friends and family, or even their health. In the long term, pressure isn't a desirable permanent fixture in working life. If you feel as if this is your organisation's preferred way of working, it may be time for you to raise the issue.

How do I maximise the benefits and minimise the downside of pressure?

Pressure can raise our performance, but sometimes it can be at the detriment of other factors such as relationships. Under pressure people often become highly task-orientated and focus on the immediate areas. Other people become very short-term orientated. Explore what happens to you, seek feedback, and evaluate whether you believe there's an issue or not. The earlier you recognise it, the easier it is to ensure that the negative impact of pressure is alleviated.

How do I know when I'm beginning to suffer from stress?

It's important to be able to distinguish between pressure and stress. Pressure is motivating, stimulating, and energising. But when pressure exceeds our ability to cope, stress is produced. Continued high levels of stress can, at worst, result in illness, depression, or even nervous breakdown. However, there are a number of warning signals that can help you detect when your levels of stress are bordering on dangerous.

Take a good look at your well-being. If you experience any number of the following behavioural and physical symptoms on a frequent or near-constant basis, it can indicate that you've crossed over the dividing line between healthy pressure and harmful stress.

Behavioural symptoms	Physical symptoms
Constant irritability with people	Lack of appetite
Difficulty in making decisions	Craving for food when under pressure
Loss of sense of humour	Frequent indigestion or heartburn
Suppressed anger	Constipation or diarrhoea
Difficulty concentrating	Insomnia
Inability to finish one task before rushing into another	Tendency to sweat for no good reason
Feeling the target of other people's animosity	Nervous twitches or nail biting
Feeling unable to cope	Headaches
Wanting to cry at the smallest problem	Cramps and muscle spasms
Lack of interest in doing things after returning home from work	Nausea
	Breathlessness without exertion
Waking up in the morning and feeling tired after an early night	Fainting spells
	Impotency or frigidity
Constant tiredness	Eczema

MAKE IT HAPPEN

Identify the sources of stress at work

Once you've admitted that you're not coping with the everyday pressures of work, the next step in the process is to identify the source(s) of the stress in the workplace. Once this is done, you can draw up a plan of action to minimise or eliminate the excess pressure or damaging source of stress.

Make a note of problem areas. The list over identifies some possible daily hassles that trouble people at work. There are, of course, more significant problem areas as well, such as coping with redundancy, dealing with a bullying boss or trying to cope with a dysfunctional corporate culture (one that demands excessive working hours or employs an autocratic management style).

Daily Hassles at Work

Trouble with client/customer
Having to work late
Constant people interruptions
Trouble with boss
Deadlines and time pressures
Decision-making
Dealing with the bureaucracy at work
Technological breakdowns
Trouble with work colleagues
Tasks associated with job not stimulating
Too much responsibility
Too many jobs to do at once
Telephone interruptions
Travelling to and from work
Travelling associated with the job
Making mistakes
Conflict with organisational goals
Job interfering with home/family life
Can't cope with in-tray
Can't say no to work
Not enough stimulating things to do
Too many meetings
Don't know where career going
Worried about job security
Spouse/partner not supportive about work
Family life adversely affecting work
Having to tell colleagues unpleasant things, e.g. redundancy

Work towards a work–life balance

Managing pressure is about achieving some balance in your life and activities. It's usually in the workplace that we're most susceptible to pressure, but be aware that it sometimes stems from home or the social environment. Pressure can make us do or say things that, on reflection, we wish we hadn't. Where possible, try to make sure that work isn't the central focus of your life. For example, take advantage of your allotted number of holidays, take exercise regularly, and maintain your relationships with friends and family. Having hobbies and interests that help you to 'turn off' is also very useful. Try to raise your concerns with your manager.

Know the causes and types of pressure

There are numerous causes of pressure in the workplace today, many of which are linked. Some of the most obvious are:

* insufficient resources—not enough time, funds, or staff to get the job done properly
* insufficient *appropriate* resources—skills gaps in certain areas
* unreasonable demands—management expecting everyone to operate constantly at 120%
* improper staffing or staff direction—failure to understand what different people are capable of
* insufficient training
* poor planning
* promising to do too much too quickly
* lack of job security

There are also many *types* of pressure. The most common is time pressure—too much to do and too little time to do it in. However, there are plenty of coping strategies to help manage it and to smooth out organisational problems. For example:

* Anticipate where the pressure may come from.
* Break up overwhelming tasks into smaller jobs.
* Draw up a 'to do' list of all the tasks you need to complete in the short term (that is, within the next week) and in the long term.
* Reserve your prime time for working, when your energy levels are high, for complex tasks, and save the trivial or routine tasks for non-prime time.
* When planning your work schedule, attempt to balance routine tasks with the more enjoyable jobs.
* Accept that risks are inevitable and that no decisions are ever made on the basis of complete information.
* Communicate progress to other stakeholders in the task and manage expectations. For example, if a task will take longer to complete than originally thought, be upfront. The sooner you alert people to potential problems, the sooner you can work together to plan for contingencies.
* Learn to say 'I don't know', when you don't know something or 'I don't understand' when you don't understand a task, a role, or an objective.
* Manage technology rather than let the technology manage you. For example, with phones, plan what you're going to say and need to know in advance; prioritise your e-mails according to their importance to your objectives; and don't keep your mobile switched on all the time because it could interrupt an important meeting or activity.

While these things may not alleviate time pressure by actually extending your deadline, it will allow you to feel more in control.

Where time pressure continues to be an issue, it may indicate that you need to re-evaluate your role and its demands and resources. Are you delegating enough? Have you prioritised your actions? Are you promising to do too much too quickly?

It's worth reading the following actionlists: *Manage Your Time*, *Make Sound Decisions*, *Delegate without Guilt*, and *Solve Thorny Problems*. These deal with the areas of everyday working life that can be most problematic for people and lead to stress when mismanaged.

Find a solution

Organisational: Where pressure exists, it could be as a result of the nature of the job, or of how the role fits in with the rest of the business. Your role or job may need to be renegotiated with different boundaries put in place. Clearer lines of responsibility, as well as better delegation and prioritisation, will help reduce pressure on individuals, teams, and departments.

Better planning, with the ability to anticipate pressure points, can help ensure that resources are in the right place at the right time. Sometimes pressure is unavoidable, but certainly more bearable if it's for short periods of time.

Personal: On a personal level (i.e. intellectual, behavioural, and physical), we may put ourselves under pressure when we lose confidence in our ability. Having a good self-awareness and understanding of our real skills is important. Building and supporting confidence is also invaluable.

Be aware of how you respond to pressure. Some symptoms you display may be positive and motivating, others not. Know your balance and how others respond. At the same time, be aware of pressure in others. No two people respond to pressure in the same way.

Physically there are things we can do to help manage pressure. Exercise is good from a health viewpoint, and may allow pent-up frustration to be exercised out. Even stretching in your chair, going for a quick walk, or talking to a friend or confidante are good remedies for relieving pressure. Try to take a break, either through regular holidays or possibly, for those who need to move further away from the situation, sabbaticals, job rotations, or study leave.

Most important to remember is that you're not alone in managing pressure. Having a sense of humour can help, as can remembering to step back from a situation. It's important to tackle the underlying causes of pressure if you can, rather than just dealing with the symptoms. Above all, remember that you're not alone. Don't hesitate to confide in a friend or colleague or seek counselling if you need help, as some causes are much more overwhelming than others. For example, you could have caring responsibilities for a sick family member, your marital status may have changed, or you may be ill yourself. In these circumstances, talking to someone may help you to see things from a broader perspective and to take the first step towards a solution.

WHAT TO AVOID

You think you can do it all alone

People sometimes take on too much, thinking that they can cope without additional support. Perhaps you think you're saving your organisation money by covering a number of responsibilities—but in reality you could be wasting money in missed opportunities or inefficiency. Often, under pressure, the one thing we become incapable of doing well is delegating work appropriately. Better communication and prioritising objectives are therefore essential. Working on identifying better resource management, prioritising the workload, building in time/slack, anticipating pressure points, and monitoring progress are all important in dealing with pressure.

You don't say 'no'

Perhaps you're one of those people who are capable of sustaining high levels of activity over a long period of time, and it has become expected that you always perform at that pitch. Your colleagues are unlikely to be aware of the sacrifice being made. There may be no reward for your sacrifice—in fact, you may have additional work dumped on you. The solution is about being assertive and saying no when the pressure is too great. Like a car, you can't stay in fifth gear all the time; you have to vary your speed and occasionally have a 'pit stop'.

You succumb to a 'long hours culture' at work

In some organisations, pressure creates status, where pressure is interpreted as accomplishment. Many people put in long hours in the hope that their hard work will be noticed and rewarded, but are secretly resentful that they have to do this. Working on outputs rather than inputs will help define your success. Find out whether others view hard work as positive or not.

You take it out on others

Pressure is no respecter of boundaries. Pressure from one aspect of your life will eventually affect all other elements of your life, too. Be aware of how these pressures may affect your work performance. Try not to transfer them to those who aren't part of the problem. Work on the causes and not the symptoms. Compartmentalisation will only work in the short term.

USEFUL LINKS

About Stress Management: **http://stress.about.com**
Mind Tools: **www.mindtools.com/smpage.html**

Maintain a Healthy Work–Life Balance

'Time flies when you're having fun' goes the adage. Time also flies when you're very busy—but rather than having fun, you can soon find yourself stressed out in a way that affects not only your mental and emotional wellbeing, but your physical health. When there isn't enough time in the day, something has to give: but is it to be your work or your personal life? Achieving a balance has become one of the burning issues of the day.

Here are some of the main reasons why more and more people are addressing the topic of work–life balance:

* **More women joining the workforce means more demands on parents to juggle job and family.**
* **More people living longer means more workers with the care demands of elderly relatives.**
* **More pressure and longer hours at work on account of modern technology (for example, overflowing inboxes, Internet information deluge, and ringing phones) mean people 'burning out' younger.**

The broad argument for greater balance and flexibility at work is that greater satisfaction among employees will lead to fewer stress-related illnesses, less time taken off for sickness, lower staff turnover, and higher productivity. People with a good balance between their work and other responsibilities and interests tend to be more motivated and productive: in other words, happy people work better.

What is work–life balance?

Work–life balance is about modifying the way you work in order to accommodate other responsibilities or aspirations in other areas of your life. Although there has been much attention of late on making things easier for parents of young children or people who care for dependents, quality of life is important for everyone, and achieving a happy work–life balance is an important part of that.

I don't know if my boss cares about my work–life balance. Do the 'people in charge' really take it seriously?
Thankfully, growing numbers of businesses are becoming aware of the importance of allowing their employees to strike a balance between their work and personal lives, and hopefully your boss will wake up to this. If you want to talk to him or her about it, explain that flexibility in the workplace is actually driven by a business need — working cultures and attitudes are changing in many parts of the world, and employers are beginning to see that they have to adapt to this if they are to recruit and retain their number one asset: their people.

I'm worried that my boss will begrudge me if I ask about flexible working. How can I get what I want without jeopardising my current position by being sidelined?
A popular way of approaching negotiations of any type is to draw up a wish list for your successful outcome that contains an ideal solution, a realistic one, and an absolute minimum. If you show that you're prepared to be flexible, your manager may be willing to meet you half-way. Be realistic but also be ready to compromise.

If you're worried that your boss may disapprove, find out if your organisation will allow you to bring a union representative with you to a meeting to discuss your application. If you do invite one along, make sure he or she has read a copy of your application and any related documents from your place of work so that he or she is up to speed. Part-time working should be attainable without becoming sidelined in the organisation or losing benefits, such as sick pay and holiday pay. If you're concerned about this, you can find out more about your rights as a part-time employee in the Equal Pay Act 1970, and get advice from the Equal Opportunities Commission (**www.eoc.org.uk**).

MAKE IT HAPPEN

Assess your work–life balance

Planning is essential in order to gain a perspective on how your current lifestyle fits in with your ambitions and requirements inside and outside the workplace. Reflect on your work situation—where you are in terms of your career, how fulfilling you find it, how much of yourself you put into it—and then set yourself some career aims, giving yourself a realistic time scale in which to achieve them.

You also need to consider your personal life. What are the most important elements? Who are the most important people to you? How much are you getting out of it? By asking yourself these profound but crucial questions, you can work out what's lacking in your life and what are unwelcome infringements upon it. Decide what you'd like to spend more time on, what you'd like to spend less time on, and then plan how to do it.

It's only once you've established what your aims are and the length of time needed to achieve them, that you can address how changing your work patterns may help you get there.

Be aware of the options

Employees now have the right to take periods of paid maternity, paternity, and parental leave, as well as the right to take time off (either paid or unpaid, depending on circumstances) to care for dependents. There are, however, several other key areas in which you can address your work–life balance needs and preferences. These are:

* **Flexi-time working.** People working on flexi-time schedules are able to vary their start and finishing times, providing they work a set amount of hours during each week or month. This is not only great for parents trying to manage a household as well as a job, but for anyone who finds working within a strict and continuous routine depressing and demotivating. Everyone's energy levels fluctuate during the day, but not necessarily at the same time, and so flexi-time is a good solution to making sure people always work at their peak. Another great advantage, particularly for city-workers and commuters, is that flexi-time gives you the opportunity to avoid rush hour—probably one of the most time-wasting and stressful parts of the day.
* **Part-time working.** Employees with a part-time arrangement may decide between working fewer days each week or fewer hours a day. This option also works well for people with parental or caring responsibilities. The other people who benefit greatly from part-time working are those returning to work after looking after young children, recovering or suffering from illness, and people who are trying to pursue other interests or careers.
* **Job sharing.** This involves two people dividing between them a full-time workload, with each working on a part time basis. This is beneficial if you want to maintain something of your career while being able to spend more time with your children or pursue other interests outside work.
* **Home working or telecommuting.** Many jobs now involve computer-based activities that can be done as easily from an Internet-linked PC at home or in a remote (telecommuting) facility. This style of working benefits not only parents and carers, but can help many people without those kinds of domestic responsibilities to work more productively, especially in tasks that require a great deal of concentration, and uninterrupted peace and quiet. It's unusual for someone to work from home or remotely full-time, but some employers do find it a cost advantage to themselves through the reduced need for fixed office space.
* **Term-time working.** This option allows employees to take time off work during school holidays in order to look after their children. This time off is usually taken as unpaid leave, although the salary can be paid evenly across the year. The sorts of employers most likely to operate this scheme are those in industries that experience seasonal peaks and trough.

The variety of opportunities being adopted by organisations to help you achieve the right balance doesn't stop there. The Department of Trade and Industry website has a fairly comprehensive list (**www.dti.gov.uk/work-lifebalance**). In addition to the options outlined above, it includes:

* Staggered hours: staff work to different start, finish, and break times.
* Compressed working hours: staff work their total weekly number of hours over fewer days.
* Annualised hours: staff have more flexibility about taking time off as working hours are calculated over the year rather than by the week
* Shift swapping: staff negotiate their working times and shifts between themselves.
* Self-rostering: staff state their preferred working times, and then shifts are organised to accommodate as many of those preferences as possible.
* Career breaks: as well as paternity, maternity, and parental leave, staff may also be allowed unpaid career breaks and sabbaticals.
* Time off in lieu: staff are given time-off when they've put in extra hours at work.
* Flexible and cafeteria benefits: staff are offered a choice of benefits so that they can pick those best suited to them.

Make an application for flexible working hours

Do your research. First of all, make sure that you qualify for flexible working arrangements. Most people apply for flexible working because of their family situation. As of April 2003 and under the terms of the Employment Act 2002, parents of children under the age of 6, or of less able-bodied children under the age of 18, may request flexible working hours, but they need to have completed six months' continuous service at the company or organisation in question before making that request. Some organisations may also consider flexible working if you need to care for a dependent adult, such as your spouse, partner, or parent.

Check the employees' handbook or with your human resources department (if you have one) to see what the preferred method of application is. The DTI has some basic forms that may be customised, so your company may be using these already. If not, most companies would expect a request for a change in working hours to be made in writing. This should be followed up within 28 days by a meeting between you and your manager. Bear in mind that only one application can be made in any 12 month period.

Once you've checked out your company's policy, speak to friends or colleagues who have applied for flexible working hours or who already are working under a new arrangement. How did the successful applicants approach their request? Are they finding it easier or harder than they'd anticipated to work in a new way? Bear in mind that if your working arrangements are changed, these changes are permanent unless otherwise agreed between you and your employer.

Make a persuasive case. Prepare your case and try to anticipate the questions your manager may ask you when you meet to talk about your application. Requests can be turned down because managers fear that flexible working arrangements may affect the business, so be prepared to give well thought-out, positive responses to questions such as:

* Will you still be able be an effective team member?
* How would a change in your working hours affect your colleagues?

* What will be the overall effect on the work you do?
* How could a change in your working hours affect the business positively?

Think about when you would want any new arrangement to start and give your company as much notice as you can. This will convey the fact that you're still committed to the company and are thinking about how the potential changes to your working life will fit in overall.

Stress that the quality of your work and your motivation will not change, even if your working hours do. In fact, you'll be more productive as you'll suffer from less stress and will need to take fewer days off sick to look after your children or dependents when they are ill. You could also explain that as part of a reciprocal arrangement whereby all parties benefit, you'd be willing to work extra or longer in times of heavy demand. Finally, but no less importantly, explain how much knowledge and expertise you've built up while you've been working there and how much the company benefits from it.

Follow up. According to the DTI guidelines, you should be informed about the outcome of your application within 14 days of your meeting. If all goes well and an agreement is reached, your new working arrangement and an agreed start date should be set down in writing and copies given to all relevant parties (you, your manager, and the HR department or representative if you have one).

If your request isn't granted, you may appeal within 14 days of receiving the decision. See the DTI website (**www.dti.gov.uk**) for further advice on this issue.

WHAT TO AVOID

You don't prepare well enough

As with all types of negotiation, you need to make sure that you've done your groundwork when you make an application for flexible working hours. First, be aware of your rights by researching the issue: visit the DTI website which sets out the rights and responsibilities of both employers and employees. Second, check your company's stance on the issue, and make sure you follow the procedures properly when submitting a written application. Think through the questions your manager might ask you about the effects of flexible working on your workload and that of your colleagues.

You aren't flexible

Bear in mind that the legislation relating to flexible working hours gives you the right to *request* them: it doesn't mean that your company will necessarily agree to your application, although they have a responsibility to consider it reasonably. If you're flexible when you meet with your manager and open to compromise if your ideal scenario isn't possible, then it's more likely that you'll end up with a result that suits everyone.

You don't think through all the financial implications

Don't forget that when you reduce your hours, it's not just your salary that may be affected. Pension contributions and other benefits may change too. Be sure that when you take the decision to apply for flexible working hours, you'll be able to cope financially if your application is granted.

USEFUL LINKS

DTI website for work–life balance: **www.dti.gov.uk/work-lifebalance**
Employers for work–life balance: **www.employersforwork-lifebalance.org.uk**
Flexibility.co.uk: **www.flexibility.co.uk/issues/WLB/index.htm**
iVillage.co.uk: **www.ivillage.co.uk/workcareer/worklife**

Manage Your Time

Time is a man-made concept. Animals don't understand the idea. They live *in* time; they are in the moment; the present is all that counts. Remembering this can be useful in the business world: being able to focus on the present is often an effective way of getting through laborious tasks and not worrying about the past or future.

In business, time is money. Paradoxically, as technology proliferates (with the promise that it will increase productivity), it simultaneously adds complexity to managers' workloads, frequently with fewer support staff to complete the work. The only realistic way out of such a paradox is to make better use of time.

How can I be a better time manager?

The *desire* to be good at time management is half the battle, but you need to be aware of the choices you have to make. These relate to your overall life balance and the values you hold.

Look at what you're being asked to do and why. If some requests are outside your area of responsibility or expertise, you may need to speak to your boss to clarify the boundaries. If you're told these new things are now a permanent part of your workload, then something else will have to give way—unless, of course, you can improve your time-management capabilities, or delegate some of the tasks.

Perhaps you'll have to be more realistic about your strengths and capabilities. Rather than deadlines being imposed, try to have input into setting realistic ones. Build some slack in the schedule to give yourself the best possible chance of meeting deadlines.

One of my team members seems incredibly disorganised. What can I do to help?

A good team leader often needs to work with individual team members to help them to understand what's expected. Set realistic goals and give them adequate time and resources to complete the work. Additionally, if possible, ask them to examine their performance objectively and identify patterns of behaviour that contribute to being disorganised. Often time management requires a change in habitual behaviour. This can only be achieved by building awareness, charting a clear route, and rewarding success.

I've recently invested in a hand-held organiser but find I am still using a diary as well. How can I get away from using redundant systems?
Plan the time it will take to learn the new technology and transfer your information. Ask for a tutorial from someone who has made the leap already. Then, over a period of a month, wean yourself off the dual system by omitting the diary. You'll soon find the computerised method more versatile and convenient than anything you've used in the past.

MAKE IT HAPPEN

Conduct a 'time audit'

You may find it useful to conduct a 'time audit' on your life. What's the balance between the demands placed upon you at work and those that define your private life? Does this balance satisfy you, or do you find yourself sacrificing one element for another? One key to good time management is being aware of the wider world in which you live and how the component parts relate to one another. Another key is prioritising—if in fact there isn't enough time to satisfy all competing demands—and then choosing how you apportion your time.

Take a large sheet of paper and write your name in the centre. Write all the demands of your life around it. Include work hours, commuting, socialising, eating, sleeping, household duties, and family commitments. Remember that taking time for family and friends, exercise, hobbies, holidays, and just plain fun is important. Mark the number of hours that you dedicate to each of these areas throughout the day, month, or year. This chart graphically represents your life, in terms of the choices and tradeoffs you have made in areas that are important to you.

Ask yourself if this how you want to live your life. You may decide to sacrifice some important areas in the short term, but be aware of what might happen when a particular phase of your life comes to an end. For example, how will you manage if you get married or divorced; when children grow up and leave home; when you get transferred to another position or take another job in another company or city; when you have an accident or long-term illness; when you retire?

Evaluate what action needs to be taken

Take a highlighter and mark those areas on your chart that need attention. If, for instance, you are spending too much time at work, you need to review your professional objectives and decide how to achieve a better balance.

Life is all about choices. You may find that you can win more time by working from home, if your employer will permit it and your family will respect the necessary home-work boundaries.

You'll probably find that there are other ways to prune hours from the day that are otherwise wasted. For instance, if you like to play sport or keep fit, consider finding a club near work where you can go early in the morning, instead of having to fit this in during the evening.

Look for patterns in the way you use your time. You may find that you're constantly in meetings that run late or that you pick up a lot of extra work because you aren't assertive enough in saying no. If you don't have enough time and your own behaviour is contributing to the shortage, change your patterns of behaviour.

Learn to use the right tools

Time-management tools and techniques are only as useful as the time you invest in using them. Some commercially available tools and techniques include:

* handheld organisers, also known as personal digital assistants (PDAs)
* organisers, both computer-based programs and paper diaries or schedulers
* 'to do' lists
* prioritising work according to its importance, and focusing only on the essential
* shared diaries—team, secretarial, professional groups

If you're a person more accustomed to focusing on 'the moment' rather than the 'big picture', it may be a good idea to learn to stand back and look at time as a continuum, in terms of past, present, and future. Doing so gives you a sense or order, structure, and perspective.

Some dos and don'ts of time management

Do	Don't
Undertake a 'time audit'	Spend time on unnecessary activities or those that don't serve your purpose
Be honest about how long things take	Try to undertake the impossible
Build in time for reflecting and learning	Blame others for your disorganisation
Build in time for yourself	Get hung up on process
Delegate wherever you can	Make commitments that you can't meet
Anticipate the pressure of commitments that you make	Expect others to make up for what you can't do
Communicate with others where you have time conflicts	Give up
Plan ahead	

If too much work is the issue, look at your workload, prioritise, and refer back to how it fits your job description. Decide, perhaps in tandem with your manager, which things you're doing that add value to your job and career potential, versus those that are better delegated to others.

The central point is that planning is essential. Bringing time into consciousness will build awareness, and awareness always precedes action.

WHAT TO AVOID

You buy a new gadget but still rely on old time-management tools

If you're going to buy a new device to help you plan your time better, you need to be disciplined in mastering it and using it daily. Don't buy something just for the sake of it and leave it to gather dust.

You expect too much of yourself and become disenchanted

Change is difficult and often requires a new set of skills. The principles of time management sound completely logical and straightforward, but in fact we lead extremely complex lives, and these simple principles are hard to put into practice. Don't overwhelm yourself by trying to change everything at once. Instead, establish a series of small, clear goals, and achieve them one by one.

You're not prepared to break bad habits, and don't ask for help

Old habits do die hard, and one of the hardest to break is the way we structure and use our time. Everyone knows people who are always late or always early, who jump right onto tasks or are terrible procrastinators, who are stressed-out workaholics or who always seem miraculously refreshed and relaxed. The choices we make in managing our time are connected to the way we view ourselves and the world: making different choices affects our sense of identity and our relationships. Take it slowly, look to family, friends, and work colleagues for support in making these changes, and don't rule out taking workshops or looking for a consultant to help you.

USEFUL LINKS

Mind Tools: **www.mindtools.com/pages/main/newMN_HTE.htm**
Time Management Guide: **www.time-management-guide.com**
Total Success: **www.tsuccess.dircon.co.uk/timemanagementtips.htm**

Delegate without Guilt

If you have a team working with you, delegation is a key skill to acquire or develop. Delegation isn't just about giving tasks to others—it's about getting people to take full responsibility for certain key functions or tasks. In order for a business to grow (and for employees to find new paths of development) new people must be employed to take over established functions, allowing others to develop different aspects of the business.

For many of us, it seems to be a natural tendency to want to be in control of everything. We find it difficult to let go of things we know we can do well ourselves. However, if we wish to be successful managers—and to preserve our own sanity—this is exactly what we must learn to do.

Why do people find it difficult to delegate?

There are many reasons why you may find it difficult to delegate. Often, it seems quicker to perform the task yourself rather than bother to explain it to somebody else and then correct his or her mistakes. You might worry that the person will make a bit of a hash of it and it'll take a long time to put right the mistakes they make. On the other hand, you may feel threatened by the competence of a person who is quick on the uptake and does well. There is a fear that the employee may take over the role of being the person the rest of the staff goes to with their problems. They may even find something wrong with the way *you* do things.

If you lack confidence, you may find it hard to give instructions and you'll put off delegating. If you do delegate, and problems arise because the employee fails to do what you've asked him or her to do, you may doubt your own ability to confront the person about his or her actions. If staff have been given increased responsibilities and have done well, you may not be confident of being able to reward them sufficiently. Conversely, you might be reluctant to delegate tasks that you think are too tedious.

Finally, you may realise that delegation is necessary, but you don't know where to start, or how to go about it. You need some kind of method to follow. The following paragraphs will help put you on the right track.

How can delegation help me?

Delegation offers many benefits. Done well, it will allow you to concentrate on the things you do best and also give you the time and space to tackle more interesting and challenging tasks in the future. You'll be less likely to put off making key decisions and you'll be much more effective. Your staff will benefit too; everyone needs new challenges, and by delegating to them, you'll be able to test their ability in a range of areas and increase their contribution to the business. Staff can take quick decisions themselves and they'll develop a better understanding of the details concerned. Done well, delegation should improve the overall productivity of employees.

It's all too tempting to withdraw into 'essential' tasks and not develop relations with your team. The bottom line is that it's wasteful for senior staff to be given big salaries for doing low-value work, and passing tasks down the line is essential if other people are to develop. Not knowing how to do this is recognised as one of the biggest obstacles to small business growth. By delegating, you'll have much more time to do your own job properly.

Delegation doesn't make things easier (there will always be other challenges), but it does make things more efficient and effective. Essentially, it represents a more interactive way of working with a team of people, and it involves instruction, training, and development. The results will be well worth the time and effort you invest in doing it properly.

When should I delegate?

Delegation is fundamental to successful management—look for opportunities to do it. If you have too much work to do, or if you don't have enough time to devote to important tasks, delegate. When it's clear that certain staff need to develop, particularly new employees, or when an employee clearly has the skills needed to perform a specific task, delegate.

What tasks should I delegate?

Begin with any routine administrative tasks that take up too much of your time. There are likely to be many small everyday jobs which you've always done—you may even enjoy doing them (for example, sending faxes)—but they're not a good use of your time. Review these small jobs and delegate as many of them as you can. Being your company's point of contact for a particular person or organisation, which is important but can be time consuming, is also an excellent task to delegate.

On a larger scale, delegate projects that it makes sense for one person to handle; this will be a good test of how the person manages and co-ordinates the project. Give the person something he or she has every chance of completing successfully, rather than an impossible task at which others have failed and which may well prove a negative experience for the person concerned. Tasks for which a particular employee has a special aptitude should be delegated.

Who should I delegate to?

Make sure you understand the person you're delegating to. He or she must have the skills and ability, or at least the potential, to develop into the role and must be someone you can trust. It's a good idea to test out the employee with small tasks that will help show what he or she can do. Also make sure that the employee is available for the assignment—beware of overburdening your effective workers. Delegation should be spread out among as many employees as possible, so think about the possibility of assigning a task to two or more people.

MAKE IT HAPPEN

Be positive

Think positively: you have the right to delegate, and you must delegate. You won't get it 100% right the first time, but you'll improve with experience. Be as decisive as you can and if you need to improve your assertiveness skills, consider attending a course or reading one of the many books on the subject. A positive approach will also give your employees confidence in themselves, and they need to feel that you believe in them.

If you expect efficiency from the person you delegate to, organise yourself first. If there's no overall plan of what's going on, it'll be hard to identify, schedule, and evaluate the work being delegated. Prepare before seeing the person (but don't use this as a ploy to delay!). Assess the task and decide how much responsibility the person will have. Assess the person's progress regularly and make notes.

Discuss the task to be delegated

When you meet the person or people you're delegating to, discuss the tasks and the problems in depth, and explain fully what's expected of them. It's crucial to give people precise objectives, but encourage them to seek these out themselves by letting them ask you questions and participate in setting the parameters. They need to understand why they're doing the task, and where it fits into the scheme of things. Ask them how they'll go about the task, discuss their plan and the support they might need.

Set targets and offer support if necessary

Targets should be set and deadlines scheduled into diaries. Summarise what has been agreed, and take notes about what the person is required to do so everyone is clear. If he or she is given a lot of creative scope and is being tested out, you may decide to be deliberately vague, but if the task is urgent and critical, you must be specific.

How much support you offer and give will very much depend on the person and your relationship with them. In the early stages you might want to work with him or her and to share certain tasks, but you'll be able to back off more as your understanding of the person's abilities increases. Encourage people to come back to you if they have any problems—while it's important to have time alone, you should be accessible if anyone has a problem or the situation changes. If someone needs to check something with you, try to get it back to him or her quickly. Don't interfere or criticise if things are going according to plan.

Monitoring progress is vital—it's very easy to forget all about the task until the completion date, but in the meantime, all sorts of things could have gone wrong. When planning, time should be built in to review progress. If more problems were expected to arise and nothing has been heard, check with the employee that all is well. Schedule routine meetings with the person and be flexible enough to changes deadlines and objectives as the situation changes.

How did it go?

When a task is complete, give praise and review how things went. If an employee's responsibilities are increased, make sure he or she receives fair rewards for it. On the other hand, there may be limits on what can be offered, so don't offer rewards you can't deliver. Also bear in mind that development can carry its own rewards. Such career development issues can be discussed with the employee in appraisals, and the results of delegated tasks noted for this purpose. If the person has failed to deliver, discuss it with them, find out what went wrong, and aim to resolve problems in the future.

WHAT TO AVOID

You expect employees to do things like you do

Managers often criticise the way things are done because it isn't the way they would have done it themselves. Remember that people prefer working in different ways and concentrate on the results rather than the methods used to obtain them.

You don't give people a chance

If you're giving someone something new to do, you must be patient. It'll take time for employees to develop new skills, but it's time that will pay off in the end. Have faith in the people around you.

You delegate responsibility without authority

It's unfair to expect results from someone with one hand tied behind his or her back. If you're going to delegate responsibilities, make sure that those involved know this, and confer the necessary authority upon the person you're delegating to.

USEFUL LINKS

Businessballs.com: **www.businessballs.com/delegation.htm**
iVillage.co.uk: **www.ivillage.co.uk/workcareer/survive/opolitics**
Jobserve.com **www.jobserve.com/news/NewsStory.asp?SID=2009**
Mind Tools: **www.mindtools.com/tmdelegt.html**

Cope with Information Overload

The amount of information available to us wherever we go is increasing rapidly, and as a result, we're all expected to absorb and respond to more information than ever before. There are a number of reasons for this.

* **There are many more means of instant communication and data access. Mobile phones, the Internet, voice-mail, e-mail, instant messaging, and tele- or videoconferencing have all contributed to the vast and fast flow of information.**
* **Despite this increased access to information, fewer people are employed to manage it. Secretaries and personal assistants have been replaced by laptops and PDAs.**
* **Everybody expects information much more quickly. For example, customers are getting used to completing transactions at the click of a button, within just a few minutes. They no longer have to wait for endless copies of paperwork to pass through several pairs of hands before they can place an order.**
* **Business structures have changed so that many projects are now outsourced, demanding clear and rapid communication between many groups of people at once. If an employee's role dictates that he or she is involved with several projects at once, he or she could be deluged with information from all sides!**
* **Globalisation and deregulation have given rise to new opportunities, but they've also increased competition and the need to understand the changing market.**

The problem is that we've all had to deal with this influx without any preparation, training, or time! Often, we find it difficult to process the flood of information—we feel as though we're drowning, struggling to find time for more important tasks. The good news is that there are steps you can take to keep your head above water.

What's the scale of the problem?

Although information overload is a fairly recent phenomenon, it's already claimed casualties. Many of us feel that we have to keep up with the information flow in order to perform well, yet increasing amounts of time are required to help us wade through the massive amounts of data available. This time pressure is resulting in stress and, in some cases, burnout. A worldwide survey conducted by Reuters found that two thirds of managers suffer from increased tension and one third from ill health because of information overload.

What's the result?

Information overload contributes significantly to workplace stress. This is turn affects all areas of your life as it manifests itself in many ways, including increased levels of anxiety, short-term memory problems, poor concentration, and a reduction in your decision-making skills.

MAKE IT HAPPEN

Take control of the problem

Information management, like time management, is a matter of discipline. To get on top of things, you need to set boundaries around how much time you're prepared to spend processing information.

First of all, decide what your limits are and create a personal information management system that works for you. This may be setting boundaries around the time you spend responding to e-mails, filtering them through your assistant (if you're lucky enough to have one), or responding only to those e-mails that hold high importance for you. Draw up some criteria to work out what you allow through your filter and what you want to screen out. This may mean putting priorities on your e-mails and deleting those that are low priority, returning calls only to those people you need to speak to, and only looking at a piece of data once before deciding what to do with it. If you miss something important, don't worry; if it's really that important, it'll come back to you in one way or another.

It's also a good idea to identify time-wasting information and eliminate it. For example, you could ask to be removed from your company's list of often unnecessary 'everyone' e-mails; request a good spam filter from the IT department; or ask for a summary of overly long minutes or reports.

Look for information efficiently

Whenever you're looking for information, keep the 'Pareto principle' in mind. This holds that 20% of what has been accessed probably holds 80% of the information you need. So much information is now at our disposal that anxiety about missing something prompts us to spend far too much time wading through every piece of data available. Remember that before the Internet, people used to make decisions in ambiguous situations; it was considered to be a management skill. Aim to develop your instincts along with your knowledge—both will stand you in very good stead.

As part of your new, efficient approach to knowledge-seeking, find your own preferred places for accessing information and discipline yourself to go there *only*. You already know the high-quality sites for your particular field of work, so why waste time elsewhere? Failing this, you could make use of the information officers in the library of your professional body, if you have one. They're experienced at finding relevant information and can often save you a great deal of time.

Finally, only look at data that is relevant to your job, the project you're working on, or the decision you're making. Bear in mind the principles of time management, as they're just as effective for dealing with information overload. For example, surfing the Web is incredibly seductive, with each link taking you further and further into fascinating but unnecessary detail. Decide how much time you'll spend in each session, print the information that is relevant, and leave the rest in the ether. You often pick up all the information you need in a few hits, the remainder being less fruitful. Remember that the more specific you make your searches, the more efficient they will be—you'll probably pick up most of the information you need in the first ten minutes or so.

Learn to say 'no'

Try not to be the dumping ground for information that others don't want to wade through. This will involve being polite but assertive and also by being sensible; if you're snowed under as it is, don't even hint at being receptive to this type of task. Take control of what passes over your desk and decide not to be held to ransom by data of any type.

Limit your availability

To give yourself some much-need space, leave your mobile phone switched off for periods during the day when you can be quiet and restful or let your voicemail field calls for you. This way you can decide who to speak to and when to schedule the conversations. Anyone who needs to speak to you urgently will always find a way of getting through.

Learn to throw things away!

Don't be a hoarder. Have the courage to throw data away or delete files when you've exhausted their usefulness. You can always access the same data again and, probably when you do, it will have been updated.

Use some tools to help

It may seem rather self-defeating to resort to technology to solve a problem that technology produced in the first place, but there are useful electronic devices that can help alleviate information overload. Hand-held organisers are one example. They have many functions that can be accessed while travelling, making use of otherwise 'dead' time: you can read your e-mails, edit documents, plan meetings, write reports, and even read the newspaper. Any changes can be automatically transferred to your PC when you get back to the office.

WHAT TO AVOID

You get bogged down in detail

Getting drawn into the detail of all the information available wastes time. People often fear they'll miss an essential piece of information if they don't comb through every available source, but in fact this rarely happens. Resist the temptation to scrutinise every piece of information that appears on your screen or arrives on your desk.

You don't prioritise

Being able to prioritise information will save you hours, and you may even find that you can delegate some of the processing to a member of your team, outlining what they should focus on and report back to you. Give your colleague clear instructions and a deadline and try not to contribute to their information overload problem!

You never switch off

Not being able to switch off from the need to absorb or generate information can be tiring and stressful. Blood pressure can rise, mental faculties can deteriorate, and any patience you may have had can disappear altogether. Just as the body needs time to relax, so does the mind—and not just when it's in the sleep state. Quieting the mind through techniques such as meditation or yoga has been proven to increase health, improve memory, and stimulate creativity. It has also been linked to increased productivity and a sense of wellbeing. If these techniques don't appeal, try other recuperative pursuits such as listening to music, reading, or taking gentle exercise. Anything that allows the mind to ' freewheel' will help a great deal.

USEFUL LINKS

Computer Bits: **www.computerbits.com/archive/1998/0200/infoload.html**
Microsoft Windows Mobile: **www.microsoft.com/windowsmobile/default.mspx**
Palm: **www.palm.com**

Manage Your Inbox

E-mail has completely changed the way we work today. It offers many benefits and, if used well, can be an excellent tool for improving your own efficiency. Managed badly, though, e-mail can be a waste of valuable time. Statistics indicate that office workers need to wade through an average of more than 30 e-mails a day, while managers or people working on collaborative projects could be dealing with a much higher figure.

This actionlist sets out steps to help you manage the time you spend dealing with e-mail so that you can get on with other tasks. It offers help on prioritising those incoming messages and deciding how quickly you need to respond. It tells you how to file e-mail according to its value or function and encourages you to clear the inbox regularly. Despite your best efforts, unsolicited e-mail or spam can clutter up the most organised inbox and infect your computer system with viruses, so this section gives guidance on protecting yourself. It also offers alternatives to e-mail that offer the same benefits of speed, convenience, and effectiveness.

Does it really matter how many e-mails I have in my inbox?

Actually, it does. Firstly, you're not making life any easier for yourself by having hundreds (or thousands!) of messages sitting there unfiled, unread, or not acted on. If you need to find something quickly, you'll have to trawl through the whole lot to find what you need; even if you search electronically, the more messages you have for the software to look through, the longer it will take. Taking control of your inbox is a way of taking control over your work as well. Secondly, if you have hundreds of e-mails you don't really need, imagine how many there are in all your colleagues' inboxes.

Hundreds of thousands if not millions, and these will clog up your company's computer systems and cause programs to crash. You know that collective groan that goes round when a system goes down? By not pruning your e-mails, you're contributing to it!

MAKE IT HAPPEN

Prioritise incoming messages

If you're regularly faced with a large volume of incoming messages, you need to prioritise your inbox—identify which of the e-mails is really important.

* **Check the names of the senders. Were you expecting or hoping to hear from them? How quickly do you need to deal with particular individuals?**
* **Check the subject. Is it an urgent issue or just information? Is it about an issue that falls within your sphere or responsibility, or is it something that should just be forwarded to someone else?**
* **Check the priority given by the senders. Do they really mean it's urgent? Remember that some people have a tendency to mark all of their messages 'important', even if they're anything but.**
* **Is it obvious spam? Can it be deleted without reading?**
* **Check the time of the message. Has it been in your inbox a long time?**

An initial scan like that can help you identify the e-mails that need your immediate attention. The others can be kept for reading at a more convenient time.

Reply in stages

Because e-mail is an 'instant' medium, it can be tempting to reply immediately but that might not always be necessary. You can reply in stages, with a brief acknowledgement and a more detailed follow-up. If you do this, give the recipient an indication of when you'll be able to get back to him or her and try to keep to this deadline wherever possible.

If the e-mail simply requires a brief, one line answer then by all means reply immediately. For example, if all you need to say is, 'Yes, I can make the 10.00 meeting', or 'Thanks, that's just the information I needed', do it. If you're unable to reply there and then or choose not to, let the sender know that you've received the message and will be in touch as soon as possible. This is a useful method of dealing with a query when:

* **you need to get further information before replying in full**
* **you need time to consider your response, rather than giving a rushed answer**
* **you're angry, upset, frustrated, or confused about a message you've received and need a cooling-off period before you make a considered response**

Taking a staged approach is useful as it allows you to maintain contact while not interrupting other work that may be more important. It also gives you a bit of breathing space if you're feeling under pressure or worried about the issue under discussion.

Set specific times for dealing with incoming e-mail

Good time management is essential in all areas of our life and e-mail is no exception. If you're completely overwhelmed by the volume of messages in your inbox, dedicate a certain amount of time each day to sorting it out.

If you don't work in a traditional office setting you may have 'dial-up' e-mail where you contact a service provider to check your inbox. Set a pattern for dialling-in that fits in well with the type of work you do and the amount of e-mails you expect, and stick to it.

If you have a broadband connection that is 'always on', your computer will let you know when you receive a new message. Think about whether to review the new messages immediately or wait till a pre-determined time. For example, if you've preferred working patterns or core working hours—times when you need to be available for contact with overseas clients, for example—you may decide to dedicate a certain portion of the day to dealing with your e-mail.

If you spend a lot of time in meetings, you may find that you have short spells between meetings (say 10 or 15 minutes) that would otherwise be wasted time. Use these breaks to catch up with your e-mail so that you don't have a flood of them waiting for you at the end of the day.

Use a filing system to manage your messages

What do you do with incoming messages once you've read them? If the information is important, you may want to keep it for future reference. However, hoarding all your messages in no particular order will not only slow you down when you're looking for information, but is also likely to make your computer system unwieldy and likely to crash.

Check whether your company has a policy for retaining and storing e-mails. Archiving may be essential for legal reasons and if there is a policy in place, you must comply with it. Your company may have a central facility for storing or accessing archived e-mails so investigate with your computer officer or helpdesk, if you have one. You'll be making their lives easier as well!

If you have a lot of important information you need to hang on to (deals done over e-mail for example, or sign-offs from partners that need to be kept), create your own filing system. For example, you could sort messages into folders arranged by:

- customer or supplier name
- project name
- date of receipt
- research topic

Using subfolders will help you keep organised too: for example, for each project it may be useful to subdivide everything into monthly or yearly folders. This will also make it easier to see what should be archived and when.

To save space in your inbox, you might want to copy important e-mails relating to a specific project or programme into other applications. For example, you could create a

Word document called 'project communications', in which all relevant e-mails or messages are held centrally. Everyone will then be able to access the information if you're away for any reason and you'll all be able to find what you need quickly.

Practise good housekeeping

If you don't file your incoming messages as described above, make sure you comb through your inbox regularly. If your inbox is chock-full of every message you've received during the course of a working week, a simple search for an important message could take an awful lot of time.

Unless you need to keep messages for legal reasons, it's generally good practice to delete them regularly. Regular 'pruning' will help you keep on top of things. To help you do this, some e-mail applications offer an option that asks you if want to empty your deleted items folder every time you exit the application. This useful option will ease you into good e-mail management practice!

Remember to:

- **set time limits for keeping messages in your inbox**
- **file or archive any messages that you need to keep**
- **make sure that you've replied if a response was necessary**
- **keep any valuable information, such as contact names or phone numbers**
- **send unwanted messages to the 'deleted messages' section of your e-mail system, but check again before you finally clear that section**

Make arrangements for e-mails when you're away

Opening your inbox after a holiday or a few days away can be an intimidating experience. 'You have 90 new messages'—where do you begin? Prioritising is a good starting point, but a few minutes spent making arrangements before you leave the office will save you a lot of time on your return.

- **Leave an 'out of office reply' on your system. This responds automatically to incoming e-mails, telling the sender that you're away and will deal with the message on your return. It won't stop the first message from a particular sender, but it may prevent further material or messages from the same person asking why you haven't replied.**
- **As part of your 'out of office reply', state when you're back in the office so that your correspondent has a rough idea of how long you'll be away. If you're expecting a lot of messages or are at a crucial stage in a big project, ask one of your colleagues if you can nominate them to be an alternative point of contact during your absence, and if your colleague agrees, give his or her e-mail and telephone number in your 'out of office reply'.**

Alternatively, ask a colleague to check your inbox regularly for particular types of message and either acknowledge them or deal with the issue, if possible. This will make sure that urgent items receive the right level of attention.

Offer alternatives to e-mail

Although e-mail is one of the most popular and convenient ways of communicating quickly, there are practical and effective alternatives:

* instant messaging, which allows short messages to be communicated between connected computers on a network. This is ideal for brief communications, such as 'meeting changed to 11.00', or 'send me the latest sales figures'.
* voicemail, which again allows the caller to leave messages that you can respond to when you're ready.
* teleconferencing, where a number of people can join in a telephone discussion and make decisions without long e-mail chains.
* introduction of informal meeting areas which promote real collaboration.

A good deal of e-mail communication comes from external sources, but think about how many e-mails you send each day to your colleagues in the office, or receive from them. Are they all absolutely necessary? If not, why not take the initiative and ask whoever is responsible for company-wide e-mail management to instigate some basic rules that will cut down on internal e-mails? The policies could cover:

* mass copies of e-mail to recipients who don't really need it (for example, sending a e-mail about a project to everyone in the business when only a small group of people need to be kept informed)
* personal e-mail
* limits on the 'thread' of a discussion which covers every point made by every recipient.

Protect against spam

Spam or unwanted e-mail, like the unsolicited direct mail that comes through your letterbox, is a tremendous waste of time and can clog up your e-mail system. It's a real and growing problem for businesses in the United Kingdom: in December 2003, the Institute for Enterprise and Innovation at the University of Nottingham found that UK office workers spent up to an hour per day deleting spam from their inboxes. That hour could be very well spent tackling other items on your to-do list, so think about the following ways to limit or prevent spam:

* Use a filter supplied by your Internet service provider. This can block e-mails that contain certain terms or other attributes that identify the message as potential spam.
* If it's practical, set rules for your incoming e-mail. Some rules block all incoming e-mail except messages from addresses you've nominated. This is helpful to a certain degree, but can cause problems for new legitimate contacts or organisations that have changed their addresses.
* Unsubscribe to any services or newsletters that that you do not wish to receive. The incoming e-mail should provide you with details of how to remove your address from their list.

* Do not give permission for your e-mail address to be passed on to other parties when you when you subscribe to or register for a new service. At some stage in the registration or subscription process, you should be asked whether or not you give permission for this to happen, normally in the form of a short statement plus a preference box that you need to tick. Read any such requests very carefully.
* As a last resort, change your e-mail address. It might take less time to send a new e-mail address to everyone on your contact list than it does to delete your daily spam load.

Not only does spam e-mail clog up your inbox, but it can pass on viruses that may spread throughout your computer system. You should immediately delete any suspicious e-mails and then empty your 'deleted items' folder. Most companies will have invested in the most up-to-date anti-virus software they can afford, but if you work from home or are self-employed, it's up to you to make sure your machine is virus-free. Scan your computer regularly for viruses and make sure you have the relevant software and security patches. The links at the end of this actionlist will help you find out more about this.

WHAT TO AVOID

You react immediately to every e-mail

Like a ringing telephone, it can be hard to ignore a new incoming message. It takes discipline to wait for a convenient moment or scan the message and reply later, but once you've decided on a new approach to dealing with e-mail, stick to it.

You don't clear your inbox regularly

The list of incoming messages can very quickly grow to unmanageable proportions. Clear the inbox regularly or develop a filing system that allows you to respond appropriately and retain useful information.

You have no protection against spam

Spam doesn't just waste your time and fill up your inbox, it can also introduce harmful viruses into your computer or your company network. Make sure you're protected against unwanted e-mail and seek advice from your computer helpdesk team or Internet service provider if you have any concerns.

USEFUL LINKS

BBC Webwise: **www.bbc.co.uk/webwise/askbruce/articles/email/index.shtml**
McAfee: **www.mcafee.com**
Norton: **www.norton.com**

Manage Successful Projects

The progress of companies has always relied on the management of projects. New plants, new methods, new ventures all require dedicated teams working to strict timetables and separate budgets. However, today, managers may spend as much time in interdisciplinary, cross-functional project teams as they do in their normal posts—project management has now become a core competence for all managers. This applies not only to projects undertaken for customers (external projects), but also to those undertaken for the development of the business itself (internal projects).

All businesses, regardless of size, have problems and opportunities they need to address. These may be related to introducing new technology, developing people, or introducing new products, processes and systems; there is always something, somewhere that needs to be created or improved.

Project management is the key tool for tackling change, and is well suited to meet the needs of modern businesses, big or small. Unfortunately it's too often thought of as something 'for techies', rather than the powerful business tool it is. In addition, it's often perceived as an expensive and lengthy exercise. Nothing could be further from the truth. Project management may be as formal or informal as you want—that is your choice. But underlying both formal and informal approaches are the same set of principles, which, if you apply them correctly, will give you the results you need.

In small projects, project management doesn't need sophisticated tools and systems—often a big wall, paper and Post-it® stickers are all you need for planning and control. This actionlist outlines techniques for effective project management.

What exactly is involved?

Understanding the scope and complexity of project management is an essential first step to achieving success. Project management involves the following key elements:

- making sure your projects are driven by your strategy
- using a staged approach to manage your projects
- placing high emphasis on the early stages
- engaging your 'stakeholders' (that is, everyone potentially involved in or affected by a project, such as staff, customers, and suppliers)
- encouraging teamwork and commitment
- ensuring success by planning for it
- monitoring against the plan
- formally closing the project

How can I make sure that a project runs smoothly?

Your project will run much more smoothly if you focus on a few basics.

* Define strategies clearly so that you're better able to eliminate low-benefit, low-value projects.
* Plan through progressive stages: proposal, initial investigation, detailed investigation, development and testing, trial, operation, and closure.
* Concentrate on the early stages of the project, when the decisions taken have a far-reaching effect on the outcome.
* Analyse the project, determine which are the intrinsically risky parts, and act to reduce, avoid, or, in some cases, insure against the risks.
* To make projects succeed, tip the balance of power towards the project and away from your company's normal management structures.
* Focus progress monitoring more on the future than on completion of activities, which doesn't predict that future milestones will be met.

MAKE IT HAPPEN

Make sure your projects are driven by your business vision

Don't waste time on unnecessary projects. Be clear about the 'vision' (that is, what you want to achieve, how, and when) or you'll risk wasting precious resources on ideas that are ultimately worthless and which will risk the business's overall performance.

Use a staged approach to manage your projects

It's very rare to be able to plan a project completely to its conclusion when you've just started work on it. However, it's usually possible at least to plan the next steps in detail and prepare a rough plan for the remainder. As you progress through the project you gather more information, risk is reduced, and confidence in delivery increases. These progressive steps are called 'stages'. Companies have their own names for these, but typically they are:

* **Proposal:** identifying the idea or need.
* **Initial investigation:** having a quick look at the possible requirements and solutions.
* **Detailed investigation:** undertaking a feasibility study of the options, choosing a solution and defining it.
* **Develop and test:** building the solutions.
* **Trial:** piloting the solution.
* **Release:** putting it into practice and closing the project.

You should use the same generic stage names **for all your projects**. This makes the use and understanding of the process very much easier, avoiding confusion and the need to learn different terms for various types of project. What differs is the content of each project, the extent to which each stage is used, the level of activity, the nature of the activity, the resources required, the stakeholders and decision-makers needed.

As a minimum you should have two stages (Plan it and Do it!). The five stage model would be for more complex projects. The 'stages' are the periods of time during which the work is done. The 'gates' are entry points to each stage and are key checkpoints for revalidating a project and committing resources and funding.

Concentrate on the early stages of the project

Decisions taken during the early stages of a project have a far-reaching effect on the outcome, setting the tone for the rest of the project. Creative thinking and solutions can cut delivery times in half and reduce costs dramatically. On the other hand, once development is under way it's seldom possible to make savings of anything but a few percent while introducing changes later can be very costly. The early stages of a project are therefore fundamental to success. Up to 50% of the project life can be usefully spent on the investigative stages before any final deliverable is physically built. Sound investigative work means objectives are clearer and plans more robust; work spent on this is rarely wasted effort.

Engage your stakeholders and understand their current and future needs

As mentioned above, a stakeholder is any person involved in or impacted by a project. The involvement of stakeholders, such as staff, customers, and suppliers, adds considerable value at all stages of the process. Viewed from a stakeholder perspective, a particular project may be just one more problem they have to cope with as well as fulfilling their usual duties; it may appear irrelevant to them, or even regressive. If their consent is required to make things happen, you ignore them at your peril!

Encourage teamwork and commitment

If you have a team of people working with or for you, involve everyone so that they all work together. This approach really will deliver the best results. If you're managing the project, be as open as you can with your team and they'll appreciate it.

Smaller business often have an advantage over larger organisations in this area as larger businesses have to draw on people in more (and necessarily separate) departments to collaborate on projects, and this can cause all manner of internal problems. As there are fewer line managers in small businesses, the projects are 'business-led' not manager-led, leading to effective delivery. In time, this will also lead to effective change which can be managed as the business grows and matures.

USEFUL LINKS

Mind Tools: **www.mindtools.com/pages/main/newMN_PPM.htm**
Project Workout: **www.projectworkout.com**

Simon Stenner—Managing Projects

Simon Stenner worked in the financial services industry for over 20 years but is now freelance. Simon has recently set up his own company, Stenner Solutions Ltd, and he has over 10 years' experience in project management.

Sorting out the essentials

'At the outset of any project, whatever your industry, you need to have clearly defined scope and objectives/deliverables. Without these how can you know what success will look like? Even when they are clear, "scope creep" can lurch in—the goalposts are changed at the last minute. This can't be helped in some circumstances, but if you *can* avoid it, for example by the project sponsor being called on to help here if the new instructions are coming from "above", so much the better.

'Close monitoring and control of all elements are also essential. If goals *do* change, it's really important to do an impact assessment so that you can judge what the knock-on effect to time, cost, and quality of the project may be. You then need to relay this back to the decision-makers so that they can make a fully-informed final decision.

'Keep a tight rein on schedules, and costs. Constantly assess and adjust them as you need to and make sure that you've built in plenty of contingency to all three. Try to design a project flexibly and build in slack everywhere. For example, when you are putting together budgets, it's advisable initially to build in up to 50% more money than you'd originally forecast you'd need. Build in up to 50% again in timescales too. Contingency levels should decrease as the project goes along, though, and as you get more of a sense of how things are going.

'Interpersonal skills are essential for project managers both within their immediate team and throughout the rest of the organisation. Most projects are based on introducing change to a company and people are naturally resistant to that, so you really need to be able to communicate clearly and persuasively the benefits of your new system, product, or way of working.

'In some cases, you'll need to form your own team. Most large project teams are "cross-functional", which means they're drawn from different departments within the company. This allows you to get the best people with the right expertise, such as budget specialists, design specialists, and so on. As project manager, you then need to meld them together into a team with a common objective.'

Understanding the general principles of project management

'Always take a step back from the detail of project and work out exactly what is needed and who wants it. Why are you embarking on the project? What are its potential benefits? Once all these elements are clear in your mind, you can then turn your attention to the nitty-gritty and the actual planning and delivery of the project. As part of your initial assessment, ask yourself 'is this really a project?'. You need to understand yourself what the project's all about, and then formulate a plan of attack in your mind.

'Know who you're working with and for and make sure that everyone's responsibilities are defined clearly. Full briefings are very important and it's worth drawing up a document that details everyone's roles and responsibilities. You can never give people too much information in terms of what you're expecting them to do and when.

'Work out milestones and be aware of how the project will be 'governed' by those in charge. As mentioned above, many large projects have a project sponsor or steering committee with controlling interests, so you need to make sure you agree progress and your next steps with the right people. Keeping in touch with the steering committee will help the business keep on-side with the project and maintain its commitment to what you're doing. Depending on timescales and the size of the project, at a minimum, it's a good idea to brief the steering committee at the end of each key stage:

* conception
* initiation
* design
* build
* test
* implementation and launch

'If people are dragging their feet about making a decision related to your project, be wary of compromising its benefits just to get a quicker solution as you may end up losing a lot of money or *all* of the project's benefits. For example, if you're introducing a new online product and you're pressurised into skimping on security features, you may run the risk of your product being exposed to fraud. Your customers will be affected, you will have to compensate them, and overall you will lose money, not to mention your good reputation.

Getting the right support

'When you are appointed project manager, it's really important to find out as much as you can about the company or organisation's structure. You need to identify the following key people:

* the project sponsor
* project team members
* stakeholders (in other words, people who will be affected in some way by the project's outcome)
* champions
* opponents

'You need to be aware of key names, places and relevant responsibilities.

'It's also essential that you have full support from all stakeholders and that there is a project sponsor in place. Normally, this would be someone at executive board level who has a hand in decision-making, and ideally, it should be someone who will fight your corner and clear obstacles if needs be. Projects can run into problems when project sponsors don't buy in to the project themselves. This could happen for a variety of reasons: for example, the project may have been delegated to them by their manager and they're unhappy about it; they may not like the way everything's going; or they may not get on with the project manager. Whatever the reason, it can make life more complicated; a good project sponsor can work wonders.

'Good project managers need to be expert and familiar with the relevant tools and techniques that help them do their job well (e.g. excellent organisation and planning skills, results focused, and adept at problem solving and issue resolution), but they also need to have strong interpersonal skills that allow them to get on with a wide range of people—a project could be seriously compromised as a result of a personality clash.'

Enjoying the highs and lows

'It's great to work with a lot of different people, assessing their skills. I enjoy getting on with people at a personal level and breaking through any corporate 'shells' that surround them. I also get a lot of satisfaction from being able to improve the way a company works. It's great to look back at a project, see the finished result, and think "I did that!". For example, when I was working for a large high-street bank, one of the services I developed was taken up by more than 500,000 people.

'I also enjoy the problem-solving side of the job. Good project managers need to adapt constantly to new challenges and think about how things could work better. Project management can be stressful at times, yes, but I think it's inevitable in most people's jobs. Nobody can avoid it completely, but one way to combat it is to try and put it into perspective. The key is to be objective, I think. Remember your achievements then look at the knock-on effects of the stressful situation you're in before reassessing your plans as necessary. Things are never as bad as they seem to be initially.

'The bulk of my project management experience has been in the financial services sector, but I've picked up lots of transferable skills along the way. Many project managers find that they have skills and knowledge which should mean that, theoretically, they can walk into any industry to do a similar job. What's key to making a success of a project, though, is building up a good knowledge of the business or industry in question so that you can put the theory into good practice.'

Avoiding the pitfalls

* Working in a vacuum. You can't do everything on your own, and neither can your team. You need to have buy-in and sign-off from the necessary people at every stage.
* Not following the process. It's essential to avoid confusion over tasks and schedules, or people will end up duplicating work and you'll end up paying for the same thing twice.
* Ignoring risks. Review them regularly so that you can plan how to deal with them should you need to.

* Not planning properly. Roughly 30% of the total time you spend on a project should be spent on assessing and planning activities. Don't think you're saving time by ignoring these stages; you're not.
* Not getting the point. You must understand why you're doing what you're doing. You need to be aware of your customer's market, what the competition is, and generally what you're up against.
* Don't think that all critics are unhelpful naysayers. You may find that some of them have really good ideas that you can incorporate into the way you're running the project, so award them your grudging acknowledgment if needs be!
* Don't underestimate the training requirements that larger projects may entail once they're rolled out. For example, if you are introducing a new product to your portfolio, you need to train staff so that they understand it and can sell it to new and existing customers, or all the money you've spent creating it will be wasted. This training is a knock-on cost, and you need to bear it in mind when you are drawing up a budget. There's no point launching something if no-one knows what it is.

USEFUL LINK

Simon Stenner: **www.stenners.co.uk**

Manage Meetings Effectively

Meetings are a necessary evil in everyone's working life. Handled well, they can help those gathered get to the bottom of a tricky situation, agree actions, and do something positive. Handled badly, they can be a terrific waste of time. Basically, you want to get in and out as soon as possible with the relevant decisions made so that you can get on with the rest of your day.
This actionlist offers advice for anyone who has to plan and chair a meeting. Special arrangements need to be followed for large meetings such as board meetings or annual general meetings, so here we focus only on the type of meeting held most commonly in an everyday work situation.

I hate going to meetings, but my boss thinks they're really important. Are there other, more time-efficient ways to get decisions made?

In some cases, meetings are not always a good use of people's time and effort. If someone suggests that a meeting be held to discuss an issue related to your project, team, or department, think hard about whether gathering the attendees in one place is really the most efficient way forward. There may be more efficient alternatives to gathering everyone together for a meeting. For example, you could try:

* conference calls or videoconferencing. If you have access to these facilities, or can afford them, they offer a good way of holding a discussion without having to disrupt the attendees' day too much.

* discussing the issue via e-mail by sending a message to all relevant parties. Your e-mail should set out the issue clearly, ask for a response, and give a deadline—and double-check that you've included everyone before sending it!

If all else fails, though, and a face-to-face meeting seems to be the best and least unwieldy way of agreeing action on the issue at hand, prepare as much as you can in advance and delegate where appropriate.

MAKE IT HAPPEN

Think carefully about who to invite

Good planning is the best way to make sure that your meeting runs to plan, and an important first step is to fix the list of invitees. Remember that the most productive meetings are usually those with the fewest number of people attending, so try to limit the numbers by only inviting those who *really* need to be there. These will be people directly involved in the decisions that need to be taken during the meeting, those significantly affected by those actions, or those who have some specific knowledge to contribute. If the agenda is lengthy and covers a variety of issues, consider asking people to drop in and out when their relevant section comes up.

Give the attendees all the relevant information in good time

Give everyone plenty of notice of the meeting's time and venue and circulate a draft agenda outlining the topics to be discussed and the time limits assigned to each topic. A good agenda will make sure that all the attendees are clear about the purpose of the meeting and why they've been called together, and should state what needs to be accomplished between the start and finish of the meeting. Time limits create a healthy sense of urgency. By stipulating the start and finish time of the meeting, as well as setting time limits for each topic on the agenda (particularly important if you're holding a lengthy meeting and asking people to drop in and out), you'll encourage people to stay focused. Sticking to these time fixtures is essential, of course, for this to work!

Other information you should provide your attendees with prior to the meeting includes:

* directions to the venue in case they haven't been there before
* information on who else is attending (this will be particularly helpful if you're going to be joined by people external to your company such as consultants, freelance contributors, or designers)
* background information or relevant documents to the meeting. For example, if you're going to discuss a long-overdue overhaul of your product catalogue, send everyone a copy of your existing brochure in case they no longer have copies of the original. You could also include other similar publications whose style you admire to see if anyone can think of new ways of presenting your products.
* your contact details and those of one other person in the office (such as your assistant, if you have one) in case of emergency

Think about catering requirements

If you think your meeting will take longer than a few hours, or if it's likely to take place over lunch, remember to ask all attendees whether they have any special dietary requirements. This will save a lot of time and stress on the day. Research shows that the best time to hold a meeting is just before lunch or towards the end of the day—this motivates attendees to focus on the agenda and keep time!

Delegate taking the minutes

Try to find someone other than yourself to take the minutes so that you're free to steer the meeting as appropriate. If the person designated as the minute-taker is new to the project or issue you're going to discuss, run through some relevant key words or acronyms so that he or she is not baffled by the jargon—you and the other attendees may be well versed in the relevant vocabulary, but don't expect the same from a 'newcomer'.

Find and prepare the venue

Once you know that a formal meeting is on the cards, find an appropriate space in which the meeting can be held. Some companies have a 'booking system' for meeting rooms, so give yourself enough time when planning the meeting date to make sure that you can get an appropriately sized room for when you want. Don't assume that it will be free as and when you're ready!

As the meeting draws near, make sure that:

* the room is tidy
* you have enough tables and chairs to accommodate everyone
* if you're using one, the flip chart has enough paper and pens ready
* there is enough light, heating, or ventilation for the time of day and year
* there are enough power points, and that they're in the right place if you're going to be using an overhead projector or laptop
* any equipment in the room is ready to use and is working properly

Make further catering arrangements once your numbers are confirmed. If your company has a canteen, book in early for someone to bring tea, coffee, and biscuits to the meeting. If you don't have a canteen, ask a colleague or assistant to stay close by at the start of the meeting and to pop out to a nearby coffee shop or café to fetch what's needed. Again, this will free you up to attend to other tasks.

Start as you mean to go on

On the day of the meeting, arrive in plenty of time so that you can double-check that everything is ready. Once the attendees have arrived, set the pace and tone of the meeting by following these steps:

* Begin on time.
* Welcome everyone, and briefly explain basic issues such as where the bathrooms are located (particularly helpful for anyone who hasn't been to your offices before) and what the catering arrangements are.

* Ask everyone to check that they've turned off their mobile phones so that the flow of discussion isn't interrupted.
* Reiterate the reason the meeting is being held, what you hope to achieve within the meeting, the time-scale and finishing time.
* Frame each item on the agenda by explaining its objectives.

Keep a tight rein on proceedings

While obviously you need to give everyone an opportunity to contribute to points raised on the agenda, there are steps you can take to make sure that you keep roughly on schedule (and on topic). For example:

* make sure that attendees keep to one agenda point at a time
* summarise at appropriate intervals and restate agreed actionpoints clearly (the person taking the minutes will be particularly grateful for this)
* firmly but politely move the discussion on if a subject has become exhausted

Don't let one person dominate the conversation

Meetings can often be hijacked by one or two vociferous attendees, so in your role as chair you need to make sure that there is only one discussion at a time. Sometimes, people start their own 'private' meeting during the main session. This may range from a few whispered asides, to notes being passed around the table, to a full-blown separate discussion taking place. Stop these diversions by addressing directly the people involved and asking them politely but assertively if there's something they'd like to raise. For example, you could say: 'I think there may be an issue you're not happy with. Would you like to raise it now? We have a lot to get through today'.

Wrap it up

Wrap up the meeting by thanking everyone for their attendance and contribution. If possible, also let attendees know when the next meeting is to be held (should you need one); this will encourage the attendees not to forget about the topics discussed the moment they leave the room.

Make sure everyone is clear on any follow-up action required

Ask the person taking the minutes to write them up as soon as possible so that they can be distributed to all the attendees promptly. Bear in mind that most of the attendees will only glance briefly at the meeting minutes, or refer back to them in order to locate a specific piece of information. This means that they need to be extremely concise and clear. The key things to note are:

* agreed actions
* the people responsible for them
* deadline (if appropriate)
* date of next meeting if you agreed to arrange another

Strategies for dealing with difficult people

The talkative	In the case of people who just like the sound of their own voice, you must be assertive enough to interject politely but firmly and remind everyone of the agenda point you're discussing and steer the discussion back to it. Also mention your target finish time and how the meeting is progressing in relation to it.
The passionate	The same goes for dealing with people who feel very strongly about the issue under discussion and who may feel that others do not share their interest and commitment. Again, make sure that they get the opportunity to voice their point of view, but also that they give others the chance to express theirs too. Interject as appropriate and summarise if you sense they're about to repeat something. Remember that a meeting is a discussion with objectives, not an opportunity for attendees to rehearse an extended monologue.
The angry	If the topic you're discussing is particularly contentious, tempers may flare. If you feel a situation is getting heated and that insults rather than well-considered opinions are being traded, step in to defuse the tension. Suggest a break outside of the meeting room for 15 minutes or so, which will give most people time to calm down and assess what has happened. If voices are being raised, match your voice to the level of other people's, then reduce the volume back down to a normal speaking pitch. This will allow the discussion to get back to a more stable footing.

WHAT TO AVOID

You leave preparations to the last minute

You're not saving time by leaving the arrangements for your meeting to the last minute—you're wasting it. If you plan in advance, you can make sure everything is in place early and spend the time you'd otherwise be wasting by rushing about aimlessly doing something more productive instead.

You think you can squeeze in taking the minutes

You're not shirking responsibility if you ask someone else to take the meeting's minutes for you. On the contrary, if you're freed up to make sure that the meeting starts and ends on time, is well organised, and achieves its objectives, you'll have made everyone's life a lot easier and you'll also end up with a set of minutes (and notes) that mean something.

You lose track of time

Don't be afraid to move things on as appropriate if the meeting seems to be getting bogged down in one particular area. Everyone else will be keen to finish on time and get on with the rest of their day, so, in your role as chair, shape the discussion and sustain the meeting's impetus.

USEFUL LINKS

It-analysis.com: **www.it-analysis.com**
Meeting Management Tips
http://users.anytimenow.com/brian/meeting_management_tips.pdf
MeetingWizard.org: **www.meetingwizard.org**
Vista: **www.vista.uk.com/Virtual_Meetings.html**

Solve Thorny Problems

Problem-solving is a key activity of management, as well as many other jobs. Without problem-solving capabilities, no organisation could exist for very long. Intelligence, common sense, and education help us solve problems in our individual lives, and those same elements can also help us with organisational problems. However, if you're attempting to do something complex, such as reorganise the business or implement a total quality management programme, you need a systematic approach to problem-solving, a process that allows people at all levels to contribute to finding solutions. This actionlist looks at a variety of issues, techniques, and resources to help you find your own best approach.

Why shouldn't I just allow people to solve problems in their own way?

In most situations, it's good to allow people to understand and then solve problems in their own way. However, using tried and tested techniques of problem-solving—ones that are plainly mapped out and used uniformly—allows others to understand the problem and areas being explored. The process ensures that, whether talking about customer service or production quotas, others can get actively involved in solving the problem at any stage.

Each problem is different; is it really possible to use the same problem-solving technique in each case?

While problems *are* always different, there are some common approaches and processes for solving them. Problems can be diagnosed and the various elements can be mapped—whether you're talking about a manufacturing roadblock or an IT systems failure. Obviously, as an organisation grows in size, so too does the need for more sophisticated techniques.

Isn't problem-solving just for those people who like to spend lots of time thinking? Surely finding a quick and ready solution is more important?
It's true that we often notice the solution more than the problem. That's because problems cause us headaches and can hold us up; solutions allow us to move forward. However, in order to be sure of having the *right* solution, spending time on using problem-solving techniques means you can be certain that you know the full extent of the problem, the possible knock-on effects, and the priorities for managing the situation.

Doesn't a structured approach stifle creativity?
Problem-solving isn't just about logical deductions; it's about finding new and alternative ways of resolving a situation. In fact, creativity can flourish through a structured process. Structure can also be limiting, though, so you must be careful not to preclude a full exploration of the possibilities. If, for example, you're working in a group, don't allow members to become judgmental about ideas and dismiss them too early in the process. Practise letting go of your assumptions, and allow everyone to contribute in a way that suits them best.

MAKE IT HAPPEN

Problem-solving is best done in groups, to ensure that a true win-win situation is achieved. Any problem-solving process requires the following steps.

Identify the problem

Understanding a problem requires an ability to see it in its entirety—in breadth, depth, and context. Here are a number of ways to evaluate the scope of a problem:

* **recognition**—can you see or feel the problem? Is it isolated, or part of a bigger problem?
* **symptoms**—how is it showing itself?
* **causes**—why has it happened?
* **effects**—what else is being affected by it?

The task then is to break the main problem down into smaller problems, in order to determine whether you're the right person or team to handle it. If not, you need to transfer the problem-solving process to those better equipped to deal with it. If the answer is yes, you need to ask additional questions, including: do you have the right resources? How long might the process take? What are some of the obstacles? What's the anticipated benefit? Once you get answers, move on to the next step.

Find the best way of gathering data

There are two important questions here: what do you need to know, and how are you going to get it? Most information can be accessed, but there are often time and resource issues involved with collecting and analysing it. Remember that data collection may involve investigating the symptoms of the problem, the underlying causes, and/or the overall effects of the problem. Each may have different implications as to how the problem is viewed. Data-gathering techniques include:

* workflow analysis
* surveys and questionnaires
* flow charts
* group and/or one-to-one interviews

Brainstorm the problem

In any problem-solving exercise, there will be a need for brainstorming. There are five golden rules of brainstorming:

* **anything goes**—no evaluation or judgment by others
* **hitchhike**—build on the ideas of others
* **quality**—strive for quality
* **be off the wall**—encourage wild and wacky ideas
* **inclusiveness**—include others and encourage participation

Explore options and solutions

Lateral thinking can play an important role in understanding the perspectives of a problem, and their implications. Look at what others have done in the past, and don't ignore what may seem a crazy idea. It's best to cast the net wide when exploring solutions, so that there is a richness of ideas and possible options.

Evaluate priorities and decisions

Taking time to identify the most appropriate solution from your range of options is very important. Suggestions need to be winnowed down to a shortlist, containing only the most realistic possibilities.

To do this, set some hard measures. Try to determine the costs and benefits of the suggested solutions. If, for example, you feel that outside investment is needed to solve a particular problem, work out the payback period. You can then assess whether your senior management team will accept it.

Always understand that each possible solution has consequences, some of which may cause additional problems themselves. Force field analysis—analysing the pros and cons of a given plan of action—is therefore crucial, so that the true benefits to the business can be evaluated. Force field analysis was developed by the management guru Kurt Lewin, as an aid to problem-solving, decision-making, and conflict prevention. It aims to promote change by identifying negative and positive factors in a situation, then working to lessen the negative by developing the positive.

Select the best solutions for the situation and context

The chosen solution needs to meet some key criteria. Do you have the necessary people, money, and time to achieve it? Will you get a sufficient return on investment? Is the solution acceptable to others involved in the situation? You should draw up:

* a rationale of why you've reached your particular conclusion
* a set of criteria to judge the solution's success
* a plan of action and contingencies
* a schedule for implementation
* a team to carry out, be responsible for, and approve the solution

Implement the solution and make it happen

Implementation means having action plans with relevant deadlines and contingencies built in. Any implementation needs constant review, and the implementation team needs to be sure it has the support of relevant management. Keep asking:

* Are deadlines being met?
* Are team members happy, and is communication strong within and from the team?
* Has the team been recognised for its achievements?
* Are the improvements measurable?
* Is the situation reviewed regularly?

Evaluate the solution

This is where the two most important questions are asked.

* How well did it work?
* What did we learn from the process?

All experience can be valuable in terms of adding to an organisation's learning and knowledge banks. Think of creating a case study that can be shared with others—either at a conference or directly.

Canvass people's opinions regarding the effectiveness of the process and its outcome. Ask for areas of improvement that could be incorporated into a second phase. Don't be scared of involving your clients in any evaluation; this can convey a positive message if handled properly, and builds trust in your ability to troubleshoot problems and implement solutions.

Be aware of the pitfalls of problem-solving

There are, of course, pitfalls that can make for ineffective problem-solving.

* Failing to involve the right people at the right time, particularly those outside the immediate group.
* Tackling problems that lie beyond the control of the team.
* Jumping to conclusions before truly understanding the depth or scope of the problem.
* Failing to gather sufficient data, either about the problem itself or some of the proposed solutions.
* Failing to 'right size' the problem; people often work on problems that are too general or too large.
* Failing fully to support the conclusions reached or the solution identified.

WHAT TO AVOID

You use too many techniques

Don't try and use too many techniques. Find one that you feel will work well in the business. Often, when running workshops, the process becomes more important than the ideas and intellectual discussion. Getting the balance right is important.

Your team is too narrow in scope

Don't limit your team to the people you like. Try and get representatives from different parts of the business to give a different angle on the problem. Always remember the following:

* Often the exciting part of problem-solving is identifying innovative solutions. But it's important to focus on the full picture, from problem identification through to final implementation and evaluation. Your ideas are only as good as the results you get.
* Creativity can often derail a problem-solving process. Getting the balance right between understanding the problem and finding imaginative solutions requires strong facilitation.
* Your solution will have an impact on other parts of the business, or the client. Make sure you think through the implications of the proposed solution and the implementation plan.

USEFUL LINKS

Buzan Centres: **www.mind-map.com/EN/index.html**
Brainstorming.co.uk:
www.brainstorming.co.uk/tutorials/creativethinkingcontents.html
Edward De Bono: **www.edwdebono.com**
Innovation tools: **www.innovationtools.com**

Make Sound Decisions

Some people are naturally more decisive than others. For them, it's relatively easy to respond to a situation, weigh up the pros and cons of various ways of tackling the issue, make the decision and move on. For the indecisive, though, the process can be nightmarish, stressful, and eat up an awful lot of valuable time. The trick here is to find a decision-making style that means you spend enough time on a decision to make sure it's a good, well-considered one, but that you cut out the procrastination. Avoid the temptation to make knee-jerk judgments: you may think you're creating a good impression by looking decisive, but it's the quality of the decision that counts in the end.

To make the best decision possible, be clear about your goals, the problem in question, the options open to you, the possible consequences, the timescale,

and the outcome of previous decisions on the matter. The process combines your intuition (to initiate your response and come up with innovative options) and your analytical ability (with which you scrutinise and quantify your options).

How can I cope with a difficult decision that comes completely out of the blue?

No one can always predict or control the everyday circumstances that you or your business faces, but there are skills you can learn that will improve how you respond. As you practise these, they'll gradually become second nature. The result will be less stress, more decisiveness, and more focus towards your long-term business goals.

You can make the best decision possible by being clear about your goals, the problem in question, the options open to you, the possible consequences, and the outcome of previous decisions on the matter. The process combines your intuition (to initiate your response and come up with innovative options) and your analytical ability (with which you scrutinise and quantify your options).

MAKE IT HAPPEN

Understand what you want your decision to achieve

When you're faced with a difficult issue, try to look past your immediate objective and take in your longer-term goals as well. For example, let's say you work in sales and have dealings with a wide variety of customers. If a customer requests that drop your price to an uneconomical level, you need to think about how important the sale is in the long run. If that customer doesn't feature in your business priorities, then you might only damage your reputation among competitors and other customers by dropping your price too low. On the other hand, if the customer is in a sector that you want to break in to, then a low-margin sale may give you an important foot in the door for future business.

Once you've defined the objectives of your decision, then you're in a position to determine its level of significance. This is important for deciding the amount of time and resources you should spend in making the right decision.

Find the information you need

Give yourself as much time as you can to research your decision, and resist the temptation to promise a quick decision to other people. You may think you're creating a good impression by looking decisive, but it's the quality of the decision that counts in the end.

Identify the sources of information you'll need and make sure they're near at hand. Get advice from experts or colleagues, and be honest about those areas where you don't have the answers. Ask colleagues for help if it looks like you might run out of time or ideas—a brainstorming session is often a good idea. Often people who are new to an issue may see a solution that you've overlooked as you're so close to it. Wherever possible, cut out assumptions: check your facts. This might look like an extra hoop to jump through, but it's a valuable one. If you base a decision around a factor or number

Different decision levels

1 Strategic	Decisions about strategy are concerned with long-term goals, philosophies, and the overall scheme of masterminding the future direction of the business. They therefore tend to be more theoretical than practical, more unpredictable in outcome, and more risky. This makes them of great importance.
2 Tactical	Tactical decisions are concerned with short to medium-term objectives, and usually involve the implementation of strategic decisions and planning. The long-term risks are fewer and the significance, therefore, more moderate. However, as tactical decisions turn strategic decisions into reality they're more likely to involve the direct and great responsibility of over-seeing and handling budgets, people, schedules, and resources.
3 Operational	Operational decisions are concerned with day-to-day systems and procedures and so tend to be more structured—to the extent that they can be routine or pre-programmed. As the third level down in the decision food chain they're used to support tactical decisions. The outcomes of operational decisions therefore tend to be immediate to short-term, and involve few risks (although a series of decision errors will mount up and cause more damage).

of factors that actually turn out to be unreliable, you'll have wasted hours of work anyway.

Six thinking hats: This powerful technique, developed by lateral thinking pioneer, Edward de Bono, will help you to look at decisions from many perspectives. Allocate each individual—alone or in a group—a series of imaginary hats, which represent different outlooks, according to colour. This forces people to move into different modes of thinking.

* White hats focus on the data, look for gaps, extrapolate from history, and examine future trends.
* Red hats use intuition and emotion to look at problems.
* Black hats look at the negative, and find reasons why something may not work. If an idea can get through this process, it's more likely to succeed.
* Yellow hats think positively. This hat's optimistic view helps you to see the benefits of a decision, providing a boost to the thinking process.

* Green hats develop creative, freewheeling solutions. There is no room for criticism in this mode; it's strictly positive.
* Blue hats orchestrate the meeting—you're in control in this hat. Feel free to propose a new hat to keep ideas flowing.

Outline the alternatives and their consequences

Get a few options down in writing, then explore the positive and negative consequences of each; give special attention to the unintended consequences that might arise, especially if you're considering a course of action that you haven't tried before. You may find it useful to list these in columns alongside the options.

Force field analysis: This is a useful technique for examining pros and cons. By looking at the forces that will support or challenge a decision (such as finances or market conditions), you can strengthen the pros and diminish the cons. Draw three columns, and place the situation or issue in the middle. The pros push on one side, and the cons push on the other. Allocate scores to each force to convey its potency. This allows you to measure the overall advantages and disadvantages of any given action.

SWOT analysis: Here's another handy grid technique that works by identifying the strengths and weaknesses of a decision, and examining the existing opportunities and threats. You can find more information on these techniques online (see **Useful links** at the end of this actionlist).

Judge each alternative by your goals

Remind yourself of what your priorities are in this situation. This will force you to always consider your longer-term goals when making your shorter-term decisions, and ensures that they're 'pointing in the same direction'.

Measure the merits and problems in each alternative—this may be a case of estimating financial costs and benefits, or it may involve less tangible factors like goodwill or publicity. This involves a forward-thinking process of predicting what will happen as a result of your decision. Make a note of these expectations, as they'll be important when you review your decision later on and judge with hindsight whether it was a good one.

Compare the alternatives to each other, and decide on which one comes out best in the light of the information available.

Decision trees: These are a great way to help you examine alternative solutions and their impact, especially when decisions are required in situations where there is a great deal of information to sift through. Start your decision tree on one side of a piece of paper, with a symbol representing the decision to be made. Different lines representing various solutions open out like a fan from this nexus. Additional decisions or uncertainties that need to be resolved are indicated on these lines and, in turn, form the new decision point, from which yet more options fan out.

Take the decision and implement it

Make sure that everyone involved is informed about the decision you've taken as soon as possible; the value of a good decision is often undermined if your staff or colleagues hear about it through inappropriate channels. You'll normally need to inform the more senior people first, but speed is often of the essence when letting people know; plan your timing carefully and control the process firmly.

Explain the reasons why the decision was made, especially if the decision is contentious. Outline what benefits you expect as a result, as well as any other implications that the business needs to anticipate. Be honest but positive if your decision will cause inconvenience of any kind, even if it's only likely to be for a short time. While news like this will never be popular, it's best to announce it openly than let it dribble out over time.

Finally, get the right people onto the job of implementing the decision, so that it gets the best possible chance of success.

Review the consequences of your decision

Estimate how long it will take before the decision will have an effect, and plan an assessment at that time to review how well it went. Make sure that some measurement is being made as you go along, as this will be helpful in any assessment you make.

For example, let's say that you've decided to invest in a promotional mailing as you're about to launch a new product. You need to make sure that:

* someone is collecting information on the impact of that mailing on daily orders
* someone is registering respondents' contact details if you asked for them and if they've given you permission to use them
* someone is fulfilling any orders that come in

When you come to review the effects of your decisions, remember that you're embarking on a learning exercise for everyone concerned with making the decision and implementing it. Try and get as many of these people as possible involved in the review process. This will help them when a similar decision needs to be taken next time; it will also advance their own decision-making skills and enhance their value to the business.

WHAT TO AVOID

You put off making a difficult decision

Procrastination will seldom lead to a decision becoming easier to make. Give the decision some thought as early as you can, and give yourself a deadline for making it—based on how long you think you need to gather the necessary information and input, and how important a decision it is.

You make snap decisions under pressure

Making any decision without enough thought is risky, but if you're in a pressurised office situation, there is the added danger of not being able to see the whole picture. If you take a very quick decision, you may not give time to seeing important consequences of your actions.

You don't consult those who will be affected

Nothing is quite as demotivating for staff as feeling like their input isn't valued or their feelings aren't respected. Before you begin to address a decision, think carefully about each of the people who are—or could later be—affected by the outcome of your decision. Make sure that you include them—not necessarily all of them at every step, but leave them in no doubt that their input is appreciated.

You let your bad decisions overshadow your good ones

Everyone makes mistakes, and there will always be the occasions when your decisions don't work out as you'd intended. Try to see these times as part of the learning process, not as indications of failure. If you learn from a bad decision, that in itself is a good outcome. Don't be too hard on yourself and remember that it's unrealistic to expect a perfect decision every time.

USEFUL LINKS

Businessballs.com: **www.businessballs.com/problemsolving.htm**
Mind Tools: **www.mindtools.com/pages/article/newTED_00.htm**
Time Management Guide:
www.time-management-guide.com/decision-making-skills.html
VirtualSalt: **www.virtualsalt.com/crebook6.htm**

Are You in the Right Job?

It's human nature to wonder, regardless of what we happen to be doing, whether we ought in fact to be doing something else. This is particularly the case with jobs; most people spend at least some of their working life questioning themselves and their careers, and speculating about whether there are other occupations 'out there' which might make better use of their time and efforts.

As with most things, it helps to analyse the situation objectively. A job is made up of many elements—it's not just the actual day-to-day work involved—and it's the combination of these elements that makes it suitable or otherwise. Your *skills*, of course, are fundamental to what you do, but are these the same as your *strengths*? And what about the company you work for . . . is it the right size, in the right industry sector, with the right culture? Then there are the questions about who you work with, what your boss is like, whether you have suitable levels of responsibility, what kind of remuneration you receive, and so on and so forth.

By looking at all these factors, you can work out whether your job is suitable for you, and if not, what needs to be put right.

I'm good at what I do. Doesn't that prove I'm in the right job?

Not necessarily. There's more to doing a job than simply being able to fulfil the requirements. You could be a very good builder because you're physically strong and fit, but you may have the soul of a philosopher, or a secret yearning to be a garden designer. It's when your interests and abilities coincide that you find yourself in the ideal job. That said, however, if you are happy in your work and don't feel the need to stretch yourself in other directions, you probably are in the right job—at least for the time being.

Every person has many facets to his or her personality. How can any job be the right one?

You're right of course; most people could do any of a number of different jobs and be equally happy and satisfied. Broadly speaking, however, there are four main areas of personality which need to be fulfilled within a work context for a person to be content with his or her job. These are: areas of interest, job strengths, behaviour under normal and stress conditions, and social perceptions and compatibility with others. If someone finds they have a mismatch between any of these four and the job being done, it is unlikely that he or she will be comfortable in that job.

MAKE IT HAPPEN

Identify your areas of interest

First and foremost, if you're not interested in what you're doing, you're never going to be able to put your heart into your work. So if your company, industry, subject, or sector doesn't engage you, it might be a good idea to go back to basics and identify one that does. Is there a topic, issue, or activity that you've enjoyed or had in your mind for a long time . . . art, maths, helping others, science, construction, the environment, for example? Or does a specific job attract you, possibly something that you've dismissed in the past for some reason, or one based on something that you do as a hobby? Maybe you'd like to be a website designer, financial advisor, music teacher, painter/decorator, or landscape gardener for instance? Or perhaps there's a specific industry that fascinates you—advertising, manufacturing, health care, electronics, entertainment, whatever—that you could explore further. Any area that piques your curiosity or makes you want to know more is a good place to start!

Pinpoint your strengths

Once you've settled on an area of interest, the most important aspect of any job is whether it makes the best use of your individual strengths. If it does, many of the other elements of satisfactory employment—self-fulfilment, motivation, a sense of achievement, and so on—fall naturally into place. So the first thing to do is to assess what your strengths are, and whether or not you're using these in your current position.

Your strengths can be defined as the areas where your interests and your abilities overlap; in other words, the business activities that you both like *and* are good at. The two aren't necessarily the same! Take a look at the table over and, being as honest as you can, put ticks against the activities you are interested in, and then against the ones you're good at. The rows where you get ticks in both 'Interest' and 'Ability' are your main strengths—and you may find there are some surprises in your results. The list of activities is by no means exhaustive, so add in any others that apply particularly to you.

Interest	Activities	Ability
	Research	
	Analysis	
	Interpretation	
	Problem-solving	
	Budgeting	
	Planning	
	Process Management	
	Leadership	
	Decision-making	
	Follow through	
	Administration	
	Mentoring	
	Innovation	
	Imagination	
	Vision	
	Project management	
	Empathy	
	Listening	
	Written presentation	
	Verbal presentation	
	Negotiation	
	Initiative	
	Flexibility	
	Teamworking	
	Facilitating	
	Installing	
	Operating	

Once you've identified your strengths, consider whether and how you're using them in your job. Could you be doing more with them? Are there other areas of the organisation which might benefit from them? Could you take on different responsibilities, or would a shift in the focus of your job suit you better? If you feel under-utilised, try talking to your boss—any sensible employer will understand the benefits of using the best strengths of employees, and value people who are proactive in the way they approach their work. Unless you know deep-down that you are going to move on, use positive language when you address this with your boss, and be as upbeat as you can so that you don't panic him or her into thinking that you are going to leave immediately.

Consider the organisation you work for

A good match between your strengths and the work you are doing proves that you are in the right *type* of job. But is it in the right place? For example, you could be an accountant in a big blue-chip corporation, when really you'd be happiest running the finances for a small family-run firm.

Think about the organisation you work for. How big is it? Would you prefer to work with more or less people? Apart from size, here's a list of other factors you might consider:

* Public/private sector
* Profit/non-profit
* National/multinational
* Academic
* Product/service
* Central/decentralised
* Financial condition
* Political climate
* Company growth, current, and future
* Stability
* Reputation
* Market dependency
* Profitability
* Vulnerability to takeover

Think about your rewards

Then think about the rewards you receive for the work you do. While these shouldn't necessarily be the most important factor about a job, obviously you need to have your needs met. This is even more the case if your circumstances mean that you require a certain level of income or security. Remember that it's not just salary that should be considered—other benefits are equally as important. A pension, life and disability insurance, health benefits, or a severance package could be vital if you have a family; a bonus scheme or other performance incentive might be a prime motivator if you're the kind of person who likes to have targets. If you're expected to travel or relocate, what provision is made for moving expenses, temporary living costs, or housing subsidy? Does the holiday entitlement give you enough time with the children? What about flexible working or study leave?

Evaluate yourself

Then there's your own personality to consider. It is extremely stressful to be trying to fill a role that simply isn't 'you'. Much of this comes down to your own personal values (see the actionlist 'Understand Your Values'), but useful areas to examine are as follows:

* **Interpersonal**—do you like working with other people? Is it essential to you that colleagues are also friends?

* **Responsibility**—how much do you like? Do you prefer to manage, or would you rather be managed?
* **Pressure**—a high-stress hospital ward could be dreadful for a postman; a peaceful publishing office might bore a sales rep to death. How much can you cope with?
* **Potential**—are you a high flier with ambitions for regular promotion, or do you want a steady job that will support your family?
* **Compatibility with lifestyle**—do you have hobbies or non-work commitments that you don't want to compromise, or would you love lots of business travel and high-powered meetings?

WHAT TO AVOID

You bail out too early

Nothing in life is ever perfect, and during a rough patch it is tempting simply to blame your troubles on your job and go hunting for another one. However, financial considerations aside, it's always worth pausing to consider before you do this. What else may be making you feel dissatisfied? Is it someone or something that could be sorted out with a little patience and effort? Could it be that you're simply bored at the moment? If you *do* decide it's time to move on, make sure you've done your homework first so that your new role brings real benefits and you don't simply move from one unsatisfactory situation into another.

You forget the importance of your own attitude

There is an old song that contains the line, 'If you can't be with the one you love, love the one you're with'. This is very useful to bear in mind in the context of your job. If it's not easy for you to leave your current working situation, your challenge is to discover its benefits rather than fretting about being stuck. Quite often, contentment comes from the way you choose to perceive things. It might be an old fashioned thing to say, but counting your blessings—rather than cursing your luck—can make all the difference to how you feel about something!

USEFUL LINKS

About Human Resources:
http://humanresources.about.com/od/careerandjobsearchhelp
Handbag.com: **www.handbag.com/careers/careerchange**
Monster.co.uk: **http://content.monster.co.uk**

Weigh Up the Pros and Cons of Looking for a New Job

Do you hate your job? Do you dread Monday mornings, feel stressed and tired, and lack motivation and enthusiasm for working? Then it's probably time to look for a new job. However, it may not be. Tempting as it might seem, handing in your resignation immediately and walking away is not always the best or most sensible option. The job market can be a cold and lonely place if you're not entirely sure what you're looking for, and simply quitting your job can have implications for your CV and the way you're perceived by other potential employers.

This actionlist aims to help you weigh up the pros and cons of whether you should stay or go, and come to a balanced decision that will improve your working life rather than causing you further problems.

Is there any good reason why I shouldn't just pack up and leave?

Technically, no. You'll always hear stories about friends of friends or former colleagues who suddenly threw in their jobs and went off to do something wildly exciting. However, many of these stories are apocryphal and at the very least, they gloss over the struggle or effort that certainly went into making dreams come true for these people. Looking for a new job is hard work, and finding the ideal post requires great determination and single-mindedness. However fed up you feel, bear that in mind and don't burn any bridges before you've considered your options carefully.

Is it true that it's easier to find a new job when you're already in a job?

Generally speaking, yes it is. A prospective employer is likely to wonder why you suddenly left your previous post and, not knowing you, they may put their own interpretations on the reasons for your departure. Existing workplaces or colleagues are also good sources of information on interesting openings, and you may also be able to use work resources to help you in your search.

MAKE IT HAPPEN

Identify the issues you might be able to address in your current job

Ask yourself whether it's the actual day-to-day work that makes you want to move, or if the problem is with other issues. If the answer *is* other issues, it is possible in many cases to resolve them. Take a look at the list below, see if your own issue is among them, and then consider whether it might in fact be possible to turn the situation around.

* **Not getting on with your boss**. This is the number one reason people cite for leaving their jobs. If your manager is nasty, abusive, bullying, or controlling, there might not be much you can do about it. However, if the situation is more subtle—

the manager fails to involve you in decisions about your work, never shows appreciation, or omits to develop your talents and abilities, for example—you should try talking to him or her about their actions. Many people don't realise the effect they have on others. If you feel as if you need some back-up, maybe you could ask a more senior manager to have a word, or maybe the HR department could intervene. Alternatively, what are the options for you to move to another department or report to a different manager?

* **Feeling stuck**. If your current position offers no hope of promotion and you see no obvious evidence of other work that you might like to do instead, there are still options to explore. Most organisations value initiative and people who want to continue to develop and learn, so talk to your manager about opportunities for lateral moves or particular assignments that will stretch your skills. Or perhaps you might find a colleague who feels the same way as you do—how about swapping jobs?
* **Feeling unappreciated**. Sadly, this is very common. If you never receive any recognition for your efforts, try telling your manager that you would value his or her input on your work, or ask for regular feedback sessions—be prepared for both good *and* bad—so you can improve. If the issue revolves around money, trying asking for a pay rise and back up your request with plenty of evidence for why you deserve one. If a rise isn't forthcoming immediately, ask for a review at a future date or see if you can get agreement for a performance-linked one. Then make sure you perform!
* **Feeling overworked**. In these days of reduced resources and lean teams, it's quite likely that you *are* overworked. Collect evidence to back up any claim that your job involves more than one person can reasonably handle, then discuss the situation with someone who can do something about it. Possible options include employing someone else to help you, whether full- or part-time; identifying tasks that you could stop doing or delegate to someone else; and analysing where you might be able to work more efficiently.
* **Disliking your employer, colleagues, or customers**. You're never going to love everyone you work with, so it's worth checking your own attitude first. Can you maintain a courteous, professional relationship and keep your personal feelings out of it? Are there steps you can take to reduce your exposure to people you find difficult (you don't *have* to spend your lunch break around colleagues who complain constantly, for example)? Could you move to a different part of the organisation?

Recognise the show-stoppers

However hard you try, there are some reasons why in fact leaving your current job *would* be your best or only option. Listed below, these are the issues which tend to be difficult, if not impossible, to solve. If any of them apply to you, it would be sensible to start planning your search for a new position. Life is too short to spend time working in a situation where you really are miserable.

* Your company is experiencing a downward spiral, losing customers and money, and closure or bankruptcy appears inevitable.
* Your relationship with your manager or other colleagues is damaged beyond repair, in spite of efforts on either side to seek help or remedy the situation. The reasons for the breakdown are not particularly important: start again somewhere else, and resolve not to let the situation arise again.
* Your life situation has changed. Perhaps you've married, had a baby, or you have a family member to care for and the salary and benefits no longer support your needs. You need to move on to better opportunities.
* Your values are at odds with the corporate culture. Maybe your company is very hierarchical and you hate having a manager breathing down your neck; perhaps you are required to travel for long periods abroad and you want to spend plenty of time with your children. It doesn't matter what's causing the clash; a lack of congruence with the corporate culture will destroy your attitude at work.
* You've stopped having fun and enjoying your job. When you dread going to work in the morning and have drawn a blank when you've explored the alternatives within the organisation, it's time to leave.
* Your company's approach is less than ethical. Perhaps you are asked to lie to customers about product quality; you discover that questionable suppliers are being used; you realise that the company is stealing information from competitors. Whatever the issue, don't stay in an organisation where you get tarred with same brush of unethical behaviour.
* For whatever reason, you yourself have behaved in ways that are considered unacceptable. You've taken too many 'sick' days on Fridays and Mondays; you haven't pulled your weight; you've failed to maintain required skills, or just generally developed a reputation as a troublemaker. Unfortunately reputations, once earned, tend to stick forever unless you make a fresh start somewhere else.
* Your stress level is so high at work that it is affecting your physical or mental health and your relationships with friends and family. Watch for the signs of burnout (such as prolonged tiredness, irritability, and weight loss) and, if they can't be cured, move on.

WHAT TO AVOID

You become paralysed by indecision

Having said that it's important to weigh up your options carefully, it should also be stressed that any decision is better than no decision. If you remain in a state of wavering for too long, you will fail to perform well and hence sap your own confidence and satisfaction levels, so the situation becomes a vicious circle. Even if you find you can't decide to leave yet, try to turn the situation round so that it becomes a positive decision *to stay*. Your mind will be easier and your tendency to fidget reduced. Nothing needs to be set in stone, and you can always reverse this decision at a later date.

You don't think strategically

We spend so much time at work that work issues tend to blend in with other areas of our lives, and hence our career decisions become charged with emotion. However, this is one area where you really must try to be objective. Say you're in your first job, and could do with getting a decent period of experience under your belt before you think about moving. Or maybe you've moved jobs frequently in the past, and prospective employers are beginning to worry that you can't stick at anything. Or perhaps you have a particular career path mapped out, which requires a number of years in this role before you can move to the next. Whatever the circumstances, take a good look at whether it's in your best overall interests to move now, or whether you should stick things out for a bit longer.

USEFUL LINKS

About Human Resources: **http://humanresources.about.com**
Career World: **www.career-world.co.uk**
Monster.co.uk: **www.monster.co.uk/**

Create a Career Plan

When jobs were for life, you decided what line of work you wanted, worked hard, and the career path was pretty much mapped out for you. The working world has changed. Now individuals wanting to maximise their potential will take a much more active part in mapping out their career. Career planning today needs to be a frequent, dynamic process of self-awareness, market and trend analysis, planning, development, and self-marketing.

The good news is that career paths are more flexible. Individuals can choose a spiral one, stepping through different fields or functions. Many employers encourage cross-fertilisation of ideas through diversity in their workforce. They also value the different perspectives offered by those from outside their industry.

As career breaks are more common today, even transitory career paths are possible. These are popular with people who like variety, novelty, or have other worthwhile priorities. If you require periods of employment, interspersed by breaks, be it for study, travel, raising family, starting a business, or caring for elderly or unwell family members, this option could be for you.

There are, however, still expert career paths for those who want to specialise in a particular field and linear careers for those who enjoy the challenge, responsibility, and status of climbing the hierarchical ladder. Whatever your set of circumstances, think about this: what does your career need to do for *you*?

What's the difference between a career plan and a development plan?
Your career plan maps out long-term objectives, your more immediate objectives, and how you want your life and work to fit together. Your development plan maps out the skills and experience gaps for the different stops along the way and how you will address those. In effect, the development plan enables the career plan to work.

How do I find out what jobs I might be suitable for?
If you are naturally curious and chatty, you could start your research by talking to people. Make use of your contacts and ask for names and contact details of people who might be able to help with each of the options you're considering. This approach not only increases your network but it also gets you the targeted information you need. It may also put you in touch with contacts who can quite often open doors for you.

On the other hand, you may prefer to get started with some Internet or library research and save the networking until you feel a little better informed about possibilities. Neither approach is right or wrong, but people who use *both* approaches are likely to be the best prepared, most knowledgeable, and 'luckiest' when it comes to opportunities.

Will frequent job moves look bad on my CV?
It depends on what is 'normal' for your market. In IT, for example, regular moves are common. A CV that shows frequent moves is less likely to be frowned on if the skills offered and achievements shown are relevant to the job you're applying for now. If it is clear that in each role you've occupied you've been promoted or selected for specific strengths or skills, then employers will see you as a sought-after individual rather than a job hopper.

MAKE IT HAPPEN

Be self-aware
Review your career so far, asking yourself some key questions. For example, what expertise do you have? What achievements are you proud of? What work have you received praise and recognition for? What were the outcomes of these achievements for your clients, team, or organisation? What flair or talents have you not yet fully used? Do you have areas of untapped potential?

Also think about the skills you've used throughout your career so far and any differences in the way you've worked from job to job. Go through a typical working week writing down each skill, strength, or knowledge area that you have used on a separate piece of paper or Post-it note. Do this for each job you've held. You can then cluster your notes, grouping those that fit together and giving each group a title, such as 'Organising', 'Communicating', or 'People skills'. Doing this will identify and organise your transferable skills and help you be clearer about what you're offering other employers.

Finally, draw other elements into the mix. What does your career need to do for you (and your family)? What do you value in work? What makes a job satisfying? What would you or do you hate in a job? Thinking about these questions will help you to identify your needs and constraints, such as financial obligations or geographical preferences.

Do a market and trend analysis

Next you need to think about the market you're working in and what way that seems to be moving. What do you like about the market you're currently in? What are the trends within this function and industry? How might these affect your prospects going forwards? Think in broad terms about who might have a need for your skills. What goals or problems could you help them with and what else can you offer them?

These are big and wide-ranging questions, so to help you focus on them, do some research. Use the Internet and your network of friends and colleagues to expand your knowledge of companies and organisations, and of their internal trends and needs. Read all you can in journals and newspapers about the markets you are most interested in and identify relevant professional bodies for information on trends and the market for relevant skills. Libraries and Chambers of Commerce can be good sources of local information. The more questions you ask, the more you will know what other information you need and research often gets easier as you go along.

Plan ahead

Be clear about how you want your research and planning to fit together. Ask yourself what you'd like your life to be like in three years' time and write down what comes to mind in as much detail as you can. Write in the present tense, as if it has already happened. Then repeat this for one year's time, six months' time and one month's time. This '3161' plan gives clarity and motivation for the long-term future. It breaks down the bigger picture of your life into an actionable plan that you can start on right now.

A 'reality check' will help you recognise the right opportunity when it arises. Spend time on this when you are job hunting. Divide a page into four quadrants, headed 'Role', 'Organisation', 'Package', and 'Boss'. Now ask yourself what you want from your next career move. Think about the 'ingredients' that make up your ideal role, putting these into the quadrants on your page. Once your criteria are mapped out in this way, you'll have a visual aid that will help you to weigh up the opportunities that come your way. When you're invited to interview for a new job, you can use the sheet to come up with strong, targeted questions about the potential role and the organisation.

Develop yourself

You have identified your own skills and your immediate and longer-term goals. Is there a direct match already or will employers see gaps? If there are, specify what those gaps are and prioritise them, working out what you need to learn. Divide each gap down into bite-sized chunks of learning or experience required.

Next think about how you learn best. Do you prefer to read books, listen to an expert, try things out yourself, or practice with supervision? Knowing your preferred learning style is important to your planning.

Finally, you have to be sure that you're motivated to do this learning. If you are, go back to your '3161' plan and write in what it will be like to have filled these gaps at the relevant stages. If, on the other hand, you have more to do than you think you'll realistically be motivated to do, your plan is unrealistic and needs to be changed. Don't think, though, that all changes need to be drastic—sometimes a realistic timescale is the only tweak needed to your plan to allow your dream to happen.

Market yourself

Identify the stage you are at and your objectives. Let's look at three examples.

* During the honeymoon period in a new job, your objective is to establish good communication channels with your new colleagues and contacts and build a practical network. Here, then, marketing yourself will focus on attracting the interest of people who will make your work easier.
* Once you feel established in your new role, your objective is to make sure that interesting work is offered to you, so self-marketing in *this* context will focus more on bringing your successes and achievements to light.
* When looking for new roles, your objective is to attract offers that meet your criteria. Your self-marketing now will focus on getting yourself noticed by the right employers.

As we can see, self-marketing is continuous but it will change in nature depending on where you are in your career and what your ideal next step is. Whatever you're doing, though, think about your 'audience' and what is important to them. You may be offering to solve problems, deliver a product or service, improve quality or develop something new. To grab and maintain their attention, you need to focus on the relevant outcomes of your activities: increased profits, customer satisfaction and retention, or improvements in efficiency.

WHAT TO AVOID

You forget to market yourself

Don't assume that your work alone will get you noticed. Self-marketing is what makes the difference between a good job well done and a good job resulting in a promotion (if that's what you want). If you are looking for a move up the ladder, keep up the momentum and don't wait to market yourself until you need your next role urgently—try to get into the habit of doing it and of raising your profile gradually but consistently.

You have unrealistic ambitions

If you can't be bothered to identify trends and their impact on your market, you'll end up with a career plan that's completely unrealistic. The wealth of information on the Internet in particular means that there's little excuse for remaining ignorant about issues that may affect your future success. Even if you're not online at home, you can use an Internet café or just visit your local library to find out what you need to know. Make it your business to be informed and don't be afraid to ask 'difficult' questions of people in the know—experts love the opportunity to shine and will be flattered that you've asked them.

You don't do anything

A plan works by provoking specific and related actions which together create the desired effect. There's absolutely no point in writing a plan, carrying out the first action, then leaving it to gather dust. You have to be ready to keep plugging away at your to-do list in order to get a good result. You may get downhearted at times—you're only human—but try to keep setbacks in perspective and to keep your goal in sight.

You're not flexible

A plan is there to make your objectives happen, and so is tied in to real life. Just as life shifts and changes all the time, so must you and your objectives. Take time to review your plans regularly so that you can take into account unexpected twists and turns at work or other areas of your life. The beauty of a '3161' plan is that it forces you to do this—each month you have to decide what to put into this month's plan so that, in turn, you can make the next 6 months' plan happen. Re-examine your chosen strategy as often as you need to make sure it still describes the future you want.

USEFUL LINKS

BBC One Life: **www.bbc.co.uk/radio1/onelife/work/index.shtml**
The Open University: **www.open.ac.uk/learners-guide/careers/**
Total Jobs.com: **www.totaljobs.com/editorial/getadvice/index.shtm**

Know When It's Time to Move On

Very few people stay in one job or at one company or one organisation for their whole career these days. Deciding to move on can be hard, though, and there's a lot to think about. The best time to go is when you feel your role will no longer meet your objectives beyond the short-term, or when you feel there are other roles out there that will bring you closer to the future that you want. Common reasons for moving on are:

- **your role turns out to be different from the one advertised**
- **your role isn't interesting**
- **there are no further opportunities for you within the business**
- **no development activities are planned**
- **you're not given enough support**
- **you disagree with the organisation's values or ethics**
- **you're treated badly by your boss or colleagues**
- **stress levels are too high**
- **grievances are not dealt with professionally**
- **grass is greener elsewhere**

Recognising the right point to leave a job is difficult. The trick is to be clear about what is important to you; once your priorities and goals are established, the decision becomes much clearer.

Is this just a blip, or am I genuinely in a rut at work?

Be sure that leaving is the right thing for you before you go ahead and do it. For financial reasons, most people wait until they have found another job to go to before they hand in their notice, but sticking it out in a nightmare situation may be the wrong thing as you may find that your confidence is sapped and your health adversely affected. Leaving in order to job hunt requires guts and isn't possible for everyone, but if you can do it, it will give you more time to find the right next role and will free your mind to focus on the future.

How can I find out what other roles are out there?

The Internet is a fantastic resource for research of this type and there are many job-related sites online these days. These allow you to target your search by industry, job title, salary, and location. Simply talking to other people can also be an effective way of exploring the job market, though. People are very good at making associations based upon partial information, that is, they can see links or patterns that you might not have noticed, and may have come across occupations that you've never even heard of. Strike up conversations with friends, family, ex-colleagues, and ex-bosses—anyone you can think of, really—and tell them you are considering the future and wondering what other options there are for you. Briefly explain your main skills and strengths and ask them what jobs they can imagine you doing well. The information you get may be interesting, stimulating, and surprising, but try not to get too carried away with it until you have followed it up with some research of your own.

MAKE IT HAPPEN

Be sure of what you feel

Take a moment to acknowledge your feelings, as decision-making is an emotional as well as a rational process. What are the main issues and how do you feel about these? Write down words that describe your reactions to the important issues facing you. When you have finished, review what you have written and try to understand what has prompted these emotions. This is important work for two reasons:

* If you decide to stay in your current job, you need to come to terms with these reactions and find strategies for coping better in the future.
* If you decide to move on, you'll need to deal with and 'park' these issues and emotions for good in order to start afresh and leave old insecurities and problems behind.

Do a reality check

Break down what you really want from a role, keeping it realistic and bearing your long-term career plan in mind. This will give you a list of the criteria against which you will weigh up your current role and any offers you get in the future.

Start with a blank sheet of paper and divide it in four. What are the elements of the ideal job? Think about:

- What kind of organisation do you want to work for? Some factors you may consider are size, sector, environment, philosophy, attitude to staff, prospects for learning, and opportunities for promotion.
- What are the ingredients of the ideal role? What would be your main focus, type of activity, travel, status (full- or part-time), and hours?
- What do you want in a boss? Someone hands-on or hands-off? A mentor with a consultative style or someone who can give a prescriptive lead?
- What will make up your ideal package? What would be your basic pay, bonus, car, and holiday allowance? Factor in what you'd want in terms of relocation package (if appropriate), flexible working options, and overtime.

As an example, below is a fully-worked reality check for someone who works in HR.

Elements of the ideal organisation:
Charismatic leader with a vision that works in reality
Communicates a clear strategy
Actually implements, rather than gives lip-service to that strategy
Tangible products/services or output
Meaningful products or services that I can take pride in
Not a status-driven organisation
HR represented on the board
Respect for employees
Nice offices
Efficiently run

Elements of the ideal role:
Working within a team, able to spark off each others' ideas
Friendly team at work (possibly socialise outside work)
Variety and novelty
Stimulating work with plenty of challenges
Opportunities for progression
Some elements familiar or drawing on processes I already know
Using my current HR expertise
Good communication between the parts of the business.

Elements of the ideal boss:
Knowledgeable
Provides clear direction, then hands-off
Supportive, able to mentor
Manages the boardroom relationships well
Imposes deadlines
Direct but caring
Empathetic, sensitive
Appreciative
Great motivator

Elements of the ideal package:
£40K salary plus:
Pension scheme
Medical insurance and life policy
Car and parking or season ticket
5 weeks' holiday
Family-friendly policies
Flexitime, so I'm not tied to 9–5 every day

Look at what you've got

Now take another sheet of paper and divide it in the same way. You've just identified the criteria you're looking for in an ideal role, so now you need to rate your *current* role on each of the criteria on a scale of 1–10, where 10 is ideal and 1 is totally unbearable.

Write comments for each rating too, such as what it would take to make things better, the extent to which you are in control of the situation, and how likely it is that things may change in the near future.

When you review this work, you may just have one or two criteria with terrible scores and recognise that if you can find a way to improve these, it may be worthwhile staying. Perhaps you can use your reality check to talk through the issue with your boss? If you're going to do this, remember to balance the discussion about what you want or need from a role with what you are giving and your employer is getting in return.

If, on the other hand, you see several areas where your current role is just not working for you, it's probably time to cut your losses and find an alternative.

Check out your options

It's time to review the market. Until you are clear about what you might be moving on to, it's impossible to weigh up the decision properly.

Start with a list of the options, asking yourself for each one: what do I need to know about this to decide if it's for me? Then decide how you will get that information: you could try the Internet, a contact, a professional body, or another way. When this list is finished use it as an actionlist so that you can target the relevant next steps. As you research the options, some will start to look more and more interesting while others may have barriers or sticking points. As you research, the list usually gets shorter as some options prove to be impracticable but you may discover more options as you go—it all depends on you, what you want, and what's available at any given time.

You may want to concentrate on options in your local area. Put out some feelers by scanning newspapers, calling two or three recruitment agencies, and visiting local companies' websites. Finally, think about the timing. You may decide to change job when the market is at its most competitive or you may decide to stick out your current job until the market picks up and your chances of getting the role you want increase.

Make the decision

Analyse the pros and cons using your BRAINS:

* Benefits: in what way would you benefit from staying where you are?
* Risks: what would you risk if you stayed?
* Advantages: what are the advantages of moving on?
* Implications: what are the implications of moving on?
* Now: is now the best time for this move?
* So . . . what do I feel about this decision?

WHAT TO AVOID

You jump from the frying pan into the fire

So you hate your job and have been offered something that looks better. Should you accept it? Accepting the first role that is offered in order to get away from an unbearable situation may seem fine at first, but if you've rushed the decision it can turn out to be a nightmare. Go carefully through a reality check and politely request enough time to get the information you need. Don't rely on the 'hype' of either the job advert or your prospective employer. Ask the new organisation if you can talk to some members of the department you'll be joining to satisfy yourself that it is the right decision for you before you sign on the dotted line.

You lack the confidence to negotiate

If you are keen to get a new job, it's easy to feel that you should just take what is offered but don't forget to ask yourself:

* Will I be happy with this package in 6 months' time?
* Is this pay above or below the average for the market?
* Is this pay similar or different to my future colleagues'?
* Given my skills and experience, is this the right level of pay?
* Will I still be happy if I work a lot of overtime?

There may also be elements other than the package that you've identified from your reality check as not quite right for you. To tackle these, wait until you get the written contract, identify what the issues are, and then call your future employer to ask what can be done to improve these elements. Make it clear how interested you are in the role so that your prospective new bosses don't feel as if they've been given an ultimatum. Remind them of what you'll be bringing in terms of skills and strengths, and of the ways in which the role fits your profile. Allow them time to come back to you with an adjusted offer.

USEFUL LINKS

BBC One Life: **www.bbc.co.uk/radio1/onelife/work/index.shtml**
Total Jobs.com: **http://jobs.msn.co.uk/LearnDirect/JobProfileSearch.asp**

Make the Decision to Take a Risky Career Move

Everything in business today is risky. There is no such thing as a safe bet. It's certainly risky to leave a familiar job with routines, expectations, and objectives that you're comfortable with to test the limits of your courage and skills in a strange environment, but, as thousands of redundant employees in global companies can attest, it's not exactly safe holding onto a job that is as dependable as a leaky lifeboat.

Whether you should decide to make that risky career move is entirely up to the nature of the risk and your ability to cope with the possible negative consequences. The risk itself may be made up of any number of factors, such as your ability to move into an unfamiliar job or your ability to move into an unfamiliar organisation. Are you jumping from an Old Economy position to a

New Economy one? Or are you leaping back into the old economy world after trying your luck in a high-tech, high-pressure, go-go new economy environment? Are you considering leaving a stable, secure position that's limited in its prospects in favour of the white-knuckle environment of a bootstrap start-up? Are you about to move from a solid public organisation into a family-owned business? Is the family that owns the business your own?

For some people, the notion of going into a shaky entrepreneurial environment after drawing a steady salary for years would be intolerable. For others, depending on only one income source, as opposed to the multiple sources of revenue available to an entrepreneur, may make them feel vulnerable.

The decision you make is entirely yours. The risk you take is entirely yours.

The following points are key questions to ask yourself while considering whether you should take the risk or not:

- **Does the benefit outweigh the potential cost of the risk?**
- **How many people depend utterly on the regular income your current job provides?**
- **Is there a back-up plan in case your gamble fails?**
- **Is it possible to return to your original position should you decide that your experiment was not as rewarding as you hoped?**

How can I be sure that I don't regret my ultimate decision?
Give yourself all the time you need to make your choice wisely and calmly. Think it through methodically, and then make the decision. Whatever the outcome, be sure to learn from it in some way.

I'm not comfortable in risky situations. Is there any way I can avoid this problem?
Not if you intend to grow in your career. Indeed, there are no guarantees in today's marketplace, so taking steps to avoid taking a risk might actually be the worst thing you could do.

MAKE IT HAPPEN

Identify what 'acceptable risk' means to you

If you're young and single (with no obligations other than to yourself), you can probably afford to take on a few risky career moves. These high-profile actions can give you early boosts that could position you for more momentum-driven rewards later in your career.

If you're older, perhaps with a family, you may not be quite as willing to try your luck with a high-risk/high-reward venture, such as a start-up enterprise.

Only you know how much risk you feel comfortable taking on.

Know your goals

Make a list of your short- and long-term objectives. Is your current position more or less likely to help you achieve them? If your position is less likely to help you achieve these goals, can you make slight adjustments to your present job in order to position yourself better for achieving your dreams? Or is it necessary to depart from your position entirely, regardless of what you're heading for?

Know what you value

List your less tangible values. Which opportunity is most likely to help you express those values? Your current job or your new possibility? Does one opportunity actually position you to behave in ways that are contrary to those values?

Conduct a risk/benefit analysis

This is the process that will help you determine whether the potential reward outweighs the potential pain. There are several methods for analysing your potential costs, but the easiest is simply to create two columns. List the potential pain in one column and the potential reward in the other. The column that has the longer list is the one that should receive serious consideration. A variation of this method is to assign points or potential pound values to each item. You can then either compare the grand totals or assess each pain/reward item on its own merit.

Consider the people you'd be working with

Who do you have the most in common with? This isn't a question of who you'd be most comfortable spending an afternoon watching television or playing tennis with. Rather, whose visions and ideals are most compatible with your own?

WHAT TO AVOID

You make the wrong choice

As there are no guarantees, there is always a chance that you'll make the wrong choice—or at least the choice that feels wrong to you as you begin to experience 'buyer's remorse'. Have faith in your risk-assessment strategy, and carefully watch how that risk plays itself out. There is always something positive to be gained from every adventure.

You don't make any choice at all

Making no choice is still making a choice. And this is the one that is almost guaranteed to net you no gain at all.

Modern business is full of risky moves. Those who relish the thrill of the risk, shift, and change will be the ones who will ultimately benefit from the growth and added self-awareness that comes from the adventure of being engaged in contemporary commerce.

USEFUL LINKS

FastCompany: **www.fastcompany.com/online/45/bounceback.html**
Monster.co.uk: **www.monster.co.uk**

Enter an Entirely New Field

It wasn't so long ago that employment stability was the hallmark of emotional maturity and reliability. Changing jobs frequently, even within the scope of a single career path, was generally frowned on, unless the transition was on a clearly upward path. Changing careers entirely was almost unthinkable. The prevailing wisdom was: 'Pick one thing, do it well, and put away your childish notions of further adventures into discovery.'

Now, however, most people are expected to change jobs several times during their working lives, and maybe their career. There are many reasons for this shift. We're healthier and more productive for longer, so we have time to build a body of several types of work, not just one. The marketplace changes so rapidly that many careers are unrecognisable from their forms even five years ago, and some have disappeared altogether. Some people are being forced into career transitions. But most can't resist the siren call of new discoveries and new opportunities to expand the frontiers of their potential.

The following points are key questions to ask yourself while considering whether you should make a career transition:

- **What aspects of your current career do you especially enjoy?**
- **What attracts you to a different career prospect? Can you isolate those elements and find ways to experience them in your current work?**
- **Where are you in your career life? Do you expect to have enough working years ahead of you to become fully functional in your new career choice?**
- **Does the time required for education and training reduce your potential for seeing a return on your investment? If so, is there an alternative choice that can give you the same satisfaction without the necessary investment of years of training before you can start?**
- **Will the career transition be the change that will give you the happiness you seek? Or are there other issues that you must address as well?**

Is it too late to change career?

This depends on what else you want to do with your life, and what you're willing to sacrifice. It's possible, for instance, to become a lawyer in your late 50s and early 60s, but that would require giving up or postponing the rewards of a leisurely retirement or the benefits of a senior position that you've earned in the years you've already invested in your current career.

What happens if I make the change and discover that I don't like it?

It's possible that you can find a way to return to your previous career. Or perhaps you can take your additional self-awareness and launch yourself into yet a third career. Continue thinking of this process as an ongoing journey.

MAKE IT HAPPEN

Focus on what goes right in the career you have now

Make a list of the elements of your current work that give you satisfaction. Is it the people you work with? The tasks you perform? The way you feel about yourself when you've achieved a goal? The geographical location of your job? The nature of the industry? How your work benefits your customers?

Isolate those things you dislike about your career

Consider the elements about your current work that you don't enjoy. Can you simply remove them or reduce them so that the positive elements are more prominent and you can renew your sense of satisfaction in your work?

Remember your earlier dreams

Think back to those careers you dreamed about when you were young. You probably had some big, idealistic ideas for your future as a child, and you might have abandoned them prematurely in favour of more seemingly practical choices. But perhaps the time to realise your dreams has arrived. Refresh your memory of what those early dreams were and how they made you feel about yourself when you imagined doing your dream work. Now that you're equipped with more world-knowledge and a more adult intellect, how many different real careers can you list that would realise those dreams?

Research your dreams

Use the vast resources available online. The Web continues to expand its content every day, so you should be able to discover the necessary information about any type of career you're interested in. Additionally, you can research the thousands of associations and professional groups that support and promote practitioners in careers that interest you. A good place to start is the European Society of Association Executives, **www.esae.org**.

Ask around

Talk to the people who are already engaged in the work that interests you. Go to association receptions. Set up interviews with practitioners in the field of your dreams. Don't be shy. Most people who love their work consider it a pleasure and a welcome duty to promote their field to others. Encourage them to discuss their work on two levels: not only the practical how-tos and to-dos, but also the intangible rewards.

Seek out the necessary financial support to help you get the education you need

It's possible that you'll need to get additional education to prepare for your career transition. That could be an expensive proposition, but there are alternatives to paying for it entirely by yourself. There are sources of financial support available to you, and the Web is a good place to research sources of scholarships, grants, and other forms of financial aid.

Don't give up

Once you've identified the next career transition that fires your imagination and your enthusiasm, keep the feeling of excitement about your future alive and well. You may go through moments of uncertainty or doubt, but try to consider those feelings as temporary dips in the transition process. Transition is a journey into the unknown, but the rewards will be well worth it.

WHAT TO AVOID

You're in such a hurry to make a change that you neglect to make an improvement

Moving from one career to an entirely different one is more than simply changing jobs. It involves changing one of the most fundamental aspects of how you define yourself. You'll be changing the environment you work in, many of your social and business contacts, much of your everyday vocabulary, your process of prioritising conflicting demands. If you're like most people, you entered your first career in a hurry, without full knowledge about all the options available to you. Take this opportunity to make this a positive adventure in discovery, as well as a way of finding a new livelihood.

You rely on the wrong help or advice

Placement agencies and search firms, for instance, are in the business of filling positions, not helping you discover yourself and your new role. Many career counsellors are underqualified and merely process you through questionable pencil-and-paper aptitude tests.

You rely on no outside help or advice

Don't try to do it all on your own. If you have a high-quality outplacement firm available to you through your employer, be sure to make full use of its services. Additionally, many colleges support alumni networking groups where you can investigate the pros and cons of possible new career paths with people already in those fields. Confer with those closest to you—people who have observed those things that have brought you satisfaction and enjoyment throughout your recent years.

You pursue careers mentioned in 'hot career' lists, thinking that they'll promise financial security

Recent history has shown that those 'hot career' lists reflect the best of limited thinking for a limited time. As those lists are published, the market experiences a flood of candidates seeking those career options, and suddenly there isn't quite the demand for qualified candidates that was originally expected. If you're fortunate enough actually to land one of those hot jobs, you may discover that, financially lucrative as it might be, you're still left with that familiar discomfort that comes with the wrong fit.

You lose heart

Try to keep in mind that you're in a far better position to seek out satisfying work the second or third time around than you were the first time you took on a new career.

You're more mature, and you're equipped with deeper self-knowledge as well as with additional marketable skills and experience.

Discovering and exploring career options that you might love should never be a once-only exercise. It should be an ongoing part of your life's journey, leading you to even more exciting revelations about your potential to contribute to the world and make a difference, while making a living.

USEFUL LINKS

iVillage.co.uk: **www.ivillage.co.uk/workcareer/survive**
Monster.co.uk: **www.content.monster.co.uk/career_change**
Workthing.com: **www.workthing.com**

Cope with Job Burnout

Job burnout doesn't occur overnight but when it does happen, it can create an increasing dread of work. In fact, it can become so strong that you can think of little else. The exact combination of symptoms varies from person to person but here are the most common ones:

- **snappiness and irritation over minor things. You may have an increasingly explosive temper with a short fuse and you may lose your sense of humour completely.**
- **overwhelming feelings of helplessness, frustration, and futility.**
- **strong and persistent negative emotions such as frustration, anger, depression, guilt, and fear. You may feel unable to pull yourself out of the cycle of negative emotions.**
- **difficulty in relating to others. You may feel increasingly hostile and react angrily towards others, with emotional outbursts that can damage relationships.**
- **withdrawal from the company of others. This is a dangerous symptom as strong social supports act as a buffer against the effects of stress.**
- **effects on your health, including 'minor' effects such as colds, headaches, insomnia, cold sores, backaches, and high blood pressure. You may have a general feeling of being tired and run-down. Heart, breathing, and stomach problems are the more serious effects of stress.**
- **problems with chemical 'solutions', ranging from coffee, cigarettes, alcohol, and sleeping pills to more addictive and dangerous substances. These can mask the root of the problem.**
- **a decline in the efficiency and quality of your work. This can often lead to increased conflict and withdrawal problems, as colleagues and managers attempt to help you reverse the trend.**

If you recognise any (or several) of these symptoms, your first step is to be honest with yourself and make a decision to change. Don't be afraid to ask for help.

What is job burnout?
Burnout is an extreme reaction to work stress. Exposure to stress produces hormonal reactions in your body. These can be divided into three stages of response, which are not specific to particular stress types and can build over time.

* **Shock and counter-shock phase**: your body reacts to perceived stress with various hormonal changes that increase your respiration and heart rate. 'Shock' can be a sudden reaction but when you are concentrating on the task in hand, you may not notice it. If stress continues, your body increases hormone production to cope and the downwards spiral continues.
* **Resistance phase**: your body resists by releasing other hormones that dampen the effects of the shock. This adaptation allows you to cope with prolonged stress.
* **Exhaustion**: if stress is continuous, your reserves of hormones drop, increasing your risk of serious illness

Why does burnout occur?
Burnout can be caused by a lack of balance between important work factors:

* **Demands**: people or tasks requiring your attention and a response
* **Supports**: available resources to help you and your team
* **Constraints**: lack of available resources or barriers to accessing support

The demands and constraints of your work increase stress and the likelihood of burn-out but your supports help you to cope and reduce stress. Each of these factors can be technical, intellectual, social, financial, or psychological. The most stressful jobs are the ones where demands are high, there is little support, and many constraints. The least stressful are not necessarily undemanding, but ones in which the three factors balance each other out.

Why am I suffering from burnout when my colleagues are not?
There are many reasons why stress may affect you more than your colleagues. The way you think or feel about things is important in determining whether stress produces a shock reaction or not. This is known as the person–environment fit. If you believe that you can cope with a particular stressor, you will be less affected by it.

Control offers a protective effect against stress. Feeling trapped will make your job more stressful and over time, you are more likely to suffer burnout than if you were in a similar role where you have choice and the opportunity to act at your discretion.

Your personality also controls the extent to which you are affected by job burnout. People who are habitually hostile and angry (known as type A personalities) react in a different way to stress from others. They are at greater risk of developing high blood pressure as a reaction to stress and are particularly coronary-prone if action is not taken.

Finally, events from all parts of your life can add to the stress that you are under, and even positive events, such as births and promotions, are major stressors. A poor balance between demands, supports, and constraints mixed together with major life events can be difficult to cope with.

Can I bounce back?

Yes. Make some immediate changes and create an ongoing stress management plan to make yourself effective in the workplace again and happier in other areas of your life. Work out clearly what stresses you, how it affects you, and what you can do about it.

MAKE IT HAPPEN

Recover your health

The first port of call is with your GP. Once you've discussed your symptoms, he or she will be able to suggest a number of ways forward. For example, you may be referred to a stress counsellor, who will help you talk about your problems in more depth and find ways to help you cope with your particular set of circumstances.

On the other hand, you may decide you'd benefit from a different tack and that you need a complete break from the demands of your job. If this is the case, you'll need to get a sick note, and if you feel that you've been treated unfairly (that you've been placed under too much pressure by your manager, for example), the wording of this can prove to be particularly important. Organisations are becoming more aware of stress links to health and are more prepared to help you if you are open about a stress-related diagnosis. When you feel ready to face work again, meet with your manager to discuss your future work regime and prepare well beforehand by coming up with some specific suggestions, such as exploring the option of working from home one day a week.

Identify the sources of stress

Stress is any factor to which you have to adapt by changing your hormone levels. To help you tackle the sources of stress in your life, follow this three-stage process:

* Identify the demands that are placed upon you now, not forgetting the positive sources of stress mentioned earlier
* Identify the supports that you currently use to help you
* Identify the constraints that hinder you from meeting expectations

Remove the sources of stress and pressure

In essence, combating job burnout effectively involves decreasing demands, increasing supports, and minimising constraints in your life, tailoring your approach to suit you best (and not everyone else). For example, you could consider:

* improving the physical work environment or redesigning your job to allow greater delegation and control. This may involve some structural reorganisation or team training, so investigate this option with your manager.
* improving role clarity and finally resolving conflicts that crop up time and again. Both of these can make a big difference. Again, this will involve more or closer communication with your boss than you're used to. You'll both need time to adjust to this more interactive style of setting objectives, but better communication and understanding are well worth fostering in the long run.
* time management training, career coaching, and/or stress counselling are good ways to help recovery and long-term comfort and satisfaction.

Minimise the outcomes of stress

Energy expenditure at work and exercise for leisure are both shown to protect against the effects of stress, so look into ways you can incorporate this into your day. For example, you could combine exercise with relaxation techniques via yoga, tai chi, and Pilates. Do check with your doctor before you begin.

Increasing the scope of your discretion through discussion with your boss can also reap plenty of rewards. Explain that having more control over *when* and *how* to achieve your objectives will reduce the impact of work stress on your life.

Increasing your support network can also have a big and positive effect on the way you're feeling: this can range from spending more time with family and friends outside of work to finding a mentor who can bring new insights to the way you live. Maintaining meaningful personal relationships and occupying different roles (such as husband, wife, mum, or dad) are important buffers to stress and will help you focus on your life outside of work.

Through good coaching or stress counselling, you can be taught to cope better with unavoidable stress by changing your perceptions or beliefs, modifying your behaviour to gain positive benefits, and negotiating more assertively with others.

WHAT TO AVOID

You go into denial

Those most at risk are the most likely to deny symptoms such as fatigue and distress, and they are unlikely to seek help or change their behaviour until a crisis dawns. Avoid this by listening to the messages from your body and allowing yourself time to recover from symptoms caused by stress and pressure.

You impose pressure on yourself

If you have a tendency to be over-enthusiastic and ambitious, if you aren't good at asserting yourself or you are a perfectionist, it may take some time to change these habits. Try not to expect too much too soon and 'rescue' yourself when you realise you have taken on too much. Pace yourself towards deadlines and map out your time, building in sufficient allowance for the other things in life.

You add to existing stress

Psychologists call this 'problems about problems': under pressure you become concerned about your work, and as pressure mounts, symptoms of your concern increase until they become more worrying than the initial trouble. For example, let's say you are finding it hard to sleep because of pressure at work. You then start to worry about the effect of the lack of sleep on your performance, so you take sleeping tablets. Now you worry about the effect of these on your health. As you can see, if you follow this pattern everything will become increasingly worse, so you need to break the cycle. Concentrate on the root of the problem and take action to balance your demands, supports, and constraints.

You relapse

When you are combating job burnout, give yourself a traffic light system to recognise 'green' comfort zone symptoms, 'amber' stretch zone symptoms, and 'red' stress symptoms. Notice what triggers you to move between these zones and set aside some time regularly to ask yourself 'how do I feel right now? What are the triggers?' Think up some strategies in advance so that you'll know what to do if you feel 'amber' or recognise the onset of 'red' symptoms. Being prepared will in itself help you to feel more in control of yourself and your situation.

USEFUL LINKS

Knowledge.com **www.knowledge.com/Top/Society/Work/Job_Burnout**
Mind Tools: **www.mindtools.com/pages/article/newTCS_08.htm**
PsychTests.com: **www.psychtests.com/tests/career/burnout1_r_access.html**

Consider Taking a Career Break

A career break is a period away from the usual working role and its routine and there are many positive reasons to consider taking one. A new parental role is the most common reason, but study, travel, trying out a business idea, or caring for a sick relative are other positive priorities that trigger people to spend a period away from work.

People may also take a break to get away from negative aspects of their career. Stress and pressure, office politics, and turbulent periods of upheaval can all make employees look for a change of scene. This allows them to recharge their batteries, get back in touch with their core values, and maintain their health.

If you do take a career break, you have some options to think about once you get back; you might return to your old job or look for a new challenge when you're ready. These days companies are more likely to look on career breaks favourably and even an enlightened employer may have a policy that goes far beyond statutory parental rights. Rather than lose the investment already made in your training and development, they agree to career breaks in the hope that their people will eventually return to employment with increased commitment, renewed loyalty, a broader perspective, and additional skills.

I've been working for quite a while now. Am I throwing away everything I've achieved if I take a break?

While time off doing nothing will be very hard to sell on your CV, having and achieving some valuable personal objectives during your time away may well affect your career for the better. You'll often be perceived with respect (and perhaps a little jealousy) for having the initiative, confidence, and determination to realise a dream. You'll need to make sure that you communicate what you've gained from your break clearly and positively, though. Stress the benefits when you describe what you've been doing and quantify your achievements if you can. For example, if you have management skills and you have been working overseas for a charity, you could say: 'I helped secure finance for a health centre which enabled it to take on three more members of staff and increase its impact in the community'.

What are the main obstacles?

Your other priorities are actually the main obstacles. The most common reasons for not taking a long career break are to do with one's partner, family, career, house, or sporting ambitions. For most people, giving up work for a period of time means a loss of income on which they have become dependant.

In general, the younger you are and the less routine your life is, the less inhibited you may feel in taking the plunge. At the other end of the spectrum, there are some lucky people for whom a career break of 12 or 24 months can be managed on savings alone, allowing them to return to pick up their previous routine without any material change.

Will my skills be downgraded?

12 months away from a role will not generally leave you with a skills issue. The more technical your role and the longer you spend away from it, though, the more time and effort you will have to put into staying in touch.

Some employers, for example in healthcare professions, find it so important to retain good workers that they will not only allow them to take a lengthy break but will fund their skills updates on their return. In other areas, it may be down to you to update yourself. For more specific advice on this area, talk to the relevant managers in your company or organisation or contact an industry body for advice. If you belong to a trade union, they may also be able to help.

Can I be made redundant while on my career break?

Yes. Your employer is expected to consult with you and your trade union in the usual way. If your employer decides to select you for redundancy *solely* because you are on a career break, though, this could be held to be unfair redundancy selection.

The length of time you've been working for your employer will have a bearing on the situation. If you have 12 months' continuous service, you are protected against unfair dismissal, including unfair selection for redundancy, and if you have two years' continuous service, you are also entitled to a redundancy payment.

A break of one week will break this continuity, except under circumstances where it is customary for such absence to count for continuity. If, therefore, you can show that absence on a career break constitutes such circumstances, you'd be protected. As this is a complex area, discuss it with your employer and ask for a statement about continuity to be added to any letters regarding your career break arrangements.

MAKE IT HAPPEN

Decide on your objectives

Step back and take some time to ask yourself why a career break holds such appeal. You need to start off with an idea of what you hope to experience or achieve. What secondary or underlying objectives do you have? Visualise the beginning, middle, and end of your time away and your eventual return to work. Make notes about how you want it to be in an *ideal* situation, but also think about how it might work realistically.

Prepare to ask your employer

When you broach the issue with your boss, be clear in your mind about everything you want. Take along some notes as prompts if you'd find that helpful. Know what you are asking for, including the length of time away, pay and benefits, continuity of employment, possibility of return to the same role, and so on. To make the idea seem as attractive as possible, you need to be able to explain what benefits your break will bring both for you and your employer, and prepare a statement about wanting to return. Make a business case that would encourage your employer to support your request. For example, let's say that you work for a large multinational organisation but that you'd like to spend some time abroad learning Spanish. You could say that the language skills you'd gain on your break would be put to good use when you return as you'd be able to liaise more quickly and effectively with your organisation's branches in both Europe and Latin America. You could also find out whether there's a policy that provides for sponsored sabbaticals. Your employer might be prepared to provide what you request, or suggest a compromise. Be ready to be flexible and to meet your employer halfway. Remember that your request may have come completely out of the blue, so he or she may feel a bit 'ambushed'.

Be ready in case the answer's 'no'

You have to be prepared for things not going to plan. If this does happen, first of all find out why you've been turned down. The provision of career breaks is purely at the discretion of your employer, but if they are made available only to women, then they are clearly behaving in a discriminatory manner. If other work colleagues have been granted similar time off for parental or study purposes and you have not been supplied with a satisfactory explanation as to why you have not, you may want to claim a grievance through your personnel department (if your company has one) or your union.

Even though you're bound to feel disappointed at first, look at the positive aspect of your company's decision: freedom. If you're that committed to the idea of the career break, you'll just go anyway, even if your employer won't keep your job open. The obvious downside to your employer agreeing to a break is that you are obligated to return. You may feel very differently about that once you've been away for a while, so in a way you've been relieved of that decision.

Consider other ways of achieving your goals

Part-time work can free you up to realise your dreams without having to take such a significant drop in earnings. If you stay with the same employer, it can also give you continuity of routine and of your social network, both of which can help to reduce the stress related to big changes in your life.

Working from home, sometimes called 'teleworking', can allow you more time in your chosen environment and it may also give you the flexibility to control when you work. Many people choose this option since it gives them fewer financial headaches than reducing their hours. There is a negative side to it, unfortunately, in that even if you do go down this route, work will still eat up reasonably large chunks of your time and attention and you may feel isolated outside of your everyday comfort zone. It may also mean that you can't spend as much time focusing on the new challenges you're hoping to explore. It's worth spending some time thinking through an average working week and seeing how that might translate to a home-office setting.

Working abroad can be a great way to satisfy a craving for novelty and variety while furthering your career ambitions at the same time. It is the best way to master a foreign language and to gain an understanding of a nation's culture, as you are totally immersed in it. Don't forget the financial benefits too: you'll still be earning something, so this is a good way to fund your itchy feet. You may choose to work within your usual field through a secondment or a change of employer, or you may go for a complete change, such as picking grapes or teaching English. If you are an EU citizen, working within other member countries is relatively easy but remember that if you want to go further afield, you'll have to apply for work permits/visas, some of which can be tricky to get hold of. Whatever you do, make sure you have all the necessary documents before you travel to your chosen destination.

Changing employer can give you the chance to negotiate terms as part of your contract, with a view to a future break. This works for study breaks and for travel abroad but may not be suitable for parental breaks, the timescale for which may already be dictated! If you (or your partner) are already expecting a baby, changing employer could result in a loss of rights to parental leave. For example, while all pregnant employees have a right to 26 weeks' ordinary maternity leave, you can only take additional maternity leave (an extra 26 weeks' unpaid leave) if you have 26 weeks' continuous service with your employer at the 14th week of your pregnancy. This may not affect you right at the moment, but it's worth bearing in mind.

Looking for a new role on return can give you complete freedom, and it's certainly a good option if you're hoping to take an extended career break. It may also be the most suitable route if you intend to retrain, take a completely new direction in your career, or care for children or other family members in the long term.

Take the plunge

Look back over the notes you took when you were daydreaming about your career break and prioritise your objectives. Which are most important to you? These are the 'core' of what you will achieve. Think about the obstacles that may stand in your way and the contingency plans you'll need to make to deal with them. Obviously you can't see all the potential events that may throw you off course, but attempting to identify the most obvious will bring your plan into the real world.

What is the gap between where you are now and where you want to be? Start breaking it up into manageable chunks and then identify milestones along the way. For example, if you are planning a trip abroad, your first 'chunk' is research about your destination(s), and the first milestone is knowing which visas and work permits are required.

Having a plan will help you move efficiently towards your goals, but don't feel you have to stick to it rigidly. You may decide to rethink your objectives as a result of experiences you have early on, so try to remain focused but be flexible too. Once you get used to planning in the way outlined above, you'll find you waste less time worrying or dithering.

Tie up loose ends

If you decide to leave your current job when you go on your career break, make sure that you leave with the best possible reputation so that you'll get a glowing reference. This will also mean that you can apply to your previous employer for work on your return, if you so wish. If you *are* planning to return to the same role after your break, it's even more important to make sure that tasks are properly completed or handed over efficiently, and that you train your successor as well as possible. Start making a list of important contacts and duties well in advance of your leaving date to act as a helpful resource to others in your absence. If at all possible, set up a hand-over period so that your successor can see what you do on an everyday basis.

WHAT TO AVOID

You don't keep in touch

Keeping in touch is vitally important if you want a smooth transition back into your previous role. It's also important if you will be moving on to a new career. Stay attuned to who's who and catch up with relevant communications in your business or industry. This is much easier to do these days, wherever you are, and websites, company publications, or trade journals can help with this. If you feel it's right for you, and you are taking some time out to complete a course of study, you could spend your holiday time back at work.

Feeling trapped by finances

Working out financial matters can be difficult, but it can be done as long as you're clear about your priorities. For example, identify where your money currently goes. What could you achieve with a different plan? Weigh up the benefits of continuing as you are, compared to spending on your career break. Are there ways to reduce spending so that you can save for a career break in advance? To release yourself from feeling 'trapped', remind yourself of your priorities and choices.

USEFUL LINKS

Careerbreaker.com: **www.careerbreaker.com**
Handbag.com: **www.handbag.com/careers/careerbreak/studyleave**
Raising kids: **www.raisingkids.co.uk/fi/fi_03.asp**
TEFL training: **www.tefltraining.co.uk**
Tefl.com: **www.tefl.com**
TEFL.Net: **www.tefl.net**
VSO: **www.vso.org.uk**

Manage Dual-Career Dilemmas

There are many arguments in favour of dual-career families. In most cases, two incomes enable partners to provide at least the basic comforts and modest pleasures of modern life. When both partners work, each is able to keep up with his or her career path, stay marketable and competitive, and contribute to post-retirement financial security. Additionally, the knowledge that one partner is securely employed gives the other partner the opportunity to resign, if necessary, and seek a better position elsewhere.

However, there are also drawbacks: one member of the couple may have to subordinate their career interests in favour of the other's. Time and energy demands can distract dual-career couples from their personal priorities: their marriage, their children, and their interests.

Fortunately, employers are increasingly recognising the need to implement policies that promote flexibility and tolerance for balancing personal needs with work. As an example, many companies are offering flexitime, teleworking, and day-care programmes for children, among other initiatives to help working parents balance their jobs with their family life. But, as a member of a dual-career couple, you and your partner must still be the ones to make the choices and decisions that best reflect the values and priorities that you've agreed on as a couple.

Only you and your partner can prioritise the elements of your life together according to your values. But the following points are key questions to ask yourselves as you plan your dual career:

- **Is each partner's career a primary career?**
- **How do family needs and career requirements conflict with each other?**
- **How do family needs and career requirements enhance each other?**
- **In the case of conflicting opportunities, how will the decisions be made equitably so that, in the long run, both partners will be able to look back with satisfaction?**
- **How can you make sure the long-term financial interests of the nonprimary career partner are protected?**

Is it possible to balance a career that I desire with a healthy relationship?
Yes, but only if you manage each carefully. Have a clear idea in advance about what you want (and agree with your partner) and you'll be able to make your choices consistently with your long-term mission. You'll know later whether you achieved that mission.

How can I have it all at once?
Work–life balance experts say that you probably won't be able to have it all at once. But if you work together with your partner, you stand a better chance of having it all, even if it's only a piece at a time. How much you truly have all at once depends on your willingness to make tradeoffs.

I have heard that dual-career divorces are more common than single-career divorces. Do I have to sacrifice my marriage for my career?
No. Communication, trust, flexibility, and creativity are important for every partnership and they're especially important for dual-career couples.

What should I do if it's not working?
Take a businesslike approach to solving the problem. Living a rough and uninspiring life doesn't necessarily mean you're falling out of love—just as a failed product launch doesn't mean necessarily that your organisation is doomed. It could merely mean that you simply need to alter the management of certain parts of your life.

MAKE IT HAPPEN

Approach your dual-career as you would a complex business

Understand there are various 'departments' in your private life, and manage them effectively. This isn't to suggest that you shouldn't manage them with love and devotion. But budgeting and compartmentalising certain aspects of your life and time could help you distribute your resources (time, money, and attention) in the most effective way.

Take advantage of technology wherever you can

Many dual-career homes have at least one computer. Install business-management software that can also automate certain aspects of the business of your life. There are calendar, organisation, and accounting software packages available for average consumers to give them the management advantages enjoyed by big business. You can even keep your shopping list on the family computer.

Consider your personal partner to be your business partner as well

Just as a company defines long-term objectives and has a mission, work with your partner to determine what your relationship's mission and long-term objectives are. Using long-term missions and objectives as reference points will help the two of you make difficult decisions when an opportunity for one partner involves great sacrifice for the other.

Communicate

You can only expect your partner to fulfil your needs and your priorities if he or she knows what they are.

Get professional help when you need it

Companies outsource services that are necessary but beyond their internal capability. Why not try this at home if you need to? The services available to you can range from chores such as housekeeping and cooking to support services such as bookkeeping, financial planning, and even marriage counselling.

Use your business skills training to help you manage your work–life balance

One skill that could serve you well into the future is negotiation. When the two of you take the same course, you'll then negotiate with each other according to the same rules and the same understanding of ultimate shared goals.

Recruit your children

There is no reason why dual-career couples with children should shoulder the burden of all the little tasks of living. Give your children age-appropriate responsibilities. Make them partners in your family's future as well as the beneficiaries of your hard work.

If there is going to be a primary career and a secondary career, agree which one is going to be which

If you aren't both going to put your careers first, make sure you both recognise this fact. With that understanding, you know who will be responsible for taking care of a sick child, while the other one attends an important meeting. If both careers are primary, it's important to understand that as well. Agreeing how your careers fit on the priority list will reduce the potential for major disagreements that could strain your relationship.

Take care of yourself

You're also the CEO of your own life. Remember to include your own needs into the larger balance of family, work, and partnership obligations. You're no good to anyone if you aren't good to yourself.

Make dates and make appointments with your partner

Dates are for romance. Appointments are for managing the business of your lives together.

WHAT TO AVOID

You find that you are 'ships that pass in the night'

It's so easy to get absorbed with the daily details of living and working that you forget to appreciate the life you've built together. Set aside time together that is exclusively for enjoying each other's company. Remember how much you like being together, regardless of what else is going on in your lives.

You lose control of the small details of life

Keeping track of minor details could seem too trivial to prioritise. However, those details could mean the difference between whether or not you'll have an argument over an empty petrol tank or milk carton—or a forgotten child still waiting to be picked up at an empty school. Keep 'To Do' and 'To Buy' lists at a central location where everyone can keep them up to date. Make sure everyone knows whose responsibility it is to complete those 'To Do' tasks.

You feel as though you're carrying the whole load, both at work and at home

Be sure you continue to communicate with your partner on both daily needs and long-term career goals. If you find one of you continually is the one to subordinate personal goals and dreams in favour of the other's, check in with your partner to make sure that this trend is acceptable to both of you.

USEFUL LINKS

Anglo Domus, International Relocation Services:
www.anglodomus.com/services/special.html#partner
Reader's Digest:
www.readersdigest.co.uk/health/ddcareer.htm
SelfhelpMagazine:
www.selfhelpmagazine.com/articles/wf/dualcar.html

Resign with Style

The way you handle your resignation depends partly upon whether you're leaving for *pull* or *push* reasons. Positive, or pull, reasons draw you towards a new future—you're taking another job perhaps, or leaving to become self-employed. Negative, or push, considerations drive you away—perhaps your job is no longer satisfying or your relationship with your boss has deteriorated irretrievably.

Either way, it's important to plan your exit carefully. An elegant exit that keeps relationships intact is always the best option, as you never know when you'll encounter former colleagues again.

I'm on six months' notice, but I'd like to leave sooner. How do I approach this?

Many employers might be prepared to negotiate an early departure if you approach them with a well thought-out exit plan. Such a plan should include the who and how of handing over responsibilities, as well as a detailed report of where you've left things, so that the knowledge you hold isn't lost. It might also include suggested training for anyone replacing you. Finally, you'd be wise to include a strategy for maintaining key relationships, where necessary, after your departure. If all this is in place, your employer may be amenable to your request.

I've handed in my resignation but have had no acknowledgment. What do I do?
You do need to ensure that your letter has been received, or you may jeopardise your plans to leave on a particular date. Ask your manager again to confirm your proposed leaving date, and whether there is any further action he or she would like you to take. If you still get no response, approach your human resources department. As long as an acknowledgment is held somewhere in the business, you have some redress if your manager claims not to have been told.

I've handed in my resignation and now realise that I've made a mistake. How do I remedy this?
Backtracking on a resignation can be sensitive, particularly if your reasons for leaving were born of an emotional outburst or a disagreement. In this case, not only do you have to build up relationships again, but you have to convince your boss to reinstate you. It'll be up to you to show how you'll avoid this happening again. It might be an idea to treat this as if you were being interviewed again for your own job! If you threatened to leave for sound reasons that have since collapsed, you may find that your employer is willing to bring you back into the fold.

I have a very difficult boss and I know it's time to move on. However, I am not sure how to resign without it affecting the rest of the team. What should I do?
It's often tempting to forewarn your colleagues of your intention to leave before informing your boss. However, if one of them should leak this information, you could simply make matters worse. It's always best to make sure your boss is the first to find out. Look for an appropriately unrushed and quiet moment to make your announcement, so that the reception you receive is more likely to be favourable. By giving your boss time to contemplate your news and how it can be managed, you'll reduce any knock-on effects for the team.

MAKE IT HAPPEN

Make sure you know your contract

Before you hand in your resignation, be clear on your responsibility to the organisation, whether spelled out in your contract of employment or in company policy. Be certain, for example, that your new position doesn't conflict with any 'non-compete' agreement you may have signed.

If you're moving to a new job, make sure you understand the basis on which that offer has been made. If it's dependent upon satisfactory references, don't hand in your notice until these have been checked and you've received your offer letter. It would be embarrassing to announce your intention to leave, only to find that your future employer decides not to offer you the job.

Be prepared for the unexpected

Your resignation may be received in a number of ways, depending on circumstances. If you're going to a competitor, you may be asked to leave immediately—a precaution that prevents you from taking 'company secrets' with you. Leaving in this manner can be a shock, as it can feel very negative, especially if you've been a loyal employee for a number of years. Try to put yourself in your former employers' shoes. They're looking out for their best interests and you're no longer part of the team.

On the other hand, your former employer may be happy for you, if, for example, you're leaving to start a new career, or are returning to education. Indeed, they may suggest that you return to see what opportunities exist when you've completed your studies. If you're becoming self-employed, they could even become a future client.

Exercise tact at all times

You can sometimes find yourself in a bind when needing a reference from your current employer before your potential new employer will offer you the job. You'll need to handle this situation carefully, perhaps by identifying someone who would be prepared to champion you. Because this could put your champion into a difficult position, you must approach the subject sensitively so that he or she doesn't feel obliged to represent you if there is a potential conflict of interests.

Throughout the process, you'll need to manage your relationships well. Even if you're leaving because of unhealthy or unsavoury situations, it's important to keep relationships intact. Try not to vent your spleen in your letter of resignation. Doing so would not stand you in good stead for the future.

Compose your letter carefully

A short, straightforward letter is all that is required, sent on paper rather than by e-mail. All you need say is that you're tendering your resignation and expect to leave on a particular date. You may like to say something about your reason for leaving, but couch it in positive language. Any further embellishments can be made verbally. If you write too much, it's bound to be contentious in someone's eyes.

Send the letter to your boss, with a copy to the human resources department. It's wise to have the letter lodged in two places so there is no possibility of it getting mislaid or ignored.

Take an interest in what will happen after you leave

Understand the implications that your resignation may have on the business. While you may not particularly care, try and show some interest in how your role could be managed after your departure. You may already have thought of a possible successor and be in the process of training him or her to replace you. However, don't make any promises or raise expectations too high—that is no longer your responsibility.

If your role is client centred, plan the hand over of your relationships carefully. Clients who are disappointed to see you go will need encouragement to build a similar rapport with your successor. The drivers for a business relationship should always be based on your product or service, not about you. Remember that if you plan to take your clients with you, you may find yourself in breach of your contract.

You may find that, as others get used to the prospect of your leaving, they stop consulting you during the final weeks of your employment. This can be uncomfortable, especially as you won't yet belong to a new team. It's a time of extraction and completion, and you may feel uncommonly sad during it.

Prepare for an exit interview

If you have an exit interview, you may be able to give feedback on what prompted you to leave. However, try to make sure that this is constructive and that you don't use it to air opinions and feelings that may be damaging—either to those you're leaving behind, or to your own professionalism and dignity.

WHAT TO AVOID

You tell the wrong people at the wrong time

Sometimes people are tempted to tell colleagues about their intention to leave before discussing this with their boss. This can cause havoc if someone is indiscreet enough to spill the beans beforehand. If you are to avoid the political fallout, make sure that you inform people in the correct way at the correct time.

You lose your cool

For those who are leaving their job as a result of personal grievances and unhappiness, it's tempting to give vent to all those pent-up emotions. This can make the leaving period very uncomfortable. Try to be clear-headed in the way you handle your resignation. It's too easy to lose your cool and develop a reputation for being ungracious.

You resign on an impulse

Some people hand in their notice in a fit of pique and regret it immediately. These impulses should be suppressed, as it's very difficult to retract a resignation, especially if it has been submitted in an intemperate manner. Make sure you approach your resignation with well-considered reasons that support your long-term career strategy.

You use the threat of resignation as leverage

Threatening to hand in your resignation as a means of getting what you want can easily backfire. It's too tempting for your boss to call your bluff. If you want something changed, try using the proper channels, presenting a rational argument for consideration. Appeal if necessary, but don't risk your job or your credibility by crying wolf.

USEFUL LINKS

About: **jobsearchtech.about.com/library/weekly/aa082001–2.htm**
I-resign.com: **www.i-resign.com/uk/resigning/how-to-resign.asp**
Reed.co.uk:
www.reed.co.uk/CareerAdvice/GenericCareerAdvice.aspx?article=Resign

Return to Work After a Career Break

People take career breaks for many reasons: to look after family members, for self-development, to satisfy an interest in other cultures, to recover from illness, to complete personal projects, or to recharge their batteries following redundancy. Whatever your reasons for stopping, there comes a moment when your attention turns back to the world of work.

You may have an agreement to return to the same employer after your break or you may be looking for pastures new. Either way, being clear about what you want, as well as what you have to offer, will move you closer to achieving it. Take some time to consider your career plan and your objectives for returning. What is the core purpose of work for you and what else do you hope to get from working? How much of this do you expect to achieve immediately and how much within three years? Think over all of these issues and then review your strengths. What knowledge, skills, achievements, facets of your personality, and potential would you like to use at work?

Will my previous experience count, even after several years away?

Many people returning to work after a break worry that their skills and knowledge will be out of date and therefore won't count. If it is a while since you worked or if you need a registration to practise, you may need to refresh your skills. In nursing and midwifery, for example, the NHS has a retraining scheme for those returning after a break. Those with technical aspects to their role will need to put extra effort into updating their knowledge. However, previous experience *does* count. It tells your employer that you are capable of success in the role that you did previously. It's also reassuring to you that you'll be able to perform, since you were successful before.

Will my self-confidence return?

Confidence in your ability to do a good job can drop when you've been away from your work for a while. This is particularly the case after illness, redundancy, or a maternity break, and returners often doubt their ability to cope with their busy and responsible job. Don't worry! Lots of people take up the challenge every year and are successful, enjoying their return to the office. Making sure you are up-to-date with all the latest policies, technologies, and skills will help you break back into the working world more easily. The best recipe for building confidence is getting out there and proving to yourself step-by-step that you can do it.

MAKE IT HAPPEN

Return to the same job

If you're planning to return to the same job, it's a good plan to keep up some regular contact with your team to reassure them of your ongoing commitment and enthusiasm and to keep yourself informed about changes. Step up this contact in the two weeks before you return and make sure that you widen this activity to all your regular working contacts.

Be sensitive in the way that you interact with your boss, colleagues, and staff. Some of them may have carried an extra workload in your absence and deserve your appreciation. Some may feel threatened by your return; others may be reluctant to give up tasks and responsibilities they have enjoyed while you've been away. Be tactful and do your best keep open good channels of communication between you.

Return after redundancy

If your job has been made redundant, try not to let it demoralise you. Take some positive action instead that will help you get back on track. Firstly, think about the market you have been working in. Is it expanding or shrinking? Your answer to this will help you decide whether to return to the same sector or try your luck elsewhere. Think about your strengths and skills and how you could transfer these to other roles. If you're not sure of current trends, ask people you know to give you a steer. Talk to your former boss and colleagues if you have a good relationship with them and ask if they have any recommendations about who you should be talking to as part of your job search. This will help keep your networks growing.

Prepare a positive statement to use if you are asked during an interview why you were made redundant. Ideally, this should be a very short description of the contraction in the market or the restructuring of your department or organisation, followed by a forward-looking statement about the skills you hope to build on and where you want to go with your career. Also prepare a description of how you spent your time away from work, how it benefited you, and how the experience will add value to your next employer's business.

Search for a new role

A gap on a chronological CV is bound to be picked up and will probably get a knee-jerk adverse reaction, so make sure that you highlight what you've been doing with your time in positive terms. If you find you are still getting negative reactions, try writing a 'skills-based' or 'functional' CV. This type of CV focuses attention on your strengths and achievements; an employer decides whether they're interested in the first few seconds of reading, well before noticing your career break on the second page. Whichever type of CV you write, you need to get across the benefits your career break has brought whenever the question arises with prospective employers. Perhaps you have demonstrated initiative, patience, people skills, planning and organising, or confidence and determination. Highlight any new skills, even if you don't feel that they are relevant to the posts you are applying for, as they demonstrate your ability to learn.

Job hunting can be tiring and deflating at times, so it's important to keep yourself feeling upbeat. Do this by making a little progress on your job search every day. Make sure that you make the most of *all* the routes to market: replying to advertisements, posting your CV on Internet job sites, registering with agencies, approaching companies direct, and networking with people you know.

Make the most of the honeymoon period in a new job

Congratulations, you've got the job! You may have a formal induction to give you a basic grounding in the information you need but it's still sensible to think about how you can make a good initial impression. In the first week, get to grips with exactly what your objectives are. Clarity is the watchword here. In some roles you'll be expected to make an impact very early, in other roles the honeymoon period is long. You need to know what's expected of you when, and how your objectives fit into those of the team and the organisation. Getting to know specifics about people, like a department head's agenda or a key client's pet hates, will help you to navigate the potential pitfalls and find the easy routes to achieving your goals. Putting all the information together will allow you to understand how and why the organisation functions best.

The second week is best spent finding out more about who's who and creating the communication channels you'll need to get your job done. Meet with as many key people as you can, as this will help you to handle any political aspects of your role well. During the third week you can begin to develop a clear picture of how to best play things in your own terms. Ask yourself:

* What am I going to be doing?
* How am I going to achieve it?
* What do people in this business need to know about me, my skills, and past achievements?
* How am I going to get that message out?

Start a role fresh, in two senses:

* Put behind you the worries that you had in your previous role. For example, if you had a difficult relationship with your boss in your last position, lay that to rest and don't dwell on it. Don't carry old insecurities into your next job—things are different now. Visualise how you want things to be and start on the first day as if they were already so.
* Be well rested, but prepared to go home feeling exhausted. If you're not taking on information like a sponge in the early weeks, then something odd is going on. Plan a very quiet first weekend or two so that you can rest, digest the information and make sense of what you have learnt.

WHAT TO AVOID

You suffer from culture shock

Humans find change stressful, and even changes that we want and actively seek out have an affect on our minds and bodies. Recognise that you may experience culture shock initially when you return to work and decide in advance how you can help yourself cope. Accentuate the positive when chatting with people at work, both about your time away and about your return. Your colleagues may feel that you are lucky to have had a break (those without children may not appreciate what hard work having a new baby is!) and may resent what they see as 'whingeing' about the difficulties of returning. On the other hand, it's important not to bottle up any negative feelings—not everyone can slot back in to their old life straightaway. Find an appropriate and sympathetic friend, coach, or mentor to share your thoughts with and to support you during this period.

You want to be the conquering hero or heroine

Some people expect to be greeted with awe and fascination by their team when they return to their old job and are surprised to be facing a very negative atmosphere, one sometimes made up of jealousy, hostility, defensiveness, and for managers, loss of authority. Try to react with understanding to your colleagues and don't expect too much attention. Throw yourself into your work and have confidence that your performance and your personality will soon bring people around. Be patient and remember that an atmosphere of this sort rarely lasts if you remain positive.

You don't 'sell' the benefits of your break

Unless you spread the word yourself, people may not recognise what a break has done for you. It may not be clear what additional skills you now have and how these can benefit your team and organisation. Whether you're chatting with colleagues or being grilled at interview by a panel of managers, it pays to have done your homework and to have really thought about what you have gained and how you can persuade others of the benefits. If you raised £X for charity and developed your organisational skills and influencing strategies in the process, say so and be proud of it.

USEFUL LINKS

CIPD: **www.cipd.co.uk/mandq/develop/cpd/careerbreaks.htm**
Total Jobs.com: **www.totaljobs.com**
Women Returners' Network: **www.women-returners.co.uk**

Survive Redundancy

No matter whether you're suddenly made redundant with no notice, or you know months in advance that your position is going to be eliminated, the actual event of losing your job can be a shock to your physical system, your emotional health, and, of course, your bank account. The steps you take as soon as you get a hint that your job is coming to an end will help cushion the impact of one of the most stressful times in your life.

The concept of 'strategy' is extremely valuable at this period in your career. It invites you somehow to rise above your sensation of panic and, perhaps, the tendency to feel worthless in the marketplace. It'll also help you take a new, bird's-eye view of your life and career, and see the potential for ultimately better work and greater success. You should consider the following questions as you take important steps to turn this upsetting news into a success story:

* **How can you benefit in the long run?**
* **What can you do to prepare yourself in advance, so you're not taken by surprise?**
* **What power do you have to decide the terms of your departure?**
* **Can you be consistent with your own dreams, in the face of a marketplace that is urging you to build a career that doesn't interest you?**
* **How do your skills, talents, and drive fit into the larger business community?**

Why is it important to have a strategy in place before I lose my job?
If you're able to design your strategy in a calm environment, you can coolly select the steps and actions to take later when you're most likely to feel panicked and diminished by the event of discovering your employer no longer wants you.

If I'm made redundant by my organisation, does that mean my relationship with my employer is over for good?
No. Many employers who are making people redundant recognise that it's very likely that they'll want to employ them back again when economic conditions improve. Even if that were not to happen, the business world is very small and you are likely to run into your employer in the future at a convention, or even at a different organisation. In fact, it's not unheard of for the redundant employee to be the one to recruit their former superior at a different organisation months or years later. For this reason, it's important never to burn a bridge!

What should I tell my family?
Hundreds of thousands of excellent employees all over the world face unemployment through no fault of their own. If you aren't completely honest with your family, they won't understand the strain and tension that is suddenly in your home and you'll rob them of the opportunity to support you in your time of crisis. Everyone—down to the smallest child—can contribute to the cause of thriving in temporarily reduced circumstances. This could be a golden opportunity to become closer through the teamwork needed to pull through.

MAKE IT HAPPEN

Try to be aware of potential redundancy long before it actually happens

Employers are often reluctant to announce to the workforce that there is going to be a cutback for fear that everyone will disappear en masse, leaving the organisation in chaos. But it's still possible to be aware of trends that might result in unemployment. Are newspapers reporting lower profits for your organisation? Is there a merger or acquisition rumoured? Is there a sudden spate of 'closed-door' meetings? Has your boss, or boss's boss, suddenly lost organisational power, no longer being invited to those closed-door meetings? Is your own job a vital link to the organisation's profitability or is it a 'cost centre'? Is your overall industry, or local economy, suffering a downturn? The answers to these questions might help you assess how secure your position really is.

Always take time to be a recognised and active member of at least one professional organisation or association

Have a large and intricate network of contacts that you can always draw from, no matter what your employment circumstances. That network could be your advance warning system, or the conduit for information about other jobs and opportunities in good times and bad. Knowing you have that resource at your disposal will reduce the anxiety and panic, should the worst-case scenario of losing your job actually come true.

Understand you're part of a network

'Old economy' market equations would place you in a value chain, where you buy from one and sell to another, almost always in your immediate sphere of commerce or expertise. But in the 'new economy' environment, you're actually one connection in an entire mesh—or network—of buyers and sellers from a wide variety of spheres and expertise. With a little imagination, what you do and what you know can be translated into a huge number of marketplaces, not just the one you're working in currently.

Don't sign the redundancy agreement while in a state of shock

Most employers will tell you the terrible news and then slide a contract under your nose for you to sign before you go away. Remember, they've had plenty of advance warning to devise a separation agreement that benefits the organisation. You deserve at least 24 hours to enable you to consider it carefully, perhaps even with a lawyer.

Remember that many redundancy agreements are negotiable

Perhaps you can convert your job to a contract position. In most cases, after all, the work still has to be done. By offering to do it on an outsourcing basis, you've found a way to generate cash flow for yourself while staying in touch and on good terms with your former employer. Other negotiable details can include the right to continue to use your office space while searching for new employment (the space may still be available whether you're there or not, and the illusion of being employed adds to your attractiveness to other possible employers); use of company equipment and services, such as the photocopier and voicemail; letters of recommendation or introduction from the organisation's senior executives; or a larger redundancy settlement.

Take advantage of company-sponsored outplacement services

The best outplacement services are highly valuable benefits, largely unavailable to the average individual. This is a once-in-a-lifetime opportunity to have free professional help in designing your job-search plan of action and to receive state-of-the-art aptitude and skills testing—as well as giving you a place to go to every day, where you'll be in a professional office environment with your peers. Outplacement counsellors also know the best and most powerful employers in the area, so you're plugged into a pipeline that's not available to individuals who aren't affiliated with organisations or outplacement services.

Keep your skills up to date

If your employer is offering free or subsidised skills training, take advantage of the offer. If you've been out of the job market for even as little as a year, it's likely that your technical and professional skills would benefit from a refresher course. Seize every learning opportunity that's placed before you. It will give you both a technical edge and the confidence to start your job search project.

Keep your spirits up

Throw a party for your fellow survivors, and invite local recruiters to enjoy the gathering as well. It's good to know you're not alone and, even if recruiters don't have any opportunities at the moment, they'll be glad to take a copy of your CV and contact information. The economy goes through cycles, and recruiters will always be glad to have a full file of excellent potential candidates.

Forget those lists of promising, 'hot' careers

They only ever promise a glut on the market of such careers in two to four years' time. Do what you love and build a career around your interests. There will always be a demand for employees who love what they do—they're the most innovative, self-starting, and constantly developing individuals.

WHAT TO AVOID

You fall into despair

Don't tie your sense of self-worth to your career or job. You are who you are, regardless of where your salary is coming from. If you go through a spell of low self-esteem, volunteer your professional expertise to a charity. The time spent with others will get you out of your gloom. Most important, you'll experience the real benefits of your gifts and knowledge, as they'll be received with no other payment than gratitude.

You don't take care of yourself physically

Without routine and regular exercise, the sofa and the remote control become increasingly enticing. But if you maintain a regular routine and exercise programme, your sense of purpose and minute-by-minute priorities will remain clear. The endorphins resulting from your physical exertion will also keep the blues and fear at bay. Eating sensibly will keep your body strong and resistant to the stress that comes with uncertainty.

You let isolation overwhelm your life

Make a point of filling your calendar with business meetings every week. Put on presentable clothes every day and go to a local coffee shop, if that's all that is available, just to be out among people. Meet at least one new person a week. Find a way to help that individual by introducing him or her to someone in your own network.

USEFUL LINKS

Citizen's Advice Bureau:
www.adviceguide.org.uk/index/life/employment/redundancy.htm
Department for Trade and Industry: **www.dti.gov.uk/er/redundancy.htm**
Laid Off Central: **www.laidoffcentral.com**
Redundancy Help: **www.redundancyhelp.co.uk**

Reinvent Yourself

'Reinvention' as a word implies a process of deconstruction, a subsequent reconstruction, and a resultant new thing or (in this case) a new person who exhibits different talents and who pursues different opportunities. The intended 'payback' for reinvention is gaining something that you currently feel is missing in your life, which could be anything from a successful career to a better financial situation, or a happier work–life balance, or a complete change of lifestyle. However, reinventing yourself as a *reaction* to something or a set of circumstances tends to result in a purely cosmetic change as it does not get to the root of *why* you want your life to be different. In order to reinvent yourself successfully and for the right reasons, you need to do it consciously and deliberately rather than as a knee-jerk reaction. This doesn't mean for a moment that spontaneity and creativity have no role in a life change—indeed, they're valuable forces in this process—but building in reality-checks as you go along will do you no harm at all.

I really dislike my current job and I'm not even sure I want to be on this career path. I do like the company I work for, though. What can I do to reinvent myself within that context?

First of all, think of a career path within your company that you *would* like to pursue and as part of that process, work out what your transferable skills and attributes are. If you feel there are gaps in your knowledge, think about how you can fill them, either by training or by gaining some experience on-site. For example, perhaps you could arrange to shadow a colleague who does have the experience you're hoping to gain. Once you've done this research and are clear about what you want to do, broach the subject with your line manager or human resources department if you have one to discuss how they can support you in making the personal changes you've identified. It's much better to tackle this situation head-on than to languish in an unrewarding role.

I am hoping to change my career direction but my CV reflects who I was, not what I want to become. How can I convince my prospective employers to back me?

There are bound to be elements in your CV that signpost the direction you'd now like to take, so draw attention to them and explain their relevance to your target job. Point out too factors in your personal life that mean you're suitable for the role. Don't be afraid to share your passions and aspirations with your prospective employers—this will help them see past any omissions in your previous experience. Remember that passion for a role is very attractive to recruiters; just think about how many uninspiring (and uninspired!) applications they have to sift through every day.

I'm feeling increasingly uncomfortable in my job as I've found that my values aren't those of my employer. I have tried to take on the organisational mindset but it isn't working. Is it worth staying on?

Values are strong personal beliefs that aren't up for negotiation. You may be able to *appear* to take on values that aren't your own but under pressure, your values will reassert themselves. It's essential that your values match those of your colleagues because otherwise you'll feel continual internal, and possibly external, conflict. Pretending to be someone you're not is too high a price to pay. It's much better to look elsewhere for a new job where your values are shared—it may be a slog, but it'll be worth it in the long run.

MAKE IT HAPPEN

Take stock

Many of us arrive at decision points in our careers unexpectedly. For most people, the planned career path is a myth and it's unusual to find people who decided what they wanted to do with their careers when they were at school and who then followed the recommended route to get there. When people talk about their jobs, it's much more common to hear how amazed they are at what they've ended up doing—listen out for how many times you hear the phrase 'I just seemed to fall into it!'. It's not surprising, then, that many of us eventually realise that we're not doing what rewards us professionally, emotionally, culturally, or spiritually.

The pressures of modern life drive us towards making choices that bring an illusion of security, status, and success. We find a 'good job' and are sucked into the promotional slipstream while being paid an increasingly large salary for taking on additional responsibilities. At the same time, we accumulate benefits such as private health care and company pension schemes which make us reluctant to change our lives radically. Once we realise we're unhappy, we try to rationalise our way out of it, convincing ourselves that we've invested too much in our employing organisation and our careers so far to risk starting again at the beginning. So we struggle on, perhaps resentfully, fantasising about how it could have been. If only . . .

Sometimes, we're 'fortunate' enough to be assisted in overcoming our resistance to change. We're made redundant, we suffer ill health, our family circumstances change, a significant relationship comes to an end, and so on. This external trigger often results in personal reinvention and often, too, is perceived to be a blessing in the long run. The challenge for most people is to arrive at the decision to make adjustments in their lives *before* such a dramatic catalyst intervenes. Being able to sense the imbalance in your life, the drawbacks of your current job, and the gulf between who you are and who you've become is key to making meaningful personal changes. In this way, you can be conscious of what you're doing, why you're doing it, and the likely pay-offs or penalties for doing so.

Below is a series of steps that may help you through the reinvention process.

Do a personal audit

This is the part of the process where you appraise your life from a personal and professional perspective. You could think of it as a 'force-field analysis', where you write your name in the centre of a clean sheet of paper and itemise your life's pressures and disappointments on the left and the pleasures and delights on the right. Write down everything you think is relevant, including the interests and aspirations that you had early in your career and all the things that have given you happiness since then. From this activity alone, you may be able to see where unacceptable pressures lie but if you cannot, highlight the 'break points' on both sides of the analysis in a highlighter pen so that you can easily identify the issues that really need to be addressed. The intention here is to find a way of swinging the balance of your life towards the pleasurable side of the diagram by drawing out the elements of your life that characterise you and your preferred role.

Explore your values and beliefs

If something is preventing you from tapping into your natural talents and living your life in line with them, write it down at the bottom of the sheet of paper. These are the barriers that you have to overcome in order to achieve satisfactory reinvention. They usually manifest as fears, for example: 'I will lose my income/pension/benefits', 'I have a dependent family and can't risk letting them down', 'I have hefty financial commitments and won't be able to meet these if I change my job', or 'I can't afford to go back and start something from the beginning at this stage of my career'. All these are fears that you hold without question. So question them. Are they *really* true? Do they *really* matter? If you live your life according to these beliefs, how will you feel at the end of your career? Is this acceptable to you?

Think about your dream scenario

Think about what you'd do if you were free from practical or financial limitations and write everything down at the top of your sheet of paper. This is a freeing exercise that may put you in touch with what it is you would prefer to be doing. Don't censor your ideas or cast them aside on the basis that you don't have enough money or security to achieve them—don't put more barriers in your way and remember that with a little imagination and inventiveness, there are ways around the perceived obstacle of money and security.

Start making changes

Now you've done the thinking, you can start making changes, small or radical. Working through the process above has allowed you to see your life laid out in front of you and should help you pinpoint the areas that need the most immediate attention. If you have a strong feeling about the need to change something that doesn't make any sense to you, don't try and reason your way out it; follow your instincts and see what happens. If you curb your impulses by rationalising them, you'll end up behaving in the same way time and time again. To others and indeed to yourself on some levels, your actions may not stand to reason but see what happens anyway—many people have benefited from taking a risk at points in their life. Taking action first and reflecting later has probably been the pattern of your career to date so try out something new, see if it works, then adopt or discard your initiative as appropriate.

Live the changes

It's no good deciding to make changes but then not doing anything about it. Even if the changes seem alien to you to begin with, practise them until they feel normal. Act as if you're the best artist in your field, the greatest writer, the most successful entrepreneur—whatever it is you want to achieve. Once you start behaving like the person you want to be, people will start treating you as if you *are* that person. You cannot change your life without changing your behaviour patterns, and this will feel strange to begin with. If you find this too hard, try starting with symbolic changes like your clothing or your car.

Reinvent yourself

You'll see that reinvention isn't really what's going on here. The *effect* is reinvention; the *fact* is that you're bringing to the surface a latent part of your character that seeks full and happy expression. Make the decision to live the way you want to fully and without apology. What's the worst that can happen?

WHAT TO AVOID

You rush it

Some people decide to make radical changes in their lives and jump in to a reinvention of themselves with tinny brashness and unattractive incompetence. This only leads to disappointment. Although enthusiasm is vital for any attempts at personal change, it needs to be balanced with considered decisions and a deep understanding of yourself. Without these, you'll make changes that don't last and end up feeling disillusioned and de-energised. Work through the process above and ask a trusted friend to help you if you feel you're getting lost along the way—someone else's perceptions and feedback can be very helpful in keeping you on track.

You feel pressurised by others

There are many pressures driving people towards feeling inadequate if they don't do something 'momentous' with their lives. There's no 'rule' for what you should be, however, so don't get pushed into reinventing yourself for the wrong reasons. Always make sure that it's your choice that is driving your desire for change and not some external pressure or some 'ideal' that you've adopted. Being happy with who you are should be your objective, not change for change's sake.

You pretend to be something you're not

Reinventing yourself isn't just a marketing exercise, although it may help you to market yourself successfully in your chosen professional area. People are quick to pick up on others who they think are just 'putting on' a new personality or way of acting, so be who you really are, for the right reasons.

USEFUL LINKS

FastCompany: **www.fastcompany.com/online/29/reinvent.html**
iVillage.co.uk: **www.ivillage.co.uk/relationships/famfri**
PsychotherapyHELP: **www.nvo.com/psych_help/reinventyourself1**

Pete Maynard – Target Car and Van Hire Ltd

When Pete Maynard left school in 1969, aged 16, he had no aspiration to set up in business on his own and he went to work for Tesco. By the age of 26, he was managing a 20,000 sq ft store and 150 staff. That was in 1979 and around that time, a close friend asked him if he was happy at Tesco. Pete scratched his head thoughtfully, and then admitted that it might be interesting to look at other options. He applied for a couple of store management jobs, was offered one by Asda, and immediately handed in his notice at Tesco. A few days later, he awoke to find a letter from Asda rescinding the offer. The financial commitments of a mortgage and a very thirsty 7.5 litre Pontiac, forced Pete to do a little grovelling in order to get his old job back. But when Tesco offered less money and a position in a new area, he started to think that maybe it was time to break free; time to start the Maynard empire.

MEET MY PARTNER . . .

'I met Sue in 1975 when I was assistant manager at the Hammersmith Tesco. She was a part-time shelf-filler. We didn't click at the time (well, I guess that's a nice way of saying that she didn't fancy me), and I was sent off to Cricklewood for six months before returning to Hammersmith as manager. Sue was about to leave to start her first full-time job at Lloyds Bank. I remember thinking, "It's now or never", and I asked her out. Nine months later, we were living together in a flat in Perivale. Sue wasn't enjoying banking and after about 18 months, she returned to Tesco for manager training. That was in 1977, and we both spent the next couple of years working at different branches, never too far from home.'

THANK YOU, AUNTIE

'After the Asda fiasco in 1979, I was moved down to Bedminster to troubleshoot a store that was struggling. The manager down there hated me – I guess he saw me as a threat – and for the first time in my working life, I experienced that terrible feeling of dreading going back to work on a Monday morning. The last straw was when my bosses started talking about sending me down to Plymouth. Sue and I were already only seeing each other at weekends and neither of us were enjoying our work. We talked about it and decided that we'd have a go on our own, doing the thing we knew best – selling groceries. We wanted to stay in a central UK location and, in 1981, we found a suitable shop in Banbury. Luckily, I had an auntie who was prepared to lend us £28K which allowed us to borrow the money we needed to buy the shop, and also keep our flat in London – an investment which provided us with additional borrowing power and a healthy profit several years later.

'As soon as we took possession, we whitewashed the windows and completely gutted the building, which until then resembled a typical corner shop. When we opened the doors a few weeks later, it looked like a mini Tesco inside, complete with baskets and trolleys. This was in the days before any of the big supermarkets had even considered opening in Banbury, and so we soon became a popular shop, if somewhat restricted by size. My partnership with Sue worked well. My strengths were in management and hers in paperwork and systems. We took it in turns to drive the van to the cash and carry, stock the shelves, operate the tills, and we worked long hours, seven days a week. 'It sounds silly, but it broke my heart to see people coming back from town, getting off the bus carrying bags full of shopping that they'd bought somewhere else. I wanted everyone to buy from our little shop but, of course, that was unrealistic. It wasn't that we weren't busy. There was plenty of cake to go around, but naturally we wanted to increase the size of our slice. In order to keep the prices on the shelves down we had to buy in bulk, but we ended up struggling with the lack of space. We had a couple of garages at the back of the shop which were always full of stock, but to be even more competitive we needed larger premises.'

PILE IT HIGH, SELL IT CHEAP

'In 1983, a supermarket became available at the other side of Banbury, on a large relatively new estate. It was a great opportunity for us and we took advantage of the fact that we had a helpful bank manager. We went about setting up the new shop in the same way as the first. We whitewashed the windows and gutted it. People were trying to see in, but we kept it all under wraps until the opening day, cleaning the windows a few hours before we opened the doors. At nine o'clock in the morning, I was rushing down the aisles, mopping the floors, and there were about 30 people outside, ready to pour in. We had room for a fresh meat counter, a big fresh fruit and veg section, a video hire department – everything you'd expect from a supermarket. Our sales went up from 3 or 4K a week to 13K a week. We were buying in bulk and offering the same deals that the big boys could offer. We'd buy 50 cases of Chum at a special promotion price of 20p a tin, and sell them at 21p. But at the end of the promotion, we'd have 20 cases left over that we could sell at full price. The margins weren't great, but the quantity of produce that we were shifting made up for that. Our 7.5 ton truck allowed us to buy six months supply of some items and that's what you need to do if you're going to make money in a supermarket. But there was always the worry that Tesco or Sainsbury would move into Banbury, and if that happened we knew that we wouldn't be able to compete.'

A BIT OF DIVERSIFICATION

'We had a couple of vans – a Transit and a 7.5 tonne truck. More often than not, they'd both be sitting outside the shop doing nothing, and so we started to let our friends hire them. It was a great way to make some extra cash without having to do very much. While we carried on exhausting ourselves working long hours in the shop, the van hire was gradually building up into a great little business. We raised the finance to buy a few more vehicles, and Target Car and Van hire was born. It felt like it was the right time to sell the shop, and that's what we did – just in time, because Sainsbury opened in Banbury shortly afterwards.

'There was a plot of wasteland in the middle of Banbury, owned by the local bus company. We parked our vehicles there, and obtained planning permission for an office. This was in about 1986 – around the time that we took advantage of our knowledge of the video rental market and opened a video shop in the town centre. We were struggling a bit, not really knowing which way to turn. In the end, it was Target Car and Van Hire that led the way, and we sort of followed it, steering a course through the pitfalls that are always to be found as a business grows.'

TWO COUPLES MAKE A COMPANY

'The first real crisis was in 1988 when Sue fell pregnant with our first son. We were still struggling with long hours and we knew that a baby would make things more difficult. My brother, John, was at a turning point in his life, and we negotiated a deal for him to come into the business. Target became Target Car and Van Hire Ltd. We also brought John's wife into the equation, with the four of us each owning 25% of the company. It became a very different business where decisions were made by four directors around a board table, as opposed to by Sue and myself at home, over a bacon sandwich. The two extra votes made it noticeably harder to reach an agreement on anything on the agenda. I had a friend who played in a band and I used to let him borrow a van overnight once or twice a week to get to gigs. Informal arrangements like that had to stop. It was a bit sad really: everything was changing and I struggled to adjust. But there were advantages in having the additional manpower, and the company grew rapidly. By 1996, we had 11 branches in Oxfordshire and neighbouring counties with between 60 and 70 full time employees and an annual turnover of five million pounds.'

MORE BUSINESS, MORE STRESS

'Target was doing fantastically well, but I'd got to the stage when I really wasn't enjoying myself any more. We'd taken on a general manager who I didn't see eye-to-eye with, and board meetings were becoming more and more argumentative. To make matters worse, the stress was beginning to take its toll on my health. My dad always used to say, "Do whatever you like, as long as it makes you happy", and I guess that's always been at the back of my mind. After lots of long conversations well away from the boardroom and over lots of bottles of wine, it was decided that I would leave, but that Sue would stay on. 'There wasn't enough money available in the company to buy back my full 25%, so I left 10% where it was. It was established as a fixed sum which attracted interest, paid monthly. The 15% that I left with was enough to set up the business that I now run, Elite Motorhomes, hiring out a range of two to seven berth motorhomes to film companies, racing teams, and private individuals. Sue stayed with Target until 2003, when it was bought out by one of the big national car and van hire companies for a number with lots of zeros. I was paid the balance owed to me and everyone went away feeling happy.'

ROUND AND ROUND WE GO

'And now, it's just Elite Motorhomes. Three years ago, we had five vehicles. Now we're running over 30. I guess it's all happening again!'

'Some people see setting up your own business as a get-rich-quick plan. In my experience, it's hard work that really counts. And, when the money starts coming in, don't make the mistake of buying expensive toys before you can afford them. It took some ten years before I could buy my first Ferrari!'

USEFUL LINK

www.elite-motorhomes.co.uk

Go Freelance

What could be more appealing than to commute to work in your dressing gown and slippers to an office only a few yards away from your breakfast table? Think of it: the idea of being your own boss, of setting your own hours and workload. After winning the lottery, being self-employed is probably the next most intoxicating idea shared by working people today.

However, before you start shopping for an executive-style dressing gown, or turning the children's bedroom into your world headquarters, you might ask yourself the following questions:

- **How much of my freelance fantasy is based on being unhappy with my current situation?**
- **What's my 'core competency', around which I will begin a freelance business?**
- **Who employs freelancers in my field of work and do I have enough experience?**
- **Who is my competition and what edge do I have over them?**
- **What are the costs of going into my own business, as well as the benefits?**

What exactly is a freelancer?

The word 'freelance' comes from the old days of knights-for-hire, but these days it refers to someone in the service of more than one employer. Nowadays, a freelancer can be a self-employed person in any number of industries, including writing, film and video, management consulting, software development, and Internet services.

What sort of personality traits and skills must a person have as a freelancer?

You must be—or quickly become—confident, resourceful, enterprising, adventurous, flexible, and organised. As a business owner, you also must be a manager, a book-keeper, and a promoter. You must be able to handle 'multi-tasking'—juggling a number of diverse projects, each with different deadlines, for your clients.

How do I decide what to charge for my services?

There are books and websites that give guidelines about the value of your profession, in terms of an hourly rate. Another way to determine your starting hourly rate is to work out what people in that field earn per hour as employees, then add 25–50% to account for the overheads you'll have (taxes, retirement savings, insurance, equipment, supplies).

Remember, too, that as a business owner, at least a quarter of your workload will involve activities you may not invoice for, such as research, marketing, promotion, and bookkeeping. If possible, find out what established freelancers in your field are charging. You may want to start at a reduced rate for the first year, especially if you're going to be competing against more established freelancers.

MAKE IT HAPPEN

Conduct your research

Making a jump to freelancing requires a kind of 'inside-out' approach. First, be honest with yourself about your motives for the move. If you feel more excitement about the future than dread of where you are now, you're on the right track. Then look at your personality assets: you'll need people skills, energy, promotional creativity, a love of your chosen profession, and a devotion to detail.

Your outside research should include canvassing the industry in which you'll offer your services. Determine how big a 'territory' you'll initially serve, and what sort of companies. Seek the advice of those already in the field, through a professional association or business group. In the best of all worlds, knowing someone at those companies who knows you from a prior work relationship is a big asset.

Develop your business plan

Once you decide to commit to a life as a freelancer—but before you leave your day job—develop a business plan. Even if you've lined up a client or two, a business plan will plot the first year's goals and activity.

It may be advisable to start your freelance business on a part-time basis, while you can still rely on your current income. This part-time approach may take on the dimensions of a second full-time job, but doing so will show you quickly if you have the determination and work ethic to persevere.

Market and promote your business

Whether or not your freelance business is in the same industry you're currently employed in, you'll need to develop a target list of companies that you wish to work for. Learn all you can about each company, its products and services, its financial health, its challenges, and its history with contract employment. Learn who in those companies makes contract decisions (executive, department manager, or contracting officer, for example). Aim your marketing and proposals at them; invite them to lunch if they happen to live nearby.

Marketing can also include letters, brochures, or e-mails sent to potential customers, as well as personal networking, advertising and promotional activities, even a website. Hopefully, you'll have built enough of a network before you start your business to reduce the amount of 'cold calling' you must do.

Focus on customer service

Staying in the freelance world is largely a matter of time: the longer you're in business, the greater the chance you'll be successful. It's far better to keep a client happy than to spend the same amount of time finding another one. Being prompt, and delivering a professional product or service for the proposed budget, are the cornerstones of a successful freelance business. And don't underestimate the value of being liked—being congenial and a good communicator often make up for the few flaws the client may eventually find in your work.

Maintain good business practices and organisation

As a freelancer, it would be rare to have a consistent client, or set of clients, for a great many years. Business climates change, and freelancers are vulnerable to shifts in policy and personnel. Get used to the idea of losing clients and gaining new ones; it's part of the nature of the business, like an animal shedding a winter coat and growing a new one.

To protect themselves against this inevitability, freelancers usually have several irons in the fire. It often takes six months to a year to secure work with a new prospective client, so discipline yourself to plan at least six months ahead. Learn to anticipate when clients need more service, but also learn to predict when your tenure may be drawing to a close. Have the foresight to build enough diversity in your client base that the loss of one won't spell disaster for your business.

WHAT TO AVOID

You're cavalier about your home office

Many freelancers begin at home and there's nothing wrong with that. But be very careful (for Inland Revenue purposes) to create a separate office that has no other purpose. Keep very good records of things you'll want to list as itemised deductions on your business tax return. The Inland Revenue doesn't mind you having such a short journey to work (actually, it does mind a little), but it has some specific guidelines under which you may deduct home office expenses.

You rely too heavily on one client

In the best sense, freelancers bring added value to a company, and companies are willing to pay handsomely for those who can deliver. But don't become complacent—valued as you may feel, freelancers are easier to lay off than employees, so when it comes to budget tightening or changes in administrative personnel be vigilant and be prepared. While having a contract may give you some security, it isn't a guarantee. For this reason, freelance work is often more volatile than being an employee, and the best advice is to insulate yourself against starvation by having a variety of clients.

You don't save for the lean times

Inevitably, there will be lean times in your freelance business. Putting aside some money for a rainy day is advisable to get you through, say, two or three months of basic expenses. Besides that, however, remember that as a freelancer, you're also responsible for paying taxes to the Inland Revenue. Make sure you're aware of what these are likely to be and create a reserve in readiness for this eventuality. However, don't forget to pay yourself including your subscription to a private health insurer and appropriate provision for your retirement.

Your business management is slipshod

Just as you must be adept and professional about what you invoice your client for, you also must become skilled at running your own business affairs. Plan to devote up to 25% of your time on various administrative and marketing-related activities. When business is booming, it's especially easy to get complacent about record keeping, credit card debt, payment of taxes, developing new business leads, and even collecting from your clients on time. If you don't stay on top of your own business details, you could be ruined very quickly when times are harder.

For tax purposes and others, it's well worth the money to have a recommended accountant look at your business. They can tell you how to avoid tax troubles and they'll often save you more in deductions than you'll pay them. They have lots of experience advising business people about a variety of issues, so feel free to pump them for information. If they're reluctant to share, ask around and find another one.

USEFUL LINKS

Freelancers.network: **www.freelancers.net**
Freelance UK: **www.freelanceuk.com/index_news4.shtml**
Inland Revenue: **www.inlandrevenue.gov.uk**
Justpeople.com:
www.justpeople.com/ContentNew/CareerAdvice/WorkingLife/Freelance.asp
Tiscali.business: **www.tiscali.co.uk/business/sme/selfemployment**

Set Up and Maintain Your Home Office

Commuting problems, being made redundant, pursuing personal freedom, bringing up children, having physical limitations, or scratching an entrepreneurial itch—there are dozens of reasons why having a home office appeals to most of us, especially those who have experienced the 'real' office world and found it lacking.

But, whether you're starting your own business at home, or you're teleworking, having an office at home calls for developing or honing skills to help you succeed there. To start, ask yourself the following questions:

* **Can I handle the social isolation of a home office on a full-time basis?**
* **Am I a self-starter?**
* **How do I rate as a decision-maker, organiser, bookkeeper, and secretary?**
* **Could I separate business and personal life if both were under the same roof?**
* **Am I a workaholic and would an office at home worsen that problem?**

Is working from home as wonderful as it sounds?

Yes and no. For convenience, cost, and comfort, there's nothing quite like a home office. Low overheads, no commuting hassles, no office politics, and setting your own hours are a few of the pluses. On the minus side, there's only you—and if you're not disciplined, you'll be spending more time with the children, the pets, or in front of the fridge than working where you belong. It can be a simple formula for failure.

How can I make a home-based business seem professional to customers?

It depends on the type of business, but start with a professional attitude and then buy some good-looking business cards and stationery. Think about adding an attractive logo and using a two-colour design on business cards, letterheads, and envelopes. Having a well-produced flier or brochure that describes your business is also a plus. Quality customer service will do the rest.

E-commerce is relatively easy to conduct from a home office, especially with a website that attracts customers. Clients need not know whether you work at home or in a sophisticated office building, so long as you get the job done for them. As with your other materials, the website should reflect the personality and professionalism of your business.

What sort of investment is necessary to equip a home office?

This, too, depends on the type of activity you'll be doing—whether it will be business or teleworking, or a personal or family office. But generally, spending between £1,000 and £3,000 should make you well equipped and comfortable. Make a list and a budget beforehand. If you're an entrepreneur, you don't want to blow your entire savings on setting up the office, then have nothing to spend on attracting business.

MAKE IT HAPPEN

Plan the layout of your office

Planning a home office involves decisions about where to locate the office, how to decorate it, and how to furnish it. Especially if the office will be the hub of a small business, you should give lots of thought to this. Some people even make a scale drawing of the room they intend to use, then place to-scale furniture in there to decide on the best layout.

Take account of tax considerations

If you plan to use the office for a small business, the Inland Revenue will allow you to deduct certain expenses connected to the business; see the next article for more information on this. For that reason, the office must be completely dedicated to the business and not merely a spare bedroom with a fold-up desk and your cordless phone. Good record keeping is very important if you plan to deduct expenses and part of the mortgage interest, utilities, and phone bills for business activity.

Make sure you're comfortable and have the right equipment

Office décor is important, whether you'll use the office for business, for a hobby, or to write your next book of poetry. Besides getting the right atmosphere (lighting, paint/wallpaper, floor covering), you may need to run more phone lines and electrical sockets into the room to support the office equipment. Beyond that, having comfortable, functional furniture will allow you to work productively.

Your package of office equipment will depend on your level of activity, but will probably include computer(s) and peripherals, software, phones and phone service for voice, fax and computer, and perhaps even a separate copier and/or scanner. Add a digital camera if you plan to put photos of yourself or your products on your website. Consider upgrading connections to the Internet, rather than relying on a computer modem to your Internet provider, especially if you're engaged in e-commerce.

Finally, there are the necessary office supplies and extra storage space for files and records to consider.

Be disciplined

One of the most difficult aspects of the home office is the home itself. How easy is it to be distracted by jobs round the house, watch TV, weed the garden, get involved with family things, have a snack in the kitchen, and otherwise avoid the work that awaits you in your office? Two factors will help avoid the home trap: being excited about your office space and the work—and discipline. Set regular office hours, have a separate business phone, organise your time, and stick to your deadlines.

Don't let yourself get isolated

Being isolated in your home office, you may develop a tendency to cocoon yourself in there or to avoid keeping in touch with the outside world, both of which can be unhealthy.

You'll still have plenty of opportunity to break away from the office to meet other people socially and professionally. Even if much of your business is conducted over the phone and by computer, it's still important to network. Invite customers and prospective customers to lunch, if they happen to do business nearby. Join a civic group or professional organisation to stay connected and also to generate local interest in your business. Get physical exercise away from the home. Join an evening class. All these things will help keep you connected, bring in new ideas, and generate lots of personal energy—things you'll value away from the office.

WHAT TO AVOID

You go halfway with the office arrangement

Starting a home office on the dining-room table isn't a good idea, nor is committing only half-heartedly to making a guestroom into a real office. If you don't treat the office seriously, there's a better than even chance you won't take your work seriously either.

Carve out a separate space and dedicate it as the office. You'll feel better and your work will benefit from that decision.

You succumb to workaholic syndrome

If, while working in an office setting, you've had a tendency to stay there until the work is done, operating from home is a workaholic's dream come true. With the office only a few rooms away, there's a temptation to 'get one last thing done' after dinner or at weekends.

It's important to be professional about your business, but it's also important that you don't let the office become your new home. Set hours, try to manage your workflow into those hours, then shut the door and leave it all behind.

You get swamped by family issues

Lots of women see working at home as the answer to two issues—making a living and raising a family. If it were easy to mix children and work, parents would have been doing it at their offices long ago.

That said, it isn't entirely impossible either. The trick is balance. You can't afford to be at the beck and call of your children, but you certainly don't want them to feel totally ignored. Racing from the office to untangle toys and do the washing every hour will soon turn your work world upside-down. Closing the door and ignoring the family completely will have an equally unfortunate effect.

Obviously, day care is an option. Consider it for the days that you might need to concentrate on your most important work. On days you set aside for more mundane tasks, such as paying bills, bookkeeping, research on the Internet, and so forth, you might find it easier to have the family there.

You lack certain office job skills

When working for other companies, you probably relied on others with jobs that complemented your own. If you decide to be your own boss, working from your home office, you have a lot more duties besides the specific ones that 'bring home the bacon'. You'll be responsible for executive and marketing decisions, financial and administrative details and deadlines, as well as clerical and reception work. Until your business becomes profitable enough to employ other people, it's all down to you.

This is where a business plan makes sense. You need to work out the details of how you'll charge for your products or services. Be careful to account for the 'cost of doing business', which includes the clerical and administrative things, too. Add in a 'fudge factor' and some profit. Assuming that you'll work a 40-hour week, set your sights on making a living in 30 hours, then use the other 10 hours to take care of the other parts of the business—marketing, promotion, billing, bookkeeping, and business errands.

If you feel you lack the skills to juggle all of these things, or don't have the interest in becoming your own secretary, perhaps you're not cut out for a home business. But if you want to give it a try, you can certainly learn what you need to know about the care and feeding of a small business from books, the Internet, or your local small-business advisory service.

USEFUL LINKS

Go Home: **www.gohome.com**
Entrepreneur: **www.entrepreneur.com/homeoffice/0,6289,,00.html**
Inland Revenue: **www.inlandrevenue.gov.uk/menus/b_taxpayers.htm**

Manage Working from Home

As we found out in the last actionlist, working from home has become much easier over recent years, especially as technology has become more sophisticated. Some people, especially those who have been used to working in larger companies, can take a while to get used to working in a less-structured setting. This actionlist offers some advice on how to get the best from working at home.

Will I be able to concentrate on my work when at home? There are so many distractions.

When you start working from home, it's crucial that you set up a suitable work environment and set boundaries. It's hopeless trying to balance your laptop on your knee in the kitchen whilst you attempt to avoid intrusions from family or friends; you need to set rules for yourself and others so that everyone can support your efforts rather than sabotage them.

I'm really looking forward to cutting down on my travelling time, but I do enjoy very much the buzz of being in the office. How can I recreate this at home?

If you're an extrovert and enjoy the energy of having other people around, it's important to recognise and cater for this. You could try planning a certain number of days in the office and balance these with quieter, more productive days at home. If you're self-employed, you may need to schedule visits and meetings sufficiently regularly for you to feel involved with and energised by others.

MAKE IT HAPPEN

Plan, plan, plan

Once people get used to working from home, they often find they prefer it to working in an office. However, to be successful, you need to plan ahead. You'll need all the elements of a 'real' office: furniture, computer, software, telephone, fax, an e-mail account, and so on. Spend some time setting up your office as you'll probably spend much more time in it than you envisage.

Make sure you have a dedicated telephone line so that calls related to work and home don't get confused. Experiment with different office layouts until you feel comfortable with your arrangements.

Create boundaries

If there are other people at home, make sure you create boundaries around the time you set aside for working. Non-work interruptions can be frustrating when you're trying to complete a task. Help yourself by establishing in advance how you're going to manage your time at home, including things like the beginning and ending of your working day. It also helps to have a separate room to call your office, with a door you can close so you won't be disturbed. Stick to your guns and people will soon get the message. If your work requires you to receive visitors, try to find an area where they won't be distracted by your domestic arrangements. Having to ignore the pile of washing on the kitchen floor can be very off-putting when the point of the meeting is anything but domestic. If you're unable to avoid these situations, find a local hotel or restaurant where you can meet for an hour or two. Again, this is about creating boundaries that will enable you to maintain focus and create an impression of professionalism.

Establish a routine

It's important to differentiate your day between being 'at work' and 'at home'. If your working and resting time becomes confused, it can feel as if you're always on duty, and when you do take a break you can feel guilty that you aren't finishing a project. This differentiation comes naturally when you have to travel to and from work, but when you're routine changes you'll need to find a way to make this shift yourself. For example, it could be signalled by a routine; making a cup of coffee, taking it to your desk, closing your door, and switching on the computer. Once you've done this a few times, this routine creates the boundary within which you can work effectively. Plan your day so that you don't find yourself wasting time. The advantage of working from home is that you have greater control over interruptions. People will no longer be able to wander past your desk at will and ask you for some information or, worse, to do something for them. A great deal of time is wasted in these 'Oh, by the way . . .' moments that happen mostly because you're accessible or visible.

Take a break

Make sure you take breaks throughout the day. Most people's concentration starts to diminish after about twenty minutes, and continuing to work after this time can lead to thinking becomes a struggle. Taking a break, perhaps a short walk, can re-energise your thinking capability. Of course, breaks need to be balanced by the need to be productive, so try not to get distracted by picking up something else that needs doing. You'll only end up wasting time and lowering your efficiency by spreading your energies too thinly.

Work at your work/life balance

Make sure you plan for the end of the day as well. When you work at home, it's all too easy to stay sitting in your workspace well into the evening and ignore the private side of your life. It can be hard to juggle these two sides of your life, but everyone needs a break from work. Try to keep some time for yourself, friends, family, and other interests; you'll be much happier in the long term.

Find out about your tax status

If your choice to work at home is linked to a decision to work for yourself, you'll find that having an office in the home may qualify you for tax concessions. Tax relief is available on your mortgage interest, heating, and telephone bills, and the cost of capital equipment and services needed to support your business. The Inland Revenue or your accountant will guide you on what tax benefits you may receive. Anyone starting a new business must register with the Inland Revenue within a strict time period, so visit their website (details below) for full information. If your income is going to reach £58,000 in a 12 month period you must register for VAT beforehand. Contact your local VAT registration office or find more information at **www.hmce.gov.uk**—remember that the upper income limit will probably change annually, so it's important to check. (HM Customs and Excise has responsibility for collecting revenue in VAT, rather than the Inland Revenue.)

WHAT TO AVOID

You lose your focus

For those who enjoy dynamic environments and the cut and thrust of being in a busy office, working from home may not be enjoyable. It's tempting for this type of person to create dynamism for themselves by finding activities that distract them from his or her own company. Flitting around from task to task can create a feeling of being in the flow but may not be very productive, though. If you worry you may be prone to finding 'displacement' activities rather than doing any work, spend a few minutes at the beginning of the day creating a 'to do' list. This will focus your energy and make sure that there's a valuable output to the day's activities.

You can't switch off

It's very easy for people to work beyond the call of duty when the office is located in the home. This is especially the case if you've started a new business; the first stages can be really hectic and long hours are often unavoidable. 'I'll just go and answer a few e-mails. . '. can become a lengthy session in front of the computer that eats into private time. Try to discipline yourself to keep to the 'rules' that you've set, with only occasional exceptions for real emergencies or key deadlines.

You lose track of the time

If you miss the energy you get from working with others, you might turn to the phone as a substitute for their presence around you. It's easy to pass a lot of the day on the phone and to find that as a result, you have to work late to actually achieve anything that day. Again, this is a question of discipline. Give yourself time to be in touch with others, but keep control of it. A large clock on the wall in front of you is a good reminder of how long you're spending on each activity!

USEFUL LINKS

Homeworking.com: **www.homeworking.com**
iVillage.co.uk: **www.ivillage.co.uk/workcareer/worklife**
Inland Revenue: **www.inlandrevenue.gov.uk**

Work as Part of a Virtual Team

Being a member of a virtual team is becoming more commonplace as organisations extend their global reach and attempt to provide integrated services to their customers. At the same time, colleagues and team members often remain physically isolated from each other due to reluctance on the part of businesses to invest time and money in bringing them together. Although tele- and videoconferencing technology and other forms of electronic communication have improved greatly over the last ten years, these media can't replicate the chemistry that teams can create as they work together to capitalise on each individual's strengths and characteristics. Building successful virtual teams is a relatively new skill that few have so far mastered, but it's one that will need to be developed if this form of co-operative working is to succeed.

I am about to take responsibility for managing a virtual team. What's the best way of getting them to bond and work as a team if they never meet?

In the absence of an opportunity to move through the team-building phases of *forming, storming, norming, performing*, you will need to co-ordinate a replacement activity. This could be an extensive briefing session run via videoconference or a training programme that encourages information sharing and collaboration. In this way, you'll put team members in a position where they have to build good communication channels and trust among themselves.

I'm a member of a virtual team with colleagues in different time zones. How can I build rapport with people who are asleep when I'm awake?

Obviously it's much easier to build trust and rapport when you can actually see someone and communicate spontaneously. You only need do this once or twice to kick-start your relationship. For this reason, it's worth having one videoconference with those members of your team who live in compatible time zones and a second with those who couldn't join you at the first conference. Encourage the others to do the same, passing real-time communication around the team like the baton in a relay race. In this way even though you can't meet everyone at the same time, you can still meet each member face to face.

I feel very isolated in my role in a virtual team. What techniques are available to create a sense of comradeship?

Try using some of the virtual group technologies that are available. Each has different attributes, so you may want to try a few before finding one that suits you. The technologies create a repository for information, advice, guidance, and war stories that bring a human element to the interaction between you all. They also create a sense of team identification, because you have to be a member to have access to them. If you go to **www.google.com** and put in the keywords: 'virtual teams', 'virtual groups', or 'egroups', you'll find lots of information about available technologies.

MAKE IT HAPPEN

Cultivate the qualities of an effective virtual team

An effective virtual team has the same qualities as a team working in close proximity. Good virtual team members are:

* collaborative in their work. They share information, knowledge, ideas, views, and experiences in order for the team to pull together as a unit.
* trusting of other members. Each member needs to know that the others will meet their promises promptly without personal agendas getting in the way.
* attentive to communication. Each member has to agree priorities and communicate progress regularly. There should be no withholding of information. Good communication only happens when every member takes responsibility for being part of the team and is committed to the team's purpose.
* skilled at building relationships. In the absence of actual face-to-face meetings, the development of strong, trusting relationships will depend even more than usual upon excellent communication.
* agreed on a modus operandi. All team members should agree on ground rules, written down or not, governing how they operate.

'Meet' all members of the team and get to know something about them

Look for similarities of values, interests, expertise, or experience so that you have a bridge into the relationship. Building rapport is the first step to being part of an effective team; without this, there is nothing to cement the team together. Share your expectations and agree the 'team ethic' or terms of your working relationship. Decide how you want to be perceived, what values you want to be known for, and what aspirations you have collectively. This may seem over-indulgent when there's work to be done, but it's time well spent. Once you've established a basis on which to build rapport, you can move on to the more concrete work assigned to the team.

Agree and assign the different roles in the team

As a group, decide who plays which part in assisting the team to meet its objectives. Outline the resources and support that you need in order to play your part effectively. This exercise demands that all members share their individual talents, capabilities, aspirations, strengths, and competence gaps.

Set boundaries around tasks and agree timescales

Decide collectively how the team will deal with failures to meet its objectives. You may need to call emergency meetings to create contingency plans, set new timescales, or realign the team's objectives.

Agree the regularity of reviews to ensure that you're on track

Reviews also act as an early-warning system if something is beginning to go wrong. Gain commitment from each team member for these very important sessions.

Discuss the possibility of conflict and decide how you'll deal with this

Many people are fearful of conflict and tend to ignore the possibility until it actually emerges and demands to be dealt with. Conflict isn't always a negative experience; it can be very creative if handled well.

Celebrate success

It's all too easy for dispersed teams to forget to celebrate their achievements, but it's important to mark the attainment of goals. Celebration allows you to release tension, enjoy your success, and move on. You can do this by organising a videoconference and agreeing to hold a virtual party. Although this may feel a little contrived, it nonetheless allows a form of togetherness and mutual appreciation. It also invites humour as you review what went well and what didn't . . .a great way of letting things go and getting them into perspective.

Learn from the experience

T.S. Eliot wrote: 'It is possible to have the experience yet miss the meaning.' If you don't learn, you don't develop and grow. Take time to reflect on how you took your part in the team and what you have learned about yourself from doing so.

Draw on electronic aids

New electronic communication systems are being developed all the time, many of which can aid the functioning of virtual teams. Most people are familiar with tele- and videoconferencing as means of bringing remote groups together, along with the mobile phone, fax, and e-mail. However, there are some other useful technologies that can assist in communicating with people who are geographically dispersed. These include:

* **Web conferencing**—This technology enables members of the team to sit at their respective computers and watch the meeting host illustrate his or her message on the screen. This technological aid requires access to two telephone lines, one for the telephone and one for the Web connection, but is otherwise easy to set up and use.
* **document storage/sharing**—There are a number of online document storage providers that enable team members to store, edit, and access common documents. This prevents the need to create multiple versions of the same document; team members can simply work on the sections they need.
* **group e-mail**—The ability to send e-mail to one or every member of the team greatly enhances the team's ability to communicate.
* **message boards**—Message or bulletin boards enable group members to go to a central place where communication can take place and information is stored.

WHAT TO AVOID

You fail to build rapport and trust

Not spending enough time on building rapport and trust will sabotage any virtual team. It's easy to assume that everyone has the same high level of commitment to the team's formation and purpose as the co-ordinator or team leader. It's important to give members an opportunity to get to know each other so that they can work out how their talents and skills will work together to reach the team's objectives. This means either a physical team-building meeting or a series of virtual gatherings.

You don't communicate enough

Forgetting to communicate with virtual colleagues is one of the main reasons that virtual teams fail. In the absence of physical proximity and the ability to pass quick messages or information over a cup of coffee in the office, out of sight can quickly become out of mind. Be sure to schedule regular meetings—and hold them without fail.

You don't establish clear understanding of roles and expectations

It's important that all members understand both their role in the team and the expectations that the team leader and the members have of each other. It's too easy to assume that this is clear. It must be unambiguous from the outset or the team will disintegrate into conflict.

USEFUL LINKS
Wally Bock: **www.bockinfo.com/docs/virteam.htm**

Martin Lee—
Working from home at Acacia Avenue

Martin Lee is one of the four founder members of Acacia Avenue, a firm of research and strategy consultants. The company was founded in September 2002 following the demise of The Fourth Room, a consultancy for whom Martin and his fellow founder members had been working.

With strengths in consumer insight, communication and marketing strategy, the team behind Acacia Avenue aims to help businesses understand their customers more profoundly and communicate with them more effectively. The company has a unique method of achieving their goals: they invite clients to their homes.

Making relationships more human

'Acacia Avenue as a company is all about understanding the lives of normal people, hence the name–Acacia Avenue as an address is synonymous with ordinary people leading normal lives. We aim to help clients develop an authentic relationship with their customers that will help them achieve a sustainable competitive advantage. Often businesses become too "internalised"–they focus too much on themselves, and don't hear the voices of their customers. Similarly, customer information is bought as data and customers end up being viewed as such. We want to humanise that relationship; we meet and interview people at home and try to bring the customer "to life" for our clients.

'When businesses run into problems and start to struggle, there's a curious paradox that often happens – businesses become more complex. Most people instinctively feel that simplicity is best, but it's also hard won. We feel that the best hope of achieving simplicity is having a vivid connection to the lives of your customers. We get businesses to put themselves in the role of the customer–how would *they* feel or react in a given set of circumstances?

'While a business's goals or profits are clearly a large part of the reason they're in business, they shouldn't be the *only* reason they're in business: they still need to be interested primarily in the product or service they are selling. Ideally, profit should be a result of what they do, not the end in itself, the point being that customers have a brilliant built in barometer for knowing when the agenda inside a company has changed.'

The benefits of semi-virtual working

'As a company, we don't have any premises—each member of staff works at home and we then meet up in one person's house once a week. We work as a semi-virtual team. This doesn't suit every business, but we've found many advantages and only trivial disadvantages to our arrangement. Granted, it is harder to switch off at night when you work at home, but the gains are tremendous. You get back so much of your day once you no longer have to commute, and all in all, we've found it to be a really efficient way of working.

'It took a while to take ourselves seriously, working from home but with major blue chip clients such as Sainsbury's, Lloyds TSB, American Express, Procter and Gamble, and Channel 4. We only took one established client with us from The Fourth Room when the business was wound up, and the rest we've found ourselves. We also get a lot of referrals via existing clients, so much so in fact, that currently we're having to turn away work and are thinking about how best to recruit and grow the team to handle the volume of work.

'As time has gone by, our confidence in our own style has increased and more recently, some clients have come to meetings in our houses rather than in their offices. Those are especially interesting encounters when they happen, because instead of being a business person with a job title, they tend to relax and be more themselves. They tend to find the exercise of seeing the world through the eyes of their customers easier without the internal frame of reference getting in the way.'

Funding a virtual team

'When we started Acacia Avenue, we wanted to fund ourselves (hence our decision to work from home). This meant that the initial set-up costs were low. We did have to pay for the IT infrastructure to support the way we work, though, and also had to forego a salary for a couple of months, but we're still fairly cheap to run and we have no plant or R & D costs to worry about, as manufacturers do—we're effectively only selling our thinking.

'The way we work also means that the time we have to spend on the day-to-day running of the business is minimal, and this gives us a competitive edge as we can get more work done. There is also a client benefit as we don't have to spend much time thinking about ourselves and can be more focused on them. We don't have to waste time on pointless meetings as meeting up is a really big deal—we all live in different parts of London. What we tend to do is meet on a Monday and do all our meetings in one day. All seven of us meet together, and then we can split off into smaller meetings as needed. We've found this a really efficient way of doing things and it also helps us set our agenda for the rest of the week. Broadband and mobiles mean that it's easy for us to keep in touch with each other.'

The future

'Our main challenge is how to grow; not in terms of clients, but how many people we can support in this virtual team setting. Our instinct is that ten is probably the maximum number of people we can have, but we're going to grow slowly and assess the impact on the company each time we add someone new to the team. The crucial thing is that we continue to defend the quality of the work we do, rather than just growing our turnover. The beauty of being a private company is that there is no pressure on us to do more than that.

'What would we do differently next time? I think it's probably too soon to tell, but on balance I think we'd take ourselves more seriously more quickly. We did feel self-conscious at first and not confident of our own stature next to that of our clients. You need a bit of success to feel successful though.

'All in all, setting up our own business and working in the way we do has been fantastic. You learn so much, especially about yourself and your own resources. In larger organisations, you have a much slower learning curve as you're not as involved in as many aspects of the business. The lack of office politics is also a joy.'

USEFUL LINKS

www.acacia-avenue.com

Apply for an Internal Vacancy

Internal job moves are considered easier to achieve than external ones. This is because the most attractive way for an employer to fill a vacancy is hiring an employee with a good and proven track record inside the business. From your point of view as an employee, internal vacancies are probably attractive if you've found an employer that you like and wish to stay with, or it could be that you want to broaden your understanding of how the business works. You may be looking for a short-term position in another part of the business before returning to your job (an internal secondment) or looking for a long-term career move.

Before you rush into looking for vacancies, it's important to consider what you really want from your career and from your next step. Your long-term goals and short-term objectives, not what is available, should drive your career path. Remember that there are a lot of jobs on the 'hidden' market, which are never advertised. These posts are filled by proactive people who seek out the right opportunity and find themselves in the right place at the right time.

Prepare for this job hunt as you would for any other by working out what you have to offer other parts of the business in terms of competence, confidence, character, and motivation.

Where should I look for internal vacancies?

Your employer may have a website, an intranet, a bulletin/newsletter, or a staff notice-board, all of which could advertise current vacancies, so check these out regularly. In some organisations the policy is to offer vacancies internally before opening them to others, but in the public sector common practice is for all posts to be advertised externally in accordance with equal opportunities policy. Your HR contact should be able to tell you where your employer advertises, both internally and externally, for the kinds of role you are looking for.

What if I can't find any that suit me?

You could make an appointment to see your HR contact and department managers. This will give you the opportunity to let them know that you're thinking of a move, what type of opportunity you're looking for, and the strengths that you feel you have to offer other parts of the business. If you feel your boss would support your move, he or she could be a great opportunity hunter and champion for you within your organisation.

My boss is leaving. What can I do to get her job?

You can increase your chances in the short-term, but a consistent long-term positioning effort will work the best. If your company has a reasonably formal work culture, always dress for the job that you want, rather than the job that you have—this goes for men as well as women. This helps people to visualise you in a more senior role, as well as creating a good impression with any senior managers and directors you come into contact with.

The higher you rise up the ladder, the more you will need to show your ability to communicate with people across the business and at all levels. Think about ways that you can achieve this within the normal boundaries of your job, and then think beyond the boundaries of your role. What can you do that would be useful experience for the future? For example, are there any jobs that your boss can delegate to you before she leaves that will allow you to develop your skills and get yourself noticed?

Without losing the ability to have fun at work, you'll also need to take your role and your development seriously. If your company invests in the development of its staff, ask for a mentor. This will communicate that you are thinking about your future within the business, and that you're working on your skills and experience for tomorrow. It will also help boost your confidence when it comes to communicating with more senior colleagues. Find out as much as you can about the strategic direction of the department and company; it's so much easier to align what you and your teams are doing if you are clear about higher level objectives and goals. Don't be humble or boastful when asked about your achievements. Lots of people aren't very good at taking compliments, but be clear about, and proud of, your achievements and take well-deserved praise gracefully. Then say, 'That was experience which will be really useful to me. How would you build on that if you were me?' This simple question gets the other person engaged in thinking about how to use your skills in the business, and often opens up new opportunities.

Not everyone is able to talk to his or her boss about ambitions, and in fact you may feel that your boss would be threatened by your plans. However, if you feel your boss is likely to support your bid to take their role when they have left, they may be able to give you some clear feedback on the areas you need to work on in order to be seen as a credible successor. Your boss may also be ready to do some groundwork on your behalf and discreetly drop your name into conversation with the right people as plans are made to fill the vacancy.

MAKE IT HAPPEN

Analyse advertised roles

If you find an advertisement, you will often see the following parts:

* **duty statement**—outlining the main responsibilities, accountabilities, and tasks
* **additional information**—perhaps about what the department does or who the customers are
* **selection criteria**—what strengths and abilities an applicant will need to perform well
* **salary guide**—this is often negotiable
* **selection process**—closing date for applications, how to apply, contact names, etc.

Two important flags to look out for are the words 'essential' and 'ideal'. For elements on the essential list, you will need to show that you fit the bill. If you don't have the exact requirements in this section, you'd better have a good alternative qualification or experience to offer as 'evidence'. The 'ideal' section gives the other desirable characteristics that the employer feels would be a bonus. As a rule of thumb, if you believe there is an 80% match between what you have to offer and the role you are considering, then apply for it.

If you are using the hidden market, don't forget to do the same analysis. It is a little harder, since you have to procure the information yourself by asking questions rather than obtain it from an advert. Even when you have an advert to start with, don't forget that you can call to clarify or to get further information that will help you decide if the job is for you. In fact, this may make you more memorable. Prepare yourself so that you make a good impression. Write yourself a list: on the left, the requirements and on the right, all the evidence that you can meet each of them. You can add to the list on the left while on the phone. Decide in advance what questions you will ask and what you will say if asked for information about yourself.

Application forms

Allow yourself plenty of time to complete application forms; it's also a good idea to photocopy the form and work on the copy. Before you start, read through the entire form, so that you can plan where to place information without repeating yourself.

Read and follow the instructions. If you don't, the person reading it may take a dim view of your application, despite your match of skills, and file it in the bin. Answer every question accurately or at least write 'not applicable' so that the recruiter knows that you haven't missed it out by mistake. Be honest in what you say and remember that application forms and CVs are often checked to ensure the information is true.

Proofreading after a day or two or getting feedback on what you have written from someone else can be well worthwhile. When you are completely satisfied, copy the information neatly onto the original form. Photocopy the final version, as it may be a month or more before you attend interview and you may want to remind yourself what you wrote. Make sure you return it in plenty of time.

Curriculum Vitae (CV)

Always keep your CV up to date, adding new achievements, skills, and qualifications, so that when an opportunity arises you can make your move without delay. Having said that, don't send it without checking that it is in the right tone of voice, and that it emphasises the skills and strengths required for the role your applying for.

Keep your CV short, one or two pages of A4. You'd actually quite like an interview, so while you need to give enough information to interest the recruiter, there is no need to tell everything now. Less sometimes has more effect than more. The trick is to get the reader thinking of questions that they would like to ask you. For example, you could talk about an achievement and the impact that it had on your department but hold back the information about how you did it, leaving this as a 'hook'.

Remember that you need to grab attention in the first half page of A4, so don't waste this section listing your middle names, marital status, and date of birth. These items can be left out or put at the end of the second page. Make the most important information readily accessible, and remove information that is not relevant to this application. An hour carefully tailoring your CV can prove to be well spent.

Cover letters

A brief covering letter or e-mail should go with every application you make, highlighting how you can meet the employer's requirements or solve their problems. The format should be the same as a formal business letter, and should fit easily on a page of A4. If you know the person in your organisation that you are writing to, the tone should reflect that fact, but remember that the letter may be shown to others—be friendly but professional. Using short, simple sentences to get across your message, write:

* an opening paragraph that immediately shows your relevance and makes a connection between you and the role you want
* the highlights of your relevant strengths or achievements
* a strong concluding paragraph that asks for a meeting to discuss the position further

Following up

People who receive applications are often inundated with replies and have to find a way to screen out those who would be good at the job from those who would not. One criteria that they may use is motivation. The theory is that good candidates are sincerely interested and excited about their role. Therefore when they apply, they are motivated to follow up their application with a phone call. Recruiters will sometimes sift through and keep the applications they are interested in on their desk and wait to see which applicants call. Those that call are invited to interview.

A follow up call is best done about a week after you sent the application. Simply call the contact and say you'd like to make sure that they received your application. If they did, you can politely inquire when you can expect to hear about interviews and close by saying you are interested in the role and hope to have the chance to discuss it further. Keep the call short, unless you are invited to say more about yourself.

WHAT TO AVOID

You 'canvas' for public sector roles

Canvassing for jobs is forbidden in local government in the United Kingdom and in some other public sector roles. What will be considered 'canvassing' is not always clear. Using your network of contacts, cold calling individuals in the relevant department or even requesting further information about the role can all be included in the definition. If you're not sure, check with the HR or personnel department.

You twiddle your thumbs while waiting for an answer

Don't put your life on hold; even if you are certain you'll be offered the job. If your current role is not right for you, look further afield, rather than putting all your eggs in one basket. If you look elsewhere you may find similar roles in other organisations that are just as suitable or even more appropriate for you.

You fall for the hype

This happens when you read the job description for a vacancy and take it at face value. Identify the issues: what would you like more of and what would you like to avoid in a new role? What elements do you expect to be different in another part of the organisation? Once you have identified the issues, check it out by talking to people in the relevant department.

USEFUL LINKS

CareerOne: **www.careerone.com.au/resources**
Guardian Unlimited: **http://education.guardian.co.uk**
Monster.com: **http://interview.monster.com/articles/internal**

Move Sideways: Benefit from a Lateral Move

Today's career environment requires more creativity, flexibility, and originality than ever before. The notion of a 'job for life' has vanished. So, fortunately, has the rigid assumption that there is only one way to succeed in a company, that is, by promotion. Previously, if you were not moving up, you were almost certainly fast-tracked in another direction: out of the door.
But today both employers and employees are discovering that lateral career moves are a creative way to build exciting companies and rewarding futures. For their part, individuals recognise that the more varied their skill sets and experiences, the more value they can bring to their employers. This translates

into increased marketability, as well as additional job security in changing times. Your willingness to move laterally may protect you from being made redundant as your company downsizes in one department while expanding operations in other more profitable divisions.

Employers, by contrast, are coming to recognise lateral moves as a way of retaining valuable employees (as well as protecting themselves from losing valued talent to their competitors). Top talent is difficult and expensive to identify, recruit, and retain. Top talent is also hungriest for new challenges and growth opportunities and will be quick to leave if not fed with them. Employers are beginning to understand that moving eager and interested employees within the organisation is an extremely valuable approach to employee development, and one which will serve them well in the future.

The following points are key questions to ask yourself when considering the option to move sideways within the organisation—perhaps, in certain circumstances, even down the ladder:

- If your company is downsizing, or if there are other elements in your life requiring more of your attention and energy, will a lateral move help you stay happily employed?
- Will a lateral move give you valuable on-the-job exposure to business functions that will help you accelerate your upward mobility?
- How receptive is your employer to the principle of recruiting from within and providing lateral experience in order to develop employees?
- Is there a monitoring system in place within the management so that your career path will be tracked and your new skills set will be expanded further later on?

Wouldn't a lateral move reflect negatively on me?

Not necessarily. As with almost every business decision, you get the best value if you make your choice for strategic reasons and then learn from the experience. A lateral move can be made for any number of reasons, and you may experience some surprising benefits in the process (understanding the ways other parts of the business are run, for example). Capture those benefits as added strategic value and you may actually boost your career prospects in the long run.

How can I be sure that my company won't just assume I belong permanently on the slow track?

Employers that support communication across the whole business and skills development are the most likely to understand the value of placing their high-potential employees in a wide variety of their business operations. After all, the best CEOs are the ones with the broadest exposure to the spectrum of corporate functions. However, if you observe that your company's most senior leaders have achieved their success via single channels of departmental experience, you might consider either staying on your departmental ladder or changing employers if your career plan involves wide variety.

MAKE IT HAPPEN

Identify the reasons why you'd like to explore the option of a lateral move

Does the next logical upward step in your career path require certain experience that you don't yet have? Have you just finished a protracted period of high-pressure productivity and need a lighter load for a short time? Are you studying hard to increase your market value in the long run and need a less strenuous set of responsibilities during your workday? Are family needs preventing you from keeping up a demanding travel schedule? Are you committed to the company in the long run and want to understand as much of it as you can? Or do you simply want some variety?

Investigate internal employment policies

Find out if there is a policy in place that supports lateral moves. Talk to employees who have made that choice to discover whether their long-term career ambitions are still being protected.

Discover which functions and divisions of your company are growing

You want to seek out opportunities in areas in which your company is thriving or continuing to expand. Talk to other employees in those divisions to discover what the environment is like and whether senior management is supportive of individual ambition and career development.

Consider the desirability of the openings that are available

Would you have to take a pay cut? How long do you think you'd remain interested in that particular work? Does the new department show promise for continued growth and opportunity? Is the management team of your chosen department well received and respected among their own superiors?

Identify what you enjoy about your current work

Think about what you like best about your job as it stands and try to work out if you'll find the same elements in your prospective new assignment. How will you stay in touch with your current team members? Would you be able to return to your present assignment when and if you desire? If not, would that make an important difference to you?

Identify your potential for success and failure in your possible new assignment

Work out roughly how long will it take to achieve your current level of proficiency in your new assignment. Are the measures of success acceptable to you? Are the requirements for upward mobility on this new ladder attractive to you?

Identify your prospects for development outside the company

Does this new ladder present opportunities for expanding your marketability in the external job market? Will it provide you with technical training and experiences to boost your competence, therefore rewarding you sufficiently for the risk you'd be taking now?

Plan for transitions

If you *do* move, be sure you and your new manager have worked out a plan to integrate you into the new team as smoothly as possible. You may have put a great deal of advance thought and work into making the transition, but your new colleagues may not be so ready for you as a new player.

Don't assume that just because you're a long-standing employee in the company, you're at home in this new division. If you're replacing a popular former colleague, you may run up against additional resistance to your presence. Do as much as you can to make yourself welcome in the group.

WHAT TO AVOID

You leave a secure position only to discover that your new job will be a casualty of a downsizing exercise

Thoroughly investigate the prospects of this new assignment, just as you would if you were applying for the job from the outside. Understand the roles that this particular post and the department play in the company's long-term plans. If you cannot see how this work serves your employer's strategic objectives, hold out for another opportunity.

You become unintentionally slow-tracked

If you take a lateral move, especially if it is to reduce your stress load temporarily for a personal reason, you may find yourself accidentally on the list of expendable employees. Be sure to invest time regularly to market yourself to colleagues throughout the business. For example, go to key meetings on a regular basis or have lunch with your former manager to stay in touch with developments in your original department. Stay up to date with your company's developments and objectives and position yourself to make another jump into a more senior job as soon as you can.

You make too many lateral moves with no apparent growth or progression

Remember that, desirable as lateral moves may be, your career path must still show regular upward mobility. When you make lateral moves, try to take a job that pays in some way, even though it's on the same level in the organisational chart. Or take a lateral move to learn more management skills elsewhere, and then return to your original department at a higher rank. Lateral career moves shouldn't be used routinely as a preventive measure against losing your job, or as a way to tread water for longer than during a very short downturn in the economy or your industry. Lateral career moves should be used as a valuable strategic career-management tool and when you're able to discuss your recent career path in those terms, you'll find that a lateral move can be an excellent springboard to an even better future.

USEFUL LINKS

Monster: **www.monster.co.uk**
PersonnelToday.com: **www.personneltoday.com**

Make Yourself Promotable

Being good at your job is not enough to guarantee a promotion these days. Being *promotable*, on the other hand, increases your chances of success and assists you in taking the career steps that you desire.
Being promotable draws together your professional skills and competences with your business sense and ability to build good relationships that create the impression of someone who will be valuable to your organisation at increasingly senior levels. When you're recognised for your specialist expertise and have a track record of success, you're no doubt likely to be seen as a candidate for the succession line. However, other personal attributes will be taken into consideration that go well beyond your current role. To get ahead, you'll need to demonstrate business acumen, political sensitivity, the ability to manage change, and loyalty to your employing organisation. These attributes go hand-in-hand with the need to communicate and network effectively and the ability to cement critical relationships with those who will sponsor and support you as you move along your career path.

I am very keen to be promoted and think I have done everything I can to get noticed. Competition is fierce, though, so how can I make sure I'm considered a suitable candidate for a new appointment?

Blowing your own trumpet too loudly isn't always the most effective way of influencing events. Being clear about what you want and why you deserve to be promoted is, of course, very important, but a subtle approach can also reap rewards. You could, for example:

- find a mentor or sponsor in the organisation with whom you can work
- approach your line manager and discuss your development plan in the light of your conviction that you have more to offer the business
- observe those that have been promoted and ask yourself if you're mirroring the same personal attributes

Try to become more visible by ensuring that you take the opportunity to mix with decision-makers and by sharing stories of your success at appropriate times. Don't make too much of your achievements or you may turn off the very people you need to court.

I am working on becoming promotable but am having difficulty becoming more visible. Do you have any ideas?

While increasing your 'visibility' within the boundaries of your organisation is important, you don't need to confine yourself to just that. Why not publish articles in your trade or professional magazine, or accept invitations (or volunteer) to speak at conferences? If you want to raise your visibility closer to home to demonstrate your commitment to the community, you could get involved in local politics.

I work in an organisation where promotion is a thing of the past for all but a very few. How can I work my way into the senior management tier?

It sounds as if you're working in a flat organisation (where there are fewer levels in the hierarchy) or in a matrix organisation (where the business is structured according to common activities rather than discrete business units. Project teams are made up from specialists across a business). In these cases, promotability takes on a new meaning as there is often no longer a clear succession route. There may be prestigious and exciting areas to be associated with, however, or some career-enhancing assignments that you could target. Take a step back and examine the patterns and trends of progressive career paths in your organisation. Once you've identified the 'hot spots', you can work out which suit you best and plan your approach to reach them.

MAKE IT HAPPEN

Making yourself promotable is not an easy task because it implies a very wide development agenda. Aspects of this include familiarising yourself with the broader business arena and general management issues, developing social and political skills that enable you to build effective relationships, and finding a personal leadership style that you're comfortable with and can develop into a distinctive personal 'brand' in the long run.

It's a sad fact that the personal skills and attributes that have carried you to the point in your career where you're looking at a more senior appointment are the very skills and attributes that can sabotage your success at this level. These include having too high a dependence on your specialist expertise, an individualistic approach that differentiates you from your peers, and an inclination to challenge the organisational status quo. Shedding some of these traits, therefore, may be the key to becoming promotable.

In addition to these features, past research has highlighted several derailment factors that can prevent an otherwise capable person from further advancement. These include: 'problems with interpersonal relationships, failure to meet business objectives, failure to build and lead a team and an inability to change or adapt during a transition'. ('Why Executives Derail: Perspectives Across Time and Cultures', *Academy of Management Executive*. 1995. Volume 9, Number 4, pp 62–72.) Two further derailment factors that were considered to reflect the changing business environment were later identified. These were the failure to *learn* to deal with change and complexity and overdependence upon a single boss or mentor. If you take each of these five factors in turn, you can be sure that you'll be building the personal capabilities that will enhance your promotability and distinguish you as a future leader.

Develop good interpersonal skills

As you progress through your career, a shift occurs in the balance between the expert contribution you make and your ability to build relationships. More senior roles demand a higher level of political sensitivity because at that level, relationships go beyond the everyday organisational setting and are more likely have an impact on the long-term viability of the business. Realising this, many potential leaders try to fake it with an over-confident communication style that conveys nothing but arrogance and authoritarianism. Good interpersonal relationships are built by people who have no axe to grind and who aren't trying to create an illusion of confidence and capability. There's no substitute for genuine self-confidence; people can generally see through bluff and blag, so it's as well to put the personal development time in to really know yourself well, understand your values, and create a clear picture of what you want. With this knowledge in place, good communication and an easy manner will follow naturally and authoritatively because it will genuinely reflect who you are.

Meet business objectives

In order to make yourself promotable, not only do you have to meet the objectives of your role, but you have to contribute to the wider business too. This means showing initiative and taking an interest in areas outside your role boundaries. You could do this by volunteering for an important project, chairing a committee, or facilitating a special interest group. If you're seen to be supportive of, and passionate for, the business, you're much more likely to be noticed as someone who could add value at a more senior level. Although it may be unpalatable to some, you may have to consider (subtle) ways in which you can broadcast your willingness to play a more committed part in the fortunes of your business, such as suggesting or volunteering for a special project. This doesn't mean that you have to be sycophantic, but if you act like someone who occupies the type of role you're aiming for, it'll be easy for others to see you in that role.

Build and lead teams

One of the essential skills of a senior executive is the ability to build and lead teams. Without this, the co-operative networks that are vital if an organisation is to achieve its objectives are damaged. Much of a person's success in this area depends on his or her ability to communicate clear objectives as well as understanding the skills, motivations, and personal values of those in their team. Relationships must be open with a healthy ebb and flow of feedback to ensure that everyone is aligned with the purpose of the team. Milestones and markers need to be part of the plan so that progress can be monitored and successes celebrated.

Learn to manage transition and change

Business and organisational models change in response to developments in the market and economy. The ripple effects of these changes are felt throughout the organisation and have an impact on everyone. Being able to field such changes and use your knowledge and insight to direct people's creative energy towards making them a success are valuable attributes of a leader. Entrenchment and other blocking types of behaviour are not perceived to be helpful, even if you feel that the change is unwise or counter-productive. If you find yourself in a situation like this, you may want to make alternative suggestions and explain the thinking behind them. If your concerns are rejected, though, demonstrate your loyalty by remaining flexible and actively seeking ways of making the changes work. Show that you're prepared to keep people motivated and learn from the new experience rather than demonstrate resentfulness or obstinacy. In short, remaining flexible and actively seeking ways of making (sometimes difficult) things happen, keeping people motivated, and learning from the new experience are all important characteristics of those in the top team. Loyalty and solidarity are values that are prized in cultures that are subject to transition and change.

Build an effective network of champions or sponsors

We've all seen people who have been promoted on the basis of who they know, not what they know, yet this is no guarantee of future success. Indeed, investing in a nepotistic relationship is all very well when your champion is in favour, but if their reputation is damaged for any reason, yours will also be tarnished because of your close association. It's important, therefore, to build a robust network of relationships that will support you purely because of your potential and personal integrity. In this way, you can be sure that you aren't reliant on the perception people have of someone else (and over whom you have no control), but that you're judged on your own talent and attributes. Think about your network and identify role models, potential coaches, and mentors for different aspects of your development plan. As you approach them, be open with your request for assistance but beware of projecting self-interest above the interests of the organisation. Frame your request in development terms stating that you feel you have more to offer the business and would appreciate their guidance.

In summary, being promotable does not rely on past success but on your ambassadorial qualities as you represent those in the upper echelons of the organisation. Neither does it rely on over-confidence or bullishness. Being promotable demands that you demonstrate an active interest in the business and an understanding of the strategic issues, an ability to reach stretch targets and build value, a genuinely confident communication style and an ability to build effective personal relationships within your team and amongst your colleagues.

WHAT TO AVOID

You irritate the people who could help you

Sometimes, people looking for a move up the career ladder make such a fuss about their ambitions that they make a lot of noise around the people who they think can promote them. This won't help their case, and in fact it's very irritating and counter-productive. There are unwritten 'rules' to being promotable and you need to work these out through observing and adopting some of the tactics of successful people who've gone before you. Find out about the interests of those in authority and reflect these back to them or make yourself known in their philanthropic circles outside the business. For example, if you know that your boss supports a local charity, society, or sports team, why not go along to one of their events?

You're not willing to change

Although a track record of being a maverick may get you noticed, this is usually not a trait that will get you promoted. You need to play down your notoriety and redirect your energies into activities that are seen to support the organisation's best interests. If you're hoping to enter a different cultural zone in the organisation, you have to make sure you're familiar with the values that operate there and demonstrate that they're part of your value set too.

You ignore your team

It's tempting to focus on yourself as you look towards your career horizon and plan for your own success. You'll be judged on your ability to develop the talent in your team, though, so it's foolish to ignore them. You won't succeed by squashing those with potential, so you must trust in your own abilities and let your team flourish too. Doing this will create a loyal group who will support you in the long run. Take care to maintain these relationships as you move through the organisation, as you never know who you'll be working with (or for!) one day.

USEFUL LINKS

OCJobSite.com: **www.ocjobsite.com/job-articles/promote-yourself.asp**
Dauten.com: **www.dauten.com/promotable.htm**

Get the Pay Rise You Deserve

You feel certain that you deserve a pay rise, but you're unsure about how to ask your boss. It's very important to think through a number of issues and to have lots of information available when you make your request. It's also important to know how to respond if you end up receiving a negative answer. Here are some questions that will help you prepare for your negotiations for a higher salary:

- **When is the right time to ask for a pay rise?**
- **How has your performance been, and what's the evidence of your accomplishments?**
- **What's the typical salary range for a job such as yours?**
- **What's the best way to make the request?**

Why should I even bother to ask for a pay rise? Won't they give me a pay rise at my annual performance review if I have performed well?

Organisations have a trade-off between paying enough money to keep people motivated to stay with the company and the need to keep down labour costs. You need to be your own agent and to promote your own case about why you should receive more money than you're currently making. It's helpful to learn about the salary philosophy of your organisation. For example, does it pay the minimum it can to keep costs down, or does it pay higher than market rate in order to attract the best employees? Does it tend to give pay rises that are close to the cost of living increase for the year (which is really not a pay rise)? Does it require managers to create a hierarchy among their staff and only give pay rises to the highest performers? If you have an understanding of the company philosophy, you can come to your performance appraisal well prepared to negotiate for a meaningful increase in salary. If you don't look out for yourself, the chances are pretty good that no one else will.

The company has not given many pay rises for quite a while. What should I do?

All companies go through boom times and difficult times, and they tend to retrench and cut costs when things are difficult financially. But that doesn't mean that you can't ask for a pay rise. If you've done a really outstanding job this past year and can point to concrete contributions, it's possible that the company might be able to find some money to reward your hard work.

I'm not good at asking for things for myself. How do I go about boosting my confidence?

If you go into the salary negotiation meeting with well-prepared documentation of your achievements (see 'document your contributions to the company' below), you'll have a stronger sense of your worth to the company and will feel more self-assured about asking for a pay rise. If you're really nervous about this, you might consider asking someone to role-play the situation with you so that you can practise beforehand. It's also helpful to visualise the meeting ahead of time and to picture what success would look like. Eliminate any negative talk in your head, such as 'No one ever appreciates what I do' or 'I never get what I want', and replace these ideas with something positive, such as 'I have worked hard for this company this past year, and I can present a strong case for why I should receive a pay rise.'

I was offered a promotion without a pay rise. Should I accept?

There are a lot of factors to take into account in this situation. If the promotion increases your skills, your responsibilities, and your visibility, and if the company is a start-up or is otherwise strapped for cash, you might agree to take the promotion. Having said that, you should also get a formal written agreement from your supervisor that you'll have a salary discussion at a predetermined time in the future, such as in three months.

MAKE IT HAPPEN

Decide on the best timing to ask for a pay rise

The most obvious time to ask for a pay rise is during your performance review discussion with your boss. However, supervisors often put off these discussions. It's one of their least favourite things to do. If it has been more than a year since your last performance review and since your last salary increase, you should approach your supervisor about your performance and your salary.

Ask your boss for a meeting

Give your boss time to prepare his or her thoughts for this discussion. Don't ask your boss for this meeting in front of other employees, because it puts him or her on the spot. Tell your boss that you'd like to have a meeting to discuss your performance, your career plans, and your salary, and plan for it to last at least 30 minutes. Don't just drop by and say, 'I'd like to talk to you about giving me a pay rise'.

Document your contributions to the company

The best way to do this is to keep a job diary or a file of your achievements regularly throughout the year. It's so easy to forget all that you've done, but if you keep track of them along the way, you'll have an excellent record of what you've contributed. When you ask for a pay rise, you need to build a business case for why the company should pay you more. You need to show what you've done for the business and document why you should be rewarded. Be sure to keep track of measurable results from your actions, such as pounds saved, sales increased, level of quality improved, or percentage of employee retention. Prepare a one-page executive briefing on your accomplishments to take into your meeting.

Know your worth in the marketplace

When companies calculate how much they typically pay for a job, they conduct wage surveys to compare salaries within the industry and geographical area. They also conduct internal pay analyses to make sure that comparable jobs within the company receive comparable pay. Such wage and salary information is now available on the Internet (see **Useful links** below). It's a little bit harder to find out information about the internal pay structure, but you can ask the human resources department for information on what jobs like yours typically pay.

Approach your meeting with your supervisor with a win–win attitude

All successful negotiations end in both parties feeling that they received something of value. Your goal is to get a pay rise. Your supervisor's goal is to have a highly motivated and productive employee. Remember that pay rises are never given for potential or for what you're 'going to do'. Pay rises are given because of meeting and exceeding performance goals. When you meet with your boss, you should be thinking about how your actions and accomplishments have helped to fulfil his or her own goals.

Discuss both performance and salary

Begin your discussion with a description of your accomplishments and contributions. Next, discuss how you intend to build on those in the coming year, and what some of your key goals are. Describe your goals in terms of how they'll support your boss and make a difference to the company. Then ask for the amount and percentage of salary increase that you think you deserve and explain why.

Listen

As your boss responds, listen to any objections that are made to your requests. Consider this discussion as a mentoring session and keep an open mind about what you can learn that will help your progress in the company. Before trying to overcome any objections, make sure that you communicate your understanding of those objections through paraphrasing what you've heard. This is the first step in negotiation and objections are a normal response. Be prepared for objections and be prepared to explain why you still deserve a pay rise.

Know what to do if you get a 'No'?

If you're told that you won't be getting a pay rise at this time, then ask what it is you need to do in order to earn one. Write down everything you're told. After the meeting, write a memo thanking your boss for his or her time, and listing the actions you need to take in order to earn a pay rise.

WHAT TO AVOID

You threaten to leave if you don't get the pay rise you deserve

Unless you're really unhappy and were thinking of leaving anyway, this strategy can do you much more harm than good. If you threaten to leave, you're sending the message that you aren't that committed to the organisation and are basically out for yourself. This approach isn't career-enhancing.

You complain to colleagues about your salary

Most organisations prefer that all salary discussions take place only with your immediate supervisor. If you complain about your salary to your colleagues, you're seen as someone who isn't a team player, and who isn't politically astute. It's very unlikely that you'd get promoted or get a pay rise under these circumstances.

You ask fellow employees how much they make

Unless you're in an 'open-book' company, most organisations insist that salary information be kept private. They're concerned that if employees begin to compare salaries with one another, it may lead some to think that they're being treated unfairly and therefore will lead to lower morale. You can get a better idea of your internal worth by benchmarking similar jobs in your organisation and then doing a search on the Internet for salary ranges for those jobs.

USEFUL LINKS

Jobsite: **www.jobsite.co.uk/career/advice/negotiate.html**
SalarySearch: **www.salarysearch.co.uk**

Learn How to Network

No matter what your organisational position, and no matter what your career goals are, you can always benefit from networking and marketing yourself. In today's world, business is driven by relationships. Networking and marketing yourself require you to build strong and meaningful relationships—many that will be long term. The following points are questions to consider as you prepare to network and market yourself:

* **Why am I networking? What's my personal or professional goal?**
* **What are my strengths that will help me to market myself?**
* **What organisations or events will be valuable places for networking?**
* **How much time do I want to spend on networking, and when will I do it?**
* **How will I know when I've been successful?**

Why should I bother to network and to market myself?
Research has shown that people who have a vast network of contacts, who are involved in professional and community activities outside their organisation, and who look for opportunities to be visible are more successful in their careers and contribute more effectively to their organisation.

Isn't networking blatant self-promotion, and won't it look bad?
No. Networking is done for the good of the organisation or your professional field, rather than for personal gain. If you're a successful networker, people are drawn to you because they know you're well connected and that you have good resources.

When is the best time to network?
Networking should become a way of life, a way of being. You should be networking all the time. As you build professional relationships, be constantly thinking: 'What can I offer this person?', 'How can I be of help?' The more you try to be of service to others, the more people will want to do things for you.

MAKE IT HAPPEN

Clarify the purpose of your networking and why you're marketing yourself

There are many reasons for networking and for marketing oneself. They can include finding a new job, seeking a promotion, or gaining support for a major project. Although it's important to build relationships continually, it's much more effective to know why you're building these relationships and what you hope to accomplish. Everyone has limited time, and this will help you to decide how to prioritise your networking activities.

Make a list of your strong points

It's important to have a sense of who you are and what your strengths are when you're networking and marketing yourself. What are your special skills and abilities? What unique knowledge do you have? What experiences will other people find valuable? What characteristics and beliefs define who you are? Once you've made this list, make copies for your bathroom mirror, for your car dashboard, and for your wallet. Knowing your strengths helps you to remember that other people will value what you have to offer.

Never network from a position of weakness. Always network from a position of strength. Have something of value to offer; otherwise people will see you as an annoyance. And remember to begin networking before you need anything from other people. Join or create a network to build relationships, and do what you can to help others or the organisation.

Make a list of organisations and events for networking

Identify professional organisations and events that may be helpful to you in your career or with your project. Look for special interest groups, like those for 'entrepreneurial women' for example. Get involved. When you're at professional events, make sure that you attend social functions, that you join people for dinner, and that you seek out volunteer opportunities. If you're networking within your own organisation, find special interest groups or social groups to join. Look for committees to be involved in, and don't be shy about asking questions and making suggestions.

If you aren't sure where to begin on this step, ask for advice from a mentor, from your boss, and from trusted colleagues.

Create a contact list

Keeping in mind your reasons for networking, brainstorm all the people you know who might be of help to you. Prioritise the list according to who is most likely to be helpful. Think about people you've done favours for in the past who might not be of direct help, but who may know someone who can be. After you've spoken to each person, ask him or her, 'Who else do you know that can be of help to me?'

Create an action plan with a schedule

Take your list of organisations and events and your contact list, and put together an action plan for making connections. Schedule networking events in your diary, along with organisational meetings, conferences, and so on. Using your contact list, set up a timetable for making a certain number of calls per day or per week.

Meet up with people and attend events

Before you meet up with someone or attend an event, review your list of strengths, and focus on your purpose for networking and marketing yourself. It helps to visualise or picture a successful outcome. Be friendly and professional, but most of all, be yourself. Spend time connecting with people on a personal level before asking for help or sharing your reason for networking. If you're meeting in person with someone on your contact list, always bring a gift—something they can remember you by.

Networking on the Net

The Internet is a valuable place to make connections and to learn fruitful information from colleagues. If you have a special interest or a special field, there is sure to be a newsgroup or threaded bulletin board on your topic. If not, start one by setting up a listserv at **http://groups.yahoo.com** or at similar sites.

Market yourself

The actions you take depend on why you're marketing yourself, but think of yourself as a brand; 'Brand You'. When marketers are marketing a product, they look for the 'Unique Selling Proposition' (USP). A USP is something relevant and original that can be claimed for a particular product or service. The USP should be able to communicate: 'Buy our brand and get this unique benefit'. When marketing yourself, you need to define who your 'customers' are and what your Unique Selling Proposition is. Your list of strengths above should give you some clues, but the USP needs to be stated in a short phrase. People who are closest to you can often give you suggestions. It might be something like: 'I help people to realise their dreams', or 'My leadership brings out the best in others', or 'I solve problems quickly and simply'.

Once you know your USP, brainstorm ways that you can market yourself and your unique qualities. The key is to let people know what you have to offer. Write an article for the company newsletter or a professional newsletter related to your USP. Volunteer to give a talk. Design a project that uses your talents and propose it to the right people. Be visible.

Assess your progress towards networking goals

You may wish to keep a notebook of your action plans and your progress. It also helps to have someone as a sounding board. That person can be a friend, your boss, a mentor, or a professional adviser. When we feel accountable for our actions to someone we trust, we're much more likely to follow through. It also helps to have someone who is willing to celebrate your successes and accomplishments with you.

Always say 'thank you'

As you network, many people will offer you information, opportunities, and valuable contacts. In your notebook, keep track of the favours that people have done for you and make sure that you write each one a short and simple thank-you letter. People are always more willing to help someone who has been appreciative in the past.

Be patient

Networking is a long-term activity. Steven Ginsburg of the *Washington Post* describes networking as 'building social capital'. You may not see results overnight, and at first should expect to give more than you get. But over time, your network will become one of your most valued assets.

WHAT TO AVOID

You don't want to bother anyone

Remember that people love to help others. Don't take up too much of their time, and come well prepared. When you ask for someone's time, be specific. Say, 'I'd like 30 minutes of your time', and then stick to it. Don't outstay your welcome. Whenever you meet up with someone, always be thinking, 'Is there something I can do to help this person?' Create a win-win situation.

You come on too strong

Networking isn't about selling someone something they don't want. You're looking for opportunities to create a mutual relationship, where there is give and take. In order for networking to be successful, you have to be interested in developing a long-term connection. Remind yourself that your focus is on relationship building, not on immediate results.

You don't come on strongly enough

You put yourself in networking situations, but never talk about your needs or interests. This may be because you aren't clear enough about why you're networking, or you're networking for reasons that aren't particularly important to you. Go back to step one and clarify your purpose.

USEFUL LINKS

Business Link: **www.businesslink.gov.uk/bdotg/action/home**
City Women's Network: **www.citywomen.org/**

Revitalise Your CV

If you're embarking on job hunt, there are lots of options open to you as you look for the right way to display your fantastic skills and experience. There are many different styles of CV, but why do you need to know how to prepare them? Because every person's career history is different, and you want a CV that puts your career history in the most marketable and attractive light. It's important to think carefully about which style to use when you apply for a job. A carefully written and targeted CV will impress a personnel officer much more effectively than a random story of your life.

Your particular job search and career goals are also unique. The stage you're at in your career is also a factor to bear in mind. As you decide which type of CV to prepare, think about whether you plan on staying in the same field or whether you're changing careers. Have you had a fairly standard career development,

or has your career been less traditional? Is this your first job? Are you aiming for a specific job in a specific company or are you on the look-out for something new and challenging? Is it a while since you've updated your CV and you feel a bit behind the times?
All these factors will help you decide which type of CV is most likely to get you the interview that will lead to your perfect job.

How many types of CV are there?
There are many different types of CV, but we'll be focusing on the following:

* chronological
* functional
* targeted
* capabilities

A chronological CV is still the most popular type of CV by far, but knowing how to put together the other types will stand you in good stead as you progress through your career and come across different job opportunities. These days people may have several different careers (not just jobs) in during the course of their working lives, so if you're thinking about changing what you do dramatically, a non-traditional CV may suit your needs best.

How do the CV types differ?
You should use a **chronological CV** when you're staying in the same field rather than making a major career change. This type of CV also works well when you've progressed steadily up a standard career ladder. For example, if you began your career as a junior designer, you moved on to become senior designer, and you're hoping to become design manager, this is the CV type for you. You would also use this kind of CV when you've worked for the same company for most of your career, even though you may have had several different kinds of job within that company. If you're starting off on your career path, looking for your first or second job, this CV is probably most appropriate to your experience.

A **functional CV** is the better choice when you're looking for your *first* professional job as it stresses your skills rather than your experience. It's also a good choice when you're making a fairly major career change, for the same reasons. If you've changed employers frequently, followed a less traditional career path, or are concerned that your career history has been a bit patchy, you may be better off this type of CV.

You should use a **targeted CV** when you're very clear about your job direction and when you need to make an impressive case for a specific job. It's hard work writing this kind of customised CV, especially if you're applying for several jobs, but it can make you and your abilities stand out from all the others in the pile.

If you're aiming for a specific job or assignment within your current organisation, the best CV to use is the **capabilities CV**. Remember, though, that you need to make time to customise your CV for the situation.

Do I need to create a CV for each of these types?
Not normally, no. The only exception to this is when you've created one of the standard formats (either a chronological or a functional CV) and a unique opportunity comes up for which one of the customised CVs (either a targeted or a capabilities CV) is better.

What's a job search 'objective'?
These were a CV must-have a few years ago. A job search objective is a short paragraph at the top of your CV that explains exactly what type of job you're looking for. It's particularly useful if you're writing to someone speculatively, but isn't always appropriate, so think carefully about whether you need to include one or not. If you want to add one to your CV, make sure it's concise, specific, and above all, honest. For example, the following objective is too general:

Seeking position in broadcasting industry.

That's not going to do you many favours. An improved version could be:

An experienced broadcasting professional is seeking a position to make full use of an in-depth background as a television producer, production manager, scriptwriter, and networker. I am looking for a challenging production manager position that will enable me to use and expand my creative skills and international experience in the broadcasting industry.

MAKE IT HAPPEN

Create a chronological CV

* Write your name and contact details at the top. Don't use your work e-mail address as part of these; it will look as if you're taking advantage of your current employer. Use your home e-mail address instead or an Internet-based one such as Hotmail, AOL, or Yahoo.
* If you're applying speculatively, you may want to include a job search 'objective' clearly.
* Write your employment history. Start with your present or most recent position, and work backwards.
* For each position listed, describe your major duties and accomplishments beginning with an action verb. Keep it to the point and stress what you've achieved.
* Keep your career goals in mind as you write and, as you describe your duties and accomplishments, emphasise those which are most related to your desired job.
* Include your education in a separate section at the bottom of the CV. If you have more than one degree, they should be listed in reverse chronological order. List any professional qualifications or training you've undertaken separately.

If you've been working for some time, you only need to write in detail about your last four or five positions, covering the last ten years or so. It's fine to just summarise the rest of your career history that goes back beyond that.

Create a functional CV

* Write your name and contact details at the top.
* As this type of CV is well suited to people starting out in their careers, you may want to state your job search 'objective' clearly.
* Write between three to five separate paragraphs, each one focusing on a particular skill or accomplishment.
* List these 'functional' paragraphs in order of importance, with the one most related to your career goal at the top.
* Provide a heading for each paragraph.
* Within each functional area, emphasise the most relevant accomplishments or results produced.
* Add in a brief breakdown of your actual work experience after the last functional area, giving dates (years), employer, and job titles only.
* Include your education in a separate section at the bottom of the CV. Again, if you have more than one degree, they should be listed in reverse chronological order.

Using this CV style means that you can include information about your skills and accomplishments without identifying which employer or situation it was connected to. This is especially helpful if you've signed a non-disclosure agreement with your current or previous employer, in which you undertake not to reveal specific information about a job or project to potential competitors. Non-disclosure agreements are particularly common in high-tech or research companies.

Create a targeted CV

* Begin by brainstorming a list of key points. For example, what have you done that is relevant to your job target? Are you proud of what you've achieved? Have you achieved anything in another field that is relevant to your job target? Think about what you do that demonstrates your ability to work with people.
* Write your name and contact details at the top.
* Think carefully about whether you need to include a job search 'objective' here; as this type of CV is best geared to an application for a specific job, you may not need to include one and could use the space more usefully.
* From your brainstormed list, select between five and eight skills/accomplishments that are the most relevant to your job target. Make sure that the statements focus on action and results.
* Briefly describe your actual work experience beneath each skills/accomplishment item, giving dates (years), employer, and job titles only.
* Include your education in a separate section at the bottom of the CV, listed in reverse chronological order.

Create a capabilities CV

- * To develop a capabilities CV, you first need to learn all you can about the internal job that you're applying for. Try to come up with between five and eight accomplishments that you've recently achieved that are relevant to this job opening.
- * List your name and contact details at the top.
- * Think carefully about whether you need to include a job search 'objective' here; as this type of CV is best geared to an application for a specific job, you may not need to include one and could use the space more usefully.
- * Next, list your five top accomplishments, focusing on actions taken and results achieved that are relevant to the post you're interested in.
- * Write a brief paragraph about any relevant work experience you've had in your current position. If you haven't been at the company for long, you should provide a complete synopsis of your work experience as described for the targeted CV.
- * Include your education in a separate section at the bottom of the CV in reverse chronological order.

Think about the look and feel

Once you've decided on the best CV type for you and the job you want, spend a little time making sure that you think about the details and present all the information to its best advantage.

- * Most CVs are submitted via e-mail these days, but if you're sending your CV by post, print the document on high-quality white or cream paper. This will make sure that your CV can be easily read, photocopied, or scanned by the recruiter.
- * Buy your own stationery. Don't use headed notepaper or address labels from your current place of work when you're printing out or posting your CV to another company or agency. Just like using your work e-mail as part of your contact details, this will give a strong impression that you're taking advantage of your present employer and his or her facilities.
- * Take care with the formatting of your CV. Use a 'clean' looking font that is easy to read (some people prefer a sans serif, such as Arial), and make sure that the type size you use isn't too small. Draw attention to your achievements by using a bold face to highlight positions you've held or qualifications you've gained. Emphasise key points in lists by using bullets.
- * Make sure you read over your CV once you've finished working on it to check for spelling or grammatical errors—these, above all, will mean your CV ends up in the bin rather than on the right person's desk. It's always a good idea to ask someone else to read over your finished CV too; he or she may spot something you've overlooked as you've become so familiar with what you've written.
- * Try not to rely on computer spellcheckers. While they'll pick up on a good deal

of mistakes in spelling and usage, remember that they won't pick up on words that are spelt correctly but used in the wrong way or the wrong place. For example, if you write 'there' when you actually mean 'their', the spellchecker won't realise that you've made a mistake.

* Unless you're *specifically* asked by a recruiter to submit a hand-written CV or covering letter, use a computer to give a more professional finish that will impress your reader.
* Follow your own instincts. By all means ask friends or family members to read through your CV but remember that if you ask 20 people what they think, you'll get 20 (probably different) opinions. In the end *you* are the one who needs to feel comfortable with it.

WHAT TO AVOID

You try to include *everything*

Like many people, you may want to tell a potential employer everything you have ever done to try to impress them. A recruiter or employer will be looking for someone who can get to the point and express him or herself clearly and effectively, though, so remember to keep it simple and focus on those things that are most likely to get you an interview.

You don't use any particular format

If you haven't had much experience of writing CVs, you may create one that is a mixture of job listings, skills, and accomplishments. This will only confuse your reader. Rather than leap straight in, work out which type of CV suits your job search or your target vacancy best.

If you're still concerned about which CV you think will suit you best, it might be worth visiting a career adviser. If you're still a student, your local further education college may well have a career adviser who can help you for free. Otherwise, the reference library may be able to suggest where to find help. If you're working already, bear in mind that you'll have to pay for this type of service, and rates can vary quite dramatically so do check them in advance.

You don't follow up

This is the commonest and most serious mistake. If you said you would phone to set up an interview in your covering letter, make a note of the date and follow up. Although it can be difficult to make the call because of fear of rejection, you'll never get the job if you don't!

You become disheartened

Sales people have learned that you have to take a certain number of rejections before you get a 'Yes'. Finding a job is the same thing. If you receive a 'No' after making a phone call for an appointment, tell yourself, 'Well, that's a shame, but it's one less "No" that I have to hear before I get a "Yes".' Keep positive and you will get the result you want eventually.

USEFUL LINKS

BBC One Life: **www.bbc.co.uk/radio1/onelife/work/cvs/cvs_intro.shtml**
Monster.co.uk: **http://content.monster.co.uk/section328.asp**
Total Jobs: **jobs.msn.co.uk/tjmsn/msn.asp**

Write a Great Covering Letter

When you send in your CV to a recruiter to apply for an advertised vacancy or to let him or her know that you're looking for work, you'll normally send a covering letter or e-mail too.

If you're applying for an existing vacancy, your covering letter should briefly describe the position you're applying for and where you saw it advertised, why you're particularly qualified for the job, and why you want to work for that specific company. If you're approaching an agency to register your CV as part of your search for a new job, you should describe the type of job you're looking for, the skills you have that would make you an attractive candidate, your current salary, and any preferences you may have in terms of location.

Writing a covering letter is a fairly straightforward process, but there are certain steps you need to follow. If you sound both interesting and interested, you're much more likely to get noticed, interviewed, and employed!

Is a covering letter still important these days? Job hunting has changed so much over the last few years.

You're quite right, the way that people look for jobs has changed a lot in a short space of time. In particular, the Internet has had a huge impact for both employers and job seekers; jobs are advertised online, applied for online, and even some pre-interview 'weeding out' is done online in some cases. However, remember that the basic premise of the job hunt hasn't changed; however you apply for a job, you have to make yourself attractive to a prospective employer, and a knock-out covering letter works with your CV to do just that.

A good covering letter can give a sense of who you are that may not come across in a CV. It's a chance for other people to see how you write, gain a sense of how you view yourself and what you understand about them. When you come to write your letter, remember to think about its tone, how you're describing yourself and your skills, and also remember to include the results of any research you've done into the company or field of work you're interested in.

How long does a covering letter need to be?

You don't need to write a long missive. An effective covering letter is usually only two or three paragraphs long; they're best kept short and to the point. Read on to find out exactly what you need to include to make the impact you're after.

MAKE IT HAPPEN

Understand what you're doing and why

The covering letter is the very first thing a recruiter or manager reads. It must grab his or her attention and make him or her want to read your CV and meet you. It's your first chance to stand out from the crowd.

One way of making an immediate good impression is by addressing your letter to the right person. Letters that are addressed to 'Dear Sir/Madam' or 'To Whom It May Concern' are usually thrown away. If you don't know the name of the precise person you need to write to, ring the company to find out, or look it up on the Internet or at a reference library. If you have a copy of the company's catalogue or annual report, it may even list key members of staff there.

There are a variety of reasons why you might write a covering letter and send a CV, such as responding to an advertisement, following up on meeting someone, or letting a potential employer know that you're available for work. Sometimes you may need to use your letter for a slightly different purpose. For example:

* when you contact a company to inquire about job openings. In this letter you would ask who you should send your CV to.
* if you visited an organisation in person and filled in a job application and want to follow up.
* when you apply for a job on the Internet. If you apply online via an agency, you may be asked to fill out a form to accompany your CV attachment. Often you'll just be asked to give your contact details, but some agencies ask for a brief supporting statement to accompany your CV.

If you're replying to an advertised job vacancy, a covering letter also gives you the opportunity to include details that the advertisement may have asked for but which can't easily be fitted into a CV format, such as:

* current salary
* desired future salary
* notice period
* preferences for geographical location
* dates you may be available for interview (you may want to include these if you are about to go on holiday for a while)

Draft the letter

First of all, you need to say why you're writing. If you're applying for an existing vacancy, begin your letter by describing the position that interests you and explain why you're writing in the first sentence. For example:

I am very interested in the position of Production Manager as described in your advertisement of 19 September on the *Daily Post* website.

Alternatively, if you're writing following a recommendation from someone already working at, or known to, the company:

I have been given your name by Ms Mary Robertson regarding the position in Human Resources.

Show how interested you are in the job

It's extremely important that you show how interested you are in the job. Take time to show that you've done your homework and that you understand what the company does and what its aims are.

Visit the relevant company's website (if it has one) and look at any recent news articles, especially its press releases. You should also read business newspapers and trade magazines. These will give you a sense of any industry issues facing the company you're interested in. They may also have particular information about the goals of your target company. Your local library will have lots of newspapers, magazines, and reference books that you can use. They also often have an Internet connection, if you don't have access to the Web at home. Save any articles or printouts on the company somewhere safe so that you can find them easily if you're asked to an interview.

To get across the fact that you've read the job advertisement thoroughly and that you've understood it, match the language you use in your letter to the advertisement itself. For example, if the job description mentions 'team leader', refer to that job title rather than using the word 'manager'.

Also, make sure you've included all the information requested in the advertisement. If the recruiters want to know your current salary and notice period, make sure you've mentioned them.

Tell them why they need *you*

Describe your qualifications early in the letter to grab the interest of the personnel officer or manager. What will really make a difference is if you explain how your qualifications will help the organisation achieve its goals. For example:

I understand that your company is planning on creating a Web presence to support your sales. In my current position as Director of Internet Sales for Speedy Sales Company, I have helped to increase our market share by 13% in the past year.

If you can, show how you and you alone can help this company deal with the challenges it faces.

Ask for an interview

Some people feel uncomfortable about asking for an interview with a prospective employer and prefer to wait and see if they're contacted by the company or person in question. A more proactive approach makes a bigger impact, however. If you want to ask for an interview, you could say in your letter that you're going to be in their area on a particular date and that you would be available for an interview. Alternatively, you can simply say something along the lines of, 'I look forward to discussing how my qualifications can help your organisation to be more successful'.

Remember the essentials

Now you've done all the planning, you can put everything together.

* Be yourself. CVs are factual records of your experiences and skills. A good covering letter is your chance to show your personality and stand out from the crowd of other applicants as the interview short-list is drawn up. Keep the letter professional, but don't be afraid to show your enthusiasm, your willingness to work hard, and your interest in the position. Potential employers want job applicants who show an interest in them and who seem eager to be a part of their company.
* Make sure your covering letter looks professional. Check that there are no grammatical or spelling errors, and read it carefully before you send it off. If possible, ask a friend to check it for you too. Don't just rely on your computer spell check!
* As with your CV, if you're submitting by post, use the highest quality paper that you can afford. Also, unless you're applying for a particularly creative post, use a plain coloured paper in ivory or white.
* Use a standard and easily readable font such as Times New Roman or Arial.
* If you're posting the covering letter and CV, send them in a large flat envelope. You may want to send two copies in case the recruiter needs to show your letter and CV to different people, and photocopies or scans will be clearer if the originals have not been folded.
* If you're e-mailing the covering letter and CV, remember to check that you've attached the files before you send the e-mail! Also tell the e-mail recipient what type of file you're attaching and be prepared to send it in another format in case they have difficulty opening it.

WHAT TO AVOID

You use a covering letter template from a book

Reading through examples of covering letters in books can help you to understand what to include, and the layout and tone for different kinds of letters. Do remember to change the letters to fit your particular needs, though. Most managers will have seen hundreds of covering letters and will not want to hear the same old phrases. Make sure you personalise each of your covering letters so that they're targeted at a particular person and company, and so that they represent you and your uniqueness. Some people literally 'fill in the gaps', and write a generic letter that they 'customise' by hand-writing the recipient's name and their own signature. It's highly unlikely that anyone will be impressed by this, so don't do it. Your correspondent needs to see clearly and unambiguously that you're interested in his or her company.

You use the same covering letter for all your job applications

A covering letter is meant to show that you really want to work for one particular company—taking the time to write a personal, company-specific letter will make all the difference to the impression you give! Using the same covering letter for all your applications also increases the likelihood of your making mistakes when you're tired or in a rush—you may inadvertently mention the wrong company in the body of your letter. It's really important to tailor your letter to the company and/or person you're applying to. It may be more time-consuming than returning to an old document, but this is your big chance to explain why you are the only person worth considering for this job. Why would you want to shoot yourself in the foot?

USEFUL LINKS

BBC One Life: **www.bbc.co.uk/radio1/onelife/work/applications/letters.shtml**
iVillage.co.uk **www.ivillage.co.uk/workcareer/findjob**

Make an Impact in Interviews

Well done! You've cleared the first hurdle in your job search with a great CV and a covering letter, and have been invited for an interview—you've already found some way to stand out from the crowd. Now you need to build on this success. This actionlist will help you prepare mentally and emotionally for your interview. Read on to find out how to make a real impact with prospective employers.

Are there any interview questions that I should prepare for whatever type of job I'm going for?

Obviously there are no hard and fast rules about what an interviewer will ask you, but there are a few things that you should get straight in your head as you start your interview preparation. Keep these questions in mind:

* Why do you think you're the best person for the job?
* What is it about this job that attracts you?
* What is it about this organisation that has made you apply for the position?
* Who will interview you and what do you know about them?
* What is the appropriate dress and/or image for this organisation?

MAKE IT HAPPEN

Refresh your memory about your CV or application form

As a first step, remind yourself thoroughly of all the information on your CV or application form (it's a good idea to keep a photocopy of anything you send to a prospective employer for this very reason). It may have been some time since you applied for the job, so it's no bad idea to look back over what you said way back when. Think about what questions you might be asked based on your education or work history. Some questions that might be difficult to answer include, 'Why did you choose to study this subject?', 'Why did you leave your last job?', or 'Why did you have a period of unemployment?'. Write notes about what you're going to say and practise your answers with a friend or family member.

Research the organisation

Finding out as much as you can about the company you're visiting will not only help you decide if it's the sort of organisation you'd like to work for, but may give you some ideas for questions to ask the interviewer. If you find an opportunity to show that you've done your research, this will signal to the interviewer that you're enthusiastic about the job, as well as knowledgeable about the market.

The best place to start looking is the company website. Focus on the annual report, news, press releases, and biographies of key members of staff. This will give you a feel for the organisation—its values, its success factor, and its people. If the company doesn't have a website, ring them and ask to be sent this information along with their most up-to-date catalogue.

If you have time, it's also a good idea to cast your net a bit wider and to research current factors that might affect the organisation. These can include industry trends, competitive issues, strategic direction, and particular challenges or opportunities.

Set yourself the challenge of finding out about these five essential questions before the interview:

* How large is the organisation?
* How is the organisation structured?
* What is its main business?
* Who are its major competitors?
* What is the organisation's work culture like?

Decide what *you* want to get from the interview

In their nerves before an interview, candidates often forget that there are two sides to the process; clearly, the prospective employer wants to suss you out, but you need to work out if you want to work with them too. It's a good idea to prepare a list of questions that will help you decide whether or not this job is a good fit for your personality and your career goals. For example, you might want to ask your interviewers what progression prospects they see for the eventual post-holder, what the company's values are, or what the professional development policy is. In general, it's a good idea to not ask about benefits and salary at a first interview, unless the interviewer brings them up. Get the offer first, then talk about money!

You also need to work out the key points you want to make about your strengths and skills. When you prepared your CV, you listed the principal strengths and skills that you thought an employer would be looking for. Look at that list again, choose a skill, and think of a recent situation you've been in that will demonstrate that strength or skill to an interviewer. If possible, include any concrete results you achieved as a result.

Even though you may feel under pressure at points, always focus on the positive in your answers, even when you've been asked to talk about a difficult situation or your weaknesses. That way, you'll come across as someone who rises to a challenge and looks for opportunities to improve and develop.

Prepare yourself mentally

Many people, including athletes and salespeople, prepare themselves for challenging situations by mentally picturing a successful result. This is a great method that can also be used to help you perform well in an interview.

Before the interview, imagine yourself being professional, interesting, and enthusiastic in your interview. Also imagine yourself leaving the interview with a good feeling about how you did. This will put you in a positive frame of mind and help you to be at your very best in the interview.

Practise!

If possible, ask a friend or family member to role-play the interview with you. If you have a career counsellor or coach, they'll also be able to help you out here. Give the other person a list of questions that you think you might be asked (and ask them to throw in a few of their own so that you have to get used to thinking on your feet!), and then role-play the interview, asking your friend afterwards for honest feedback. Role-play the interview and then ask for the other person's feedback. Videotape the role-play if you can so that you can watch your body language; this is often more telling than you realise.

Start the ball rolling with some standard questions that interviewers often ask.

* Tell me a little bit about yourself.
* Where do you see yourself in your career five years from now?
* What are you most proud of in your career?
* What is your greatest strength?
* What is your biggest weakness?
* Describe a difficult situation and how you handled it.
* Can you tell me about a time when you had to motivate a team?

You don't need to go right back to your junior years if someone asks you to tell them a bit about yourself: use it to give a very brief overview of yourself including a short history of recent employment.

Create a positive impression on the day itself

When the day of the interview dawns, be punctual. Better still, be early to give yourself some preparation and relaxation time. If you're not sure of the location of the company, you might want to do a practice run of the journey so you can be sure to leave yourself enough time. Once you're there, have a glass of water, flick through company magazines if they're available, and try to get a feel for the atmosphere, as this will help you to decide if it's the sort of place you can see yourself being happy working in. It will also give you an idea of what to expect in the interview, and the sort of candidate the interviewers will be looking for. If he or she isn't too busy, take some time to talk to the receptionist. They are often asked by recruiters to act as an extra 'screen' during the recruitment process; if candidates are rude to the receptionist, they often don't get much further.

Be enthusiastic

You know why you're interested in this job, and you need to convey that interest to the recruiters—interviewees who are excited about the organisation get job offers! Even if it's true, don't say that you're keen on the job because it pays well. Instead, be ready to talk about what you can offer the company, how the position will expand your skills, and why this kind of work would be satisfying and meaningful to you. Be sensible and don't overdo it, though, as this may come across as insincere or overconfident.

Be honest

The overall impression you're trying to create is of an enthusiastic, professional, positive, and sincere person. These things will come across from the word go if you follow the basic rules of giving a firm handshake, a friendly smile, and maintaining good eye contact throughout the interview.

Never lie in the interview or attempt to blag your way through difficult questions—it's just not worth it. Good preparation should ensure that you don't have to resort to this. Speak clearly and respectfully to the interviewers and remember that swearing and flirting are definite no-nos.

Wherever possible, back up your responses to questions with evidence-based replies. For example, if an interviewer asks you how you manage conflict within a team, it's best to give a brief general response and then focus on a specific example of how you've done this in the past. Illustrating your answers with real examples gives you the opportunity to focus on your personal contribution, and will be more impressive than giving a vague, hypothetical reply.

Look *and* sound the part

Even though what you're saying in an interview is the main thing, it's important to look professional as well. You should feel comfortable in what you wear, but it's better to turn up 'too smart' than 'too casual'—people will take you seriously if you dress respectably. If you're applying for jobs in media or the arts a suit may not be necessary, but dressing smartly will always give the impression that you care about getting this job.

It's always a good idea to take some anti-perspirant with you to an interview, as when people are nervous they tend to sweat. You may also find yourself a bit hot and dishevelled if you had to rush to get to the interview in good time (although if you've prepared your journey well, this shouldn't happen!). Make sure you have time to freshen up before the interview. This will help your confidence, and spare the interviewers from a sweaty handshake or, worse still, a bad odour when you enter the room. And remember, don't go overboard on the perfume or aftershave—that would count as a bad odour, too.

WHAT TO AVOID

You 'misread' the interviewer

People tend to underestimate the level of formality and professionalism required in an interview, and some interviewers even create a more social than professional situation to catch you off guard. If you find yourself in an interview with a more casual approach than is appropriate, change your behaviour as soon as you notice. The interviewers are more likely to remember your behaviour at the end of the interview than at the beginning. On the other hand, if the environment or the interviewer is more casual than you realised, don't worry. You're *expected* to look and act in a highly professional and formal way in an interview. Use your instincts to judge how much you need to change your behaviour to show that you'd fit into the company culture.

You use humour inappropriately

To make a situation less tense, people sometimes use humour to lighten the mood. If you've said something you think is funny and received a negative reaction, though, it's best not to call attention to the situation by apologising. Try to act as if nothing happened and go back to behaving professionally. Whatever you do, don't follow inappropriate humour with more humour.

You didn't do your homework

You get to the interview and realise that you really know nothing about this organisation. Hopefully, you arrived early and have some time in reception. Often, booklets and leaflets found in receptions provide quite a bit of information about the company, its industry, its products and services. Look at them, look around, and learn everything you can. Talk to the receptionist and ask him or her questions that may be helpful to you in the interview. It's possible to learn quite a bit about the organisation on the fly, but nothing works better than doing your homework.

You criticise your former employer

Avoid this at all costs. It gives the interview a very negative feeling, and will leave the interviewer wondering if you would criticise this organisation when you left. This kind of criticism usually happens when someone is asked why they're leaving (or have left) their last position. The best way to answer this is to talk about the future rather than the past, and to show your keenness to take on challenging career opportunities.

USEFUL LINKS

iVillage.co.uk: **www.ivillage.co.uk/workcareer/findjob**
Monster.co.uk:
http://content.monster.co.uk/Job_hunting/articles2/coping_with_interviews

Prepare for Different Types of Interviews

Looking for a new job can be a long and tiring process, but when you get to the interview stage, you know that the end is in sight, whatever happens. Quite understandably, some people find interviews nerve-wracking; it's not easy to see your professional life laid out before you on your CV and then have a series of questions fired at you. Preparation can help, though, and part of that process is being aware of the different types of interviews that you may be asked to attend. Some of them are industry-specific, some are more suitable for experienced employees, and some are designed to root out the best first-jobbers. This actionlist gives you an overview of the different types of interview out there and what you need to do to let your natural talent shine.

I feel much more comfortable talking to one person than a group of people, but I've been asked to attend a panel interview. I'm really nervous. What can I do to help myself?

First of all, don't panic. You'll just tire yourself out. Keep calm and remember how well you've done to get to this stage—lots of other candidates won't have got this far! Next, find out as much as you can about who you'll be meeting and then plan what you need to say to impress them. This doesn't mean pretending to be someone you're not; rather that you're good at what you do, on top of your game, and you'd like to work with them. If you feel nervous, take plenty of deep breaths before you go in and before you speak. If you don't hear a question clearly or aren't sure if you understand it, don't be afraid to check. Read on for more help!

MAKE IT HAPPEN

Deal with telephone interviews

Initial interviews by telephone are becoming more common, but they're quite challenging for both parties. You probably normally use the phone either to talk with friends whom you know, and can visualise, or for business calls with people you don't need to know. Getting to know someone on the phone can be awkward: the absence of visual feedback is disconcerting. As always, preparation and practice will provide some help.

Be well equipped

* Have everything ready before you start: papers, pen, information you'll need to put across accurately, dates, and so on.
* Think carefully about the likely shape of the interview. What information do you need to give? What questions do you need to ask?
* Make sure you find a quiet room to take the call in, where you won't be interrupted or have any distractions. You may need to refer to some notes, but try not to rustle your papers too much. It may be best to arrange to take the

call at lunchtime or at home after work. Most HR professionals are used to having to interview clients later in the day, so this may be a good option for you.

Be aware of your own voice

* It may sound strange, but don't talk too much! Pauses—even very short ones—are awkward on the phone and with no visual cues to guide you it's tempting to fill spaces with words. You may end up saying more than you mean to.
* Take care not to become monotonous—your voice is important because you cannot make an impression visually. As you would in any face-to-face interview, sound positive, friendly, and business-like.

Listen to the interviewer

* Since you get no visual information on the phone, you should pay careful attention to the non-verbal aspects of speech—tone, pitch, inflection, for example—to pick up clues about what the interviewer is interested in.
* Make notes of important facts and agreements—it's easy to forget things when there is no 'picture' to reinforce them

Cope with competence-based interviews

The idea behind competence-based interviews (often called behavioural interviews) is to determine how well suited you are to a job based upon what you've learnt from situations in the past. Most interviews incorporate some competence-based questions, because research shows that they seem to be the most effective form of assessment—your knowledge and experience are being judged against the specific criteria of the job. Competence-based questions usually start with 'Give me an example of when . . .' or 'Describe a situation where . . .'.

As a rule of thumb, there are certain competences that almost all employers will be interested in. A shortlist of favourites is: planning and organising; decision-making; communicating; influencing others; teamwork; achieving results; leadership.

Prepare examples

Given that the interview will focus on past experience, it's useful to think about examples you could use to show how you've developed the core competences outlined in the list above. When you look back at these experiences, ask yourself the following questions:

* What did you do personally?
* How did you overcome barriers or pitfalls?
* What did you achieve?
* Is there anything you would have done differently?
* What did you learn from the experience?

Whilst you may not be asked precisely these questions, they'll prepare you for areas of questioning that you're very likely to encounter in the interview.

Know the job

Before an interview of this type, read the job description very carefully and focus on the specific requirements of the post. Think about the issues and responsibilities related to the job. You can try to anticipate the sorts of questions you may be asked based on those requirements and responsibilities. Also think about your present job and in particular how your role fits within the team.

Cope with internal interviews

Some companies like to use an interview process for filling internal vacancies or making career plans. Within an organisation there can be all sorts of assumptions that may complicate this process. For example, some people feel that the company should know them well enough from experience and appraisals to make an interview unnecessary. Others worry about the politics of the situation, and the consequences of failure. Some may be inclined to treat it too informally or lightly.

The general rule is to treat these interviews as you would an external application until you have definitive information that things are different. It's much better to err on the side of formality until you're sure what is required.

As ever, remember to do your homework beforehand and find out as much as you can about the job. If you have a human resources department, they'll probably be the best source of information. It's also a good idea to:

- talk to your boss about your intended move if your interview is for a job in a different department. It could create a very nasty atmosphere if he or she finds out from someone else.
- find out what's required from you and how the decision-making process works.
- anticipate what the interviewer knows already and what he or she will want to know about your experience and competence. Don't take too much for granted in this area.

Don't panic in stress interviews

Stress interviews involve putting the candidates under pressure to see how they respond to difficult people or unexpected events. Organisations should only use this technique when they can clearly show the need for it, and even then they should be careful how it is handled, taking account of the sensitivities of the interviewee. It can be an unnerving experience, but being aware that this is a recognised interviewing technique for some firms will help you to cope should you come across it. The sorts of industries that may employ this technique include banking and some security firms.

Stress questions often come in the form of a role play, when the interviewer, *in his or her role*, may say something like: 'I think your answer is totally inadequate: it doesn't deal with my concerns at all, can't you do better than that?' The interviewer is testing your ability to manage surprises and ambiguity. He or she will want to see you keep the initiative and take responsibility for dealing with the situation appropriately.

The trick is not to take the remarks personally but to recognise that you're required to play a role. Take a deep breath, pause, keep your temper, and respond as naturally and accurately as you can.

Keep your wits about you because the technique is designed to catch you off guard. Create time for yourself to balance logic and emotion calmly in framing your response. If you can, try to anticipate what the next problem will be and keep ahead of the game.

Make your mark at assessment centres

This method of selection usually involves a group of candidates performing a number of different tasks and exercises over the course of one to three days. Assessment centres were traditionally used at the second stage of recruitment, but nowadays candidates are often asked to one at the first stage.

Assessment centres usually include:

1 Group exercises: role-playing, discussion, leadership exercises
2 Individual exercises. For example:

- written tests (such as report writing based on case studies)
- in-tray exercises (a business simulation where you're expected to sort through an in-tray, making decisions about how to deal with each item)
- presentation of an argument or data analysis
- psychometric tests
- interviews

3 Social events
4 Company presentations

You'll be assessed most of the time—the administrator should clarify this for you—so there's rarely an opportunity to let down your guard.

You can make these events a little less stressful with a few simple rules:

- The organisation will probably tell you what they're looking for in their career literature or their invitation. Make sure you've read this, thought about it, and worked out how you show the behaviour they're interested in.
- Behave naturally but thoughtfully. Do not attempt to play an exaggerated role—it's never what the assessors want to see!
- Make sure that you take part fully in all activities: assessors can only appraise what you show them.
- Don't be over competitive. The assessors are likely to be working to professional standards, not looking for the 'winner'. Unnatural behaviour quickly becomes inappropriate and boorish.
- Take an overview. Most of the exercises have a purpose wider than the obvious. Try to stand back and look at things in context rather than rush

straight in. With the in-tray exercise, for example, you'll probably find that some items are related and need to be tackled together.

Tick all the boxes at technical interviews

In this type of an interview you'll be asked specific questions relating to technical knowledge and skills. As you'd imagine, this approach is common and extremely useful in research and technology companies' selection processes.

The organisation will normally tell you in advance that they have a technical interview or if they want you to give a presentation on your thesis or experience. You need to be prepared for 'applied' questions that ask for knowledge in a different form from the way you learned it at college. For example, ' How would you design a commercially viable wind turbine?' or 'How would you implement the requirements of data protection legislation in a small international organisation?' Consider the 'audience' and how your knowledge fits with their likely interests and priorities. What questions are they likely to ask?

Sometimes these presentations go wrong when interviewers ask very 'obvious' questions; or one of them has a favourite or 'trick' question. It's easy to be irritated by these, but you should remain calm and courteous. Try to see the interviewers as your 'customer' and respond with patience.

As always, preparation and anticipation are the keys to success. Work out what your interviewers will want to know and make sure your knowledge is up to scratch in the correct areas.

Think on your feet in panel interviews

When you're looking for a job, sooner or later you may be asked to attend a panel interview. These are becoming more popular as they:

* save time and are efficient. Several interviewers meet in one place at one time, so the applicant does not need to be shuffled around from office to office and there is no schedule to follow or overrun.
* provide consistent information. You, as the job applicant, only need to tell your story once instead of repeating it over and over again in private meetings with interviewers.

Although it can be quite daunting to walk into an interview where several people are present, a panel interview is also an excellent opportunity to show your strengths to a number of interviewers at once. A successful panel interview is one in which you come across as cool and confident and able to handle whatever is thrown your way.

To take the sting out of panel interviews, find out about the organisation as well as the position you're applying for. Start with the company's website, if it has one, and try to get a copy of its annual report. Talk to people who may be familiar with the organisation. Go to the library and see if any recent articles have been written about it.

Next, begin to prepare mentally for the possibility of a panel interview. Ask yourself what your major selling points are. How can you get these across to each member of the panel? This is particularly useful if you know beforehand who you're going to meet and what their responsibilities are. If, for example, you'll be meeting a sales director and a finance director, you might want to explain how you can do things in such a way that you achieve maximum sales of a product or service cost-effectively. If you like, see the panel interview as a type of presentation, and keep your audience in mind at all times.

If the prospect of this type of interview makes you nervous, try to combat your nerves with 'visualisation'. This is a very good way of helping you feel and appear relaxed and confident. Before your interview, imagine what a panel interview might be like. Visualise yourself in a conference room with several people sitting around a large table. Imagine answering each question easily, bonding with each interviewer and having a successful interview.

Some people are uncomfortable using the visualisation technique, but it's a really effective method. Remember, Jack Nicklaus claims that much of his golf success comes from mentally rehearsing each shot before he actually picks up a club. What has worked so well for him can work for you, too.

Answer the questions

Sometimes in a panel interview it can feel as though questions are coming at you from all directions. Try to take the first question, answer it, then build on that answer to respond to the second interviewer. Make sure you answer every question so that none of the interviewers think you ignored his or her question. Ask for a question to be repeated if you didn't quite hear it properly at first.

If you need to, clarify questions if necessary. If you find a question confusing, don't be afraid to ask for further explanation; it shows that you're coping under pressure and also it will save time all round. Phrases such as, 'Just to clarify . . .' or, 'If I understand correctly, you want to know . . .' can help you understand exactly what information the interviewers are looking for. If you're still unsure, you might want to check that you answers were understood and that you've answered the question fully. Simply ask the appropriate person, 'Did I answer your question?'.

As you're talking, make eye contact with each member of the panel in turn. This means catching the gaze of a particular member of the panel, holding it for about three seconds, and then moving to the next panel member. In reality, it's actually very difficult to look someone in the eye, count to three, and then move on, all while answering a challenging question, but with some practice it will become second nature. It's a really useful skill to develop for meetings of all types and public speaking and will help you in your future career.

Resist the temptation to take the less pressurised route by letting members of the panel do all the talking. Remember, you're there to sell yourself and to do that you need to get your point across. If the people on the panel do all the talking, all they will remember about you is that you may be a good listener. Of course, you should certainly not interrupt members of the panel, but do make sure you discuss your strengths and the reasons they should employ you. Sell yourself as you would in an individual interview.

Keep calm in 'scenario-based' interviews

Most interviewers have been carefully trained to look only for evidence and facts from the candidates past and therefore *never* to ask hypothetical questions. But sometimes—and especially with younger candidates who don't have much past work experience—an organisation will be more interested in what the person can become in the future rather than what he or she is now.

There are techniques for doing this. They normally focus on exploring how you think and act when confronted with problems you haven't experienced before—*how* rather than *what* you think and do. The logic is that in order to learn from a new experience you must be able to understand the experience thoroughly. These interviews assess the level of complexity at which you can think—and therefore understand the issues and learn how to deal with them.

Typically you'll be asked in these interviews to take part in a conversation that gets more complex and wide-ranging as it progresses. You build a scenario further and further into the future. There are no right answers of course: the interviewer is looking for an ability to spot the right questions.

Knowing that the interview will take this form is some help, but there is really little that you can do to prepare for it. Being well rested and alert, relaxing and enjoying the challenge are the best tips.

WHAT TO AVOID

You think you can wing it

You can't. You have to prepare for interviews if you want to do well. The amount of preparation you do will depend on the type of interview you're having or the type of job you want, but you have to show that you not only understand what the prospective job is about, but what you can bring to it, what challenges the business faces, what the state of the relevant industry is, and so on. You must be professional and show that you're the complete package.

USEFUL LINKS

Monster.co.uk career advice: **http://content.monster.co.uk/section323.asp**
University of Bradford: **www.careers.brad.ac.uk/student_hunt_interview**

Get Your Head Round Psychometric Tests

Large organisations often use tests as a way of working out whether or not a candidate has the knowledge, skills, and personality needed for a particular job. These tests are called psychometric tests. They can help identify those people who may be suitable for future leadership positions. Psychometric tests are also often used to help in career guidance and counselling.

Can psychometric tests help me* as well as *employers?
Yes, they can. If you're just beginning your career, or if you're thinking about a major career change, psychometric testing can help you work out which careers would best fit your interests and personality. (If you're about to leave university, talk to your career development officers about the range of tests they can provide.)

How many types of psychometric test are there?
There are many different types of test. Let's look at those grouped as 'attainment and aptitude tests'.

Attainment tests are designed to find out how much you've learned from your past training and experience—much like school exams. If you're applying for your first real job you might be confronted with a test of maths, English, or IT skills, for example.

General intelligence tests, along with **special aptitude tests** (see below) are concerned with your ability to learn new skills. Intelligence tests measure your capacity for abstract thinking and reasoning in particular contexts. The items usually cover numerical, verbal, and symbolic reasoning, often in the familiar forms, such as: 'What is the missing number in this series . . .?' The tests in most common use are the AH series, Raven's Matrices, and NIIP tests. The first two have 'advanced' forms for use with graduates and managers.

Special aptitude tests. Some types of work clearly require you to have—or be able to learn—particular skills at a high level. This group of tests is designed to reveal general or specific aptitudes that the employer needs to develop. The most usual types of test are:

* **verbal ability**, including verbal comprehension, usage, and critical evaluation. An example is the VA series.
* **numerical ability**, involving numerical reasoning or analysis of quantitative data. You might meet the NA series of tests, NC2, or the GMA numerical test.
* **spatial ability**, relating to skill at visualising and manipulating three dimensional shapes, for example. Frequently used tests are the ST series.
* **analytical thinking**, relating to the way in which candidates can read and process complex arguments. These tests are very common among graduates and those applying for MBAs. An example is the Watson-Glaser Critical Thinking test.
* **IT aptitude**, including various tests for technical programming ability and word processing.
* **manual dexterity**, testing special manipulation or hand to eye co-ordination linked to the special requirements of a job. If you're applying for a modern apprenticeship, especially in engineering or technology you may meet these.

Other tests are grouped as 'personality and interest tests'. There are four types in general use.

Personality questionnaires are used widely and are the type of test you're most likely to meet, especially if you're a graduate. The tests are designed to measure particular personality traits or characteristics that are important in general or specific work contexts. Examples are motivation, sociability, resilience, and emotional adjustment. Most of these inventories are 'self-report': they ask you to say how you respond to a variety of situations by choosing from a list of possibilities. You may find that they ask very similar questions several times over to judge the fine detail of your responses, and in many cases to check that you're answering straightforwardly and not trying to create a particular impression! The majority of the inventories you'll come across compare your responses with those of other people like you, or groups of people who are successful in the type of work you're applying for. These are called *normative* tests. A few will measure the relative strengths of different traits within your make-up, independent of other people. This type is called *ipsative* (literally, 'oneself'). The inventories you're most likely to meet are Savile and Holdsworth's OPQ, Myers-Briggs Type indicator, Cattell's 16PF, or Gordon Personal Profile.

Interest inventories are designed to find out where your career interests lie and the areas of work at which you're likely to be most successful. You'll find them being used for career guidance in any careers service office, in some selection processes, and for later development of people within an organisation. You may come across the Strong-Campbell or Rothwell-Miller Interest blanks (mostly for career guidance), or the SHL Occupational Interest inventories.

Values questionnaires deal with values, motives, or life goals. These guide your choices and are very important in determining the types of work and work-contexts in which you're most likely to succeed. These questionnaires explore collections of values that are relevant to the workplace such as the need for achievement, order, and belonging. The Gordon Survey is a typical example.

Other more specialised tests that might be met include:

* **Sales aptitude**. Various tests concerned with the special skills and attitudes needed for selling are in use.
* **Leadership**. While most of the Personality inventories will have a leadership dimension, there are some specialised tests, such as LOQ, that focus on leadership behaviours like planning, communication, and implementing ability.
* **Alternative methods**. Though not widely accepted in the UK, many European employers use graphology and sometimes astrology, as means of appraising personal characteristics. If you're asked to hand-write your application letter the former is probably being used.

MAKE IT HAPPEN

Prepare for the test mentally and physically

As with any type of test, good preparation is the key to a great result. As you prepare for a psychometric test, think about the following:

* How should I prepare for the different types of psychometric test?
* Are there resources that can help me prepare for a particular kind of test?
* Are there test-taking skills that I can learn?
* What can I do if I don't like the results of the test?

It's important to be physically prepared for taking a psychometric test. Research has shown that people perform better in all kinds of psychometric tests when they're well rested and in good physical shape. And, strangely, people do better in tests when they're slightly hungry, so eat lightly before taking one!

Get ready for attainment and aptitude tests

These tests have 'right answers', so you can improve your score with practice. Before you go for the test, find out exactly what skills and knowledge are being tested. It is a really good idea to practise the kind of test you're taking and there are hundreds of test preparation books available. These books explain how the questions are structured, provide test-taking tips, and contain sample tests so that you can evaluate your own level of skills and knowledge. It's best to:

* take a sample test
* use the book's study guides to help strengthen your weaker areas
* retest yourself to see if you've improved

Get ready for personality and interest tests

Since these tests measure your interests, personal preferences, and your ability to learn new skills, you can't really prepare for these tests in the same way that you would for a maths or history exam. Career-related aptitude tests are based on self-awareness, so the more you know yourself, the more likely the test results are to be useful to you.

Having said that, it's a good idea to:

* spend time thinking about your life and career goals, and the things you most like to do.
* look up the Strong-Campbell Index. This is a widely-used and popular career test which suggests career choices based on the interests of the person being tested.
* be well rested and relaxed so that you can focus clearly on the questions and provide your best answers.
* find copies of the test that will be used, or a similar one. Familiarity with the style of the test will give you confidence.

Brush up on test-taking skills

Whatever type of test you're doing, there are some general skills that are good to bear in mind.

Firstly, read the instructions very carefully and make sure you understand them completely. People often misread things when they're nervous; they focus on a few key words but don't read the sentence as a whole. If there is anything you don't understand, ask for clarification from the person administering the test.

Many people dive right into the test, and so get a much lower score than they deserve because they missed some important information. For example, in some tests, unanswered questions do not count against you. In others, however, the instructions may tell you that wrong answers will be subtracted from right answers to provide a final score for the test. In this case, you should skip over questions where you're not sure of the answer—don't just guess. Some tests are timed and, if so, it's important to know how much time you have left so you can focus on the questions that you're most likely to answer correctly.

When taking a 'personality' test, it is usually a mistake to spend too long thinking about your responses—generally speaking, the response that comes immediately to mind will be the best one.

As a general good test-taking strategy:

* first go through the whole test, answering only the questions you're absolutely sure of
* go back over the unanswered questions and tackle the ones that you're confident about
* if you still have time left, go through the remaining questions once again, really think them through, and provide your best answer

Remember that different companies will administer tests in different ways, so don't let this put you off. You may find yourself taking the test on your own or in a roomful of other people. Not everyone in there will necessarily be applying for the same job as you, however; some companies hold 'testing days' in which they test all applicants for all vacancies at the same time. Try to focus on your own performance rather than on the venue or potential 'competition'.

Reflect on the results

If you're taking a test for career guidance, take the results as an indicator—extra information to add to what you already know about yourself. Think carefully about the results but remember that no test is completely accurate, and no one knows you better than you do yourself. If the career advice provided by the test seems too far off the mark, trust your intuition. You may want to take a different kind of career test as a second opinion.

If you're taking an attainment or aptitude test as part of a job application, the organisation should give you an indication of how you did, even if they don't give you more detailed results. For some companies, that indication may be an invitation to interview (if the test took place as an initial screening process), for others, an invitation to a second interview (if the test took place as part of your initial interview).

In any case, you have the right to ask for feedback if you have any questions about the whole process. In most organisations, a lot of effort has been made to make sure the tests measure what they're supposed to. If you're in any doubt ask for an explanation of how the test results are used and what the organisation has done to see that they're fair to all applicants.

It is usually the human resources department of a company that is responsible for the tests, so if you have questions about your results you should contact them first.

WHAT TO AVOID

You make a major career shift based on your test results

Test results are meant to be used for guidance and should only be *part* of a comprehensive career-planning process. This process should include self-assessment exercises, plenty of personal soul-searching, talking to trusted friends and family, and possibly chatting things through with a professional career coach.

You don't take the test seriously

Your CV looks good, you know some people in the organisation and you have a lot of confidence in your ability to charm the recruitment manager—so you don't give much thought to the test you're asked to take. But, even though the results can be taken with a pinch of salt, you should adopt a serious attitude towards taking the test. Organisations that use testing often use the results at the very beginning of the recruitment process. If you don't pass the test, you will not even be considered for an interview. If there *is* a test, be as prepared as possible to do it and to do it well.

You take the test *too* seriously

Many people get extremely worried about psychometric tests, but the fact is that they can have such a varied predictive validity that some are only slightly better than chance. Don't feel you've failed if tests don't go to plan, and remember that the company is measuring itself as well as you.

You stay up all night the night before, cramming for the test

This, and a lot of caffeine, may have been how you got yourself through tests and exams before, so perhaps it has become the way you tackle all tests. But it wasn't a good strategy then, and it's not a good strategy now. The students who did best in final exams were those who began preparing right at the beginning of term—slow and steady wins the race. So if you know you'll be taking a psychometric test, find out as much as you can about the test and study over a period of time on a regular basis. If you have to take a 'personality test' there is little you can do to prepare, so don't worry about it!

USEFUL LINKS

GraduateCareersOnline:
www.graduatecareersonline.com/advice/employability
Mind Tools: **www.mindtools.com/page12.html**
Support4Learning: **www.support4learning.org.uk/jobsearch/assess.htm**
University of Sussex: **www.sussex.ac.uk/Units/CDU/psycho.html**

Negotiate the Best Deal in Your New Job

When you start a new job, you have a unique opportunity to position yourself as a valuable asset in the organisation and to set your level of pay accordingly. To achieve this you need to establish an appropriate asking price. On one hand, you don't want to oversell yourself and price yourself out of the market. On the other, you need to avoid selling yourself short, for it's extremely difficult to change your position significantly once you're placed in a complex pay structure.

There are no hard and fast rules about how or when to conduct your negotiation. Every situation is different and each employer will have their own set of thresholds. Understanding the context in which your negotiation is going to take place and being sensitive to the culture of the organisation is therefore essential. Having said that, there are some practical steps you can take to position yourself sensibly.

I am in the process of applying for a new job. How should I prepare for the negotiation of the package?

You need to do your research before entering the negotiation so that you're supported by accurate, current information. This means familiarising yourself with the company itself, as well as the range of salary and benefit options that are being offered. You may be able to tinker with the combination of benefits, if not the salary itself. Don't assume you'll be offered more than your former salary, especially if you're competing with someone who is equally qualified but willing to work for less. If the salary offered is less than you had hoped for, you can discuss the benefits package and make provision for an early salary review.

I feel extremely uncomfortable talking about how much I'm worth. What can I do to make this easier?

Many people dislike the negotiation phase of finding a new job. However, here are some simple steps you can take to make this easier.

* Try and avoid discussing your package until you've been offered the position.
* When you start negotiating, make sure you have in mind the minimum acceptable salary to you. (Don't reveal this figure, though!)
* Try and elicit the salary information first. If you're offered a range, go high or even slightly above the top end. If you're offered a specific figure, assume this is mid-range and try to push it up.
* If you're asked to name a figure, don't lie, but offer a range within which you'd be prepared to negotiate.

* If you're successful in your negotiations, ask for the agreed terms and conditions confirmed in writing—before you resign from your current position.

I am applying for a position that is a dream come true, and I don't want to put off my prospective employer by asking for too much. How can I safely work out my worth?

You can put off a prospective employer by pitching too high *or* too low, so it's important to get your level right. Look at the job pages to get a feel for the market rate, and draw information from your professional network. You'll also find some listings on the Web that will help you. Some of these are indicated below.

MAKE IT HAPPEN

Position yourself well

When you're going for a job, you are effectively a salesperson promoting a product, and it's up to you to demonstrate that the 'product' is valuable, high-quality, and superior to anything a competitor could offer. Potential employers, or 'buyers', are looking for the best value for their money, so will be driving the deal in the opposite direction. However, if you've positioned yourself well, they won't risk losing you and will be prepared to settle at the top of the market rather than at the bottom.

Leave the salary discussions as late as possible

It's preferable to leave salary discussions until the point at which you're offered the job. However, it isn't always the case that this will be left until the final stages of the process. Many recruiters ask for salary expectations and details of current salary early in the process. Some even screen people out on this basis. If this is the case, you may need to spend some time researching the question of salary at the application stage or before the first meeting. This will require you to think about your aspirations and be absolutely sure of the territory you'd like to cover, the experience you'd like to gain, and the context in which you'd like to work.

If you're forced to answer a question about your salary hopes at the beginning of your interaction, have a figure ready that is at the higher end of the scale. You can always supplement this with a request for a particular benefits package.

Consult the right sources

When seeking an entry point for your salary, there are several sources that will help you find an appropriate figure.

* Look at the range of packages offered for similar positions in the adverts on the jobs page.
* Ask for advice from people in your professional and personal network.
* Ask your mentor, if you have one, to advise you—or use his or her own network to access the information.
* Approach your local Training and Enterprise Council.
* If you're a member of a union, it will have information on acceptable salary ranges for your profession.

* Go to some of the Web-based salary information services, like the one listed at the end of this actionlist.

Consider the package, not just the salary

Some employers have fixed-scale salaries, in which case there is little room for negotiation. However, you may find that the total package of pay and benefits raises the worth of the salary to an acceptable level. For instance, you may be offered private health cover, a non-contributory pension, a fully financed car, and significant bonus potential. You may be able to negotiate a cash equivalent in place of a benefit, particularly in a smaller organisation that doesn't have inflexible systems in place. When bonuses are mentioned, you may want to discuss the basis on which the bonus is paid so that you're absolutely clear of the terms and conditions attached to it. Some bonus schemes spread the payments over several years as an incentive to stay with the business. Such complexities can be very off-putting.

Remember the tax implications

It's worth remembering that all the benefits included in a package are taxed as 'benefits in kind'. Company cars are taxed on the basis of the price of the model when first registered. You may want to consider whether you need a car with a large capacity, or whether running a car with a smaller engine could improve your income tax situation. As a result of the rapid depreciation of new cars, many people are now opting for a salary increase instead of a car allowance. Private health insurance is taxed at its cash value. This would make another impact on your tax bill.

Explore the boundaries

Adverts usually carry salary ranges to give applicants an idea of the boundaries of the negotiation. You can be sure, however, that the negotiation will start at base level. If you find that potential employers aren't responding to your sales pitch, you could negotiate an early pay review instead: for instance, if you demonstrate your worth against certain criteria in the first six months of employment, they'll agree to a particular salary increase. Ensure that the criteria are clearly set, though, and make sure this is included in your contract of employment.

Some adverts state that the salary is 'negotiable'. The onus is then on you to move in with an offer. Again, try and leave it to the end of the recruitment process, and be sure that you've studied the equivalent packages for the type of role and industry sector you're applying for.

Stay calm

When negotiating for a package, try to do it calmly and assertively. Appearing too eager can defeat your negotiation. Being too laid back or diffident can portray a lack of professionalism or self-confidence. Either extreme can damage your case.

WHAT TO AVOID

You don't do your research

Thinking that requesting a high salary will convey your worth is often misguided. Your prospective employer will naturally look for reasons to back up your assertion that you're worth so much. If you don't have a rational argument, you will look ill-prepared and unprofessional. Time spent in research is always well spent. In this way, you can argue your case logically and professionally.

You try to bluff

Don't bluff in your negotiation and try to play off fictitious job offers against the real one you're hoping to get. Employers generally don't respond to this kind of pressure, and instead of receiving a speedy offer you're likely to be left with nothing.

You show too much interest in the package

Behaving as if you're more interested in your package than in the role you're being recruited for is a mistake. Every employer knows that you will want a fair package, but you need to demonstrate that your financial concerns are balanced with a genuine desire for the job.

USEFUL LINKS

iVillage.co.uk: **www.ivillage.co.uk/workcareer/survive/prodskills**
Low Pay Commission: **www.lowpay.gov.uk**
UNISON: **www.unison.org.uk/bargaining/pay.asp**

Handle Office Politics

Life would be wonderful if you could work in an office without worrying about other people and what they're up to. However, everyone has a network of relationships throughout the organisation, and if you don't handle those carefully, you could be heading for a career disaster.

You don't have to work somewhere long to work out whether or not is has a highly political culture, where *who* you know tends to matter more than *what* you know. Friendships and casual conversations take on a new significance—one wrong word to the wrong person could end up scuppering that promotion. The context in which people have come to know each other is also important, as that can imply certain kinds of loyalty (or perceived obligations). Family, school, or social networks that intrude into professional territory can embroil people in all sorts of Machiavellian manoeuvrings that eventually create an overly politically-charged workplace. If you find yourself in this sort of minefield, this actionlist offers advice on how to pick your way through. It also suggests ways for managers to avoid and discourage negative 'politicking'.

I have unwittingly become involved in a political situation which I fear will compromise my reputation in the business. What should I do?

If you're unable to confront the situation directly, it's important to go through the correct channels to avoid compromising yourself further. Explain what's happened with your supervisor or manager. If the political situation involves your boss, you may want to approach your human resources department or mentor, if you have one, to ask their advice.

I am weary of the politics of large organisations, yet I love what I do and want to carry on doing it. How can I find an environment where I can just get on with my work?

You may find that a change of context meets your needs. This doesn't necessarily mean a move out of the organisation entirely, but perhaps you could consider a move to a small-business unit or specialised department where the likelihood of a different political culture exists. Smaller work units are very often structurally simpler and less political than large ones.

MAKE IT HAPPEN

Watch for signs of office politics

Politics plays a part in all organisations; it's an inevitable effect of putting human beings together in some sort of hierarchical arrangement. Indicators of office politics are often fairly easy to pick up—just hang around near the kettle, water cooler, or canteen in any organisation.

Listen out for clues about how the business works under the surface. Perhaps you might hear comments from people who have been passed over for promotion in favour of the recruiting manager's former golf partner. Also watch out for those who succeed by publicly supporting their boss, or by ensuring that they are always in the right place at the right time. Such successes again indicate that hidden agendas may be at play.

Ensure your own survival

Self-preservation is always desirable, but don't use political dirty tricks to survive, whatever your level of responsibility—they'll only create new nightmares. If your organisation is rife with politics, you can survive by following some simple rules.

First of all, observe the organisation's political style without getting involved until you're sure that you know what is going on. You may have started to notice coincidences or inconsistencies. Bide your time and watch the process so that you can begin to understand what the patterns and motivations are. You should keep your own counsel during this period and work according to your own values. Don't try to change your values to match those of the organisation; under pressure your own values will reassert themselves forcefully. You can't please everyone all the time, so use your own integrity to make decisions.

Try to build a network of trusted allies. During your observation phase you will have identified who these people could be. It's also a good idea to build a network outside the organisation to create options and opportunities for yourself. This will take the focus off work for a while and gives you time to reconfirm or realign your values.

It's important to expose other people's politically motivated behaviour. When colleagues say one thing and do another, or seem to be sabotaging your decisions or work relationships, use your assertiveness skills to challenge their motivation: 'You seem to be unhappy with the decisions I've made; would you like to discuss them?' They'll either have to deny your assertion or confront it, but at least the issue will be out in the open.

If you can find a mentor with whom you can discuss your observations and concerns, so much the better. You may gain a deeper understanding of the political processes at work and some insight into how you can manage these more effectively.

Discourage negative political behaviour

In any working environment, decision-making based on self-interested politics will encourage hypocrisy, double-dealing, cliques, and deception. These must be reined in if the business is to survive in the long term. Here are a few tips for those in managerial positions on how to create change and avoid potential nightmares:

* Give promotions to the candidates who've demonstrated a relevant track record of success. Conduct structured, formal interviews and consult with others affected by the decision. Match the successful candidate to the job description. Remember that although a good working relationship is necessary, the talents and values of the candidate don't have to match those of their new line manager exactly.
* Offer rewards and recognition solely for good performance, not in return for favours. All promotions or pay rises must be based on the individual's ability to reach or exceed the key performance indicators set during the performance review. Performance data should be available to those it concerns, with no hidden judgments or decisions.
* Communicate openly and transparently. Only unhealthy organisations hide information and spring unpleasant surprises on their employees. Communicate anything that affects your employees and their performance, including bad news, challenges, and initiatives for change.
* Introduce new initiatives, projects, and ideas on the basis of their value to the business, not on the basis of favouritism or possible personal benefit. Setting up a formal process for proposing new initiatives and tracing their evaluation and implementation will create confidence in an unbiased outcome.
* Don't be tempted to indulge in 'politicking', even when you can see an opportunity to benefit either yourself or the organisation as a whole. For example, you might want to offload a member of your team in order to attract someone you feel may perform more effectively. However, this is where the rot sets in. If you manage people on this basis, you'll destroy any trust your team has in you and their collective performance may deteriorate.

WHAT TO AVOID

You misread a situation and wade in with an accusation of politicking

At best this reveals your navety, at worst your own politicking or neuroses. If you think a colleague is politically motivated, observe their behaviour until you're sure that you understand it. You may wish to share your thoughts with someone you trust or, if it serves a purpose, confront the situation. Sometimes it's best to leave things alone. You will be the best judge of this.

You build a network purely for your own ends

Some people try to short-circuit the path to promotion by cultivating what they believe to be essential relationships. However, there's a big difference between building professional networks and using your contacts shamelessly in a headlong pursuit of your own selfish ends. Remember that if you launch yourself into an early promotion without having developed the skills to be successful, you may be setting yourself up for a very public and career-damaging failure. Build your networks prudently and use them to help develop your skills and deliver new opportunities. It may take a little longer, but it will pay off in the end.

You get involved in the politics too early

When you join a new organisation, try not to get embroiled in the politics at an early stage. Your newness in the business will allow you to ask naive questions that will help you create a picture of the political environment. Keep your relationships open and friendly and build your network with a diverse range of people. Observe the patterns of relationships closely to see where the information lies and where the power sits. After a few months you'll probably have a fairly accurate idea of what's going on and you can then make your own decisions about the extent to which you should get involved in organisational politics.

You communicate badly

Poor communication is probably the most common cause of a destructive political culture. In the absence of information or explanation, people will fill the gaps with speculation and rumour, which circulate around the office grapevine very fast. Clear communication, leaving people in no doubt about plans or decisions, helps protect an organisation from becoming a breeding ground for politics. Newsletters, bulletin boards on an intranet, and company-wide meetings are all useful vehicles for disseminating information, along with more local activities such as team meetings, departmental get-togethers, and personal briefings.

USEFUL LINKS

Doctor Job: **http://doctorjob.com/lifesupport/view.asp?ID=78**
Guy Browning's office politics: **www.officepolitics.co.uk**
iVillage.co.uk: **www.ivillage.co.uk/workcareer/survive**

Cope with a Nightmare Boss

Many people have a difficult or challenging relationship with their boss. Of all the difficult relationships you may have at work, this will probably be the trickiest and most stressful because of the inherent political dynamic of your relationship. It can be tempting to lay the blame for this unhappy type of situation at the boss's feet due to his or her unreasonable, negative, awkward, or unhelpful behaviour. Whether justified or not, the good news is that, as a significant party in the relationship, there is much you can do to end the bad boss nightmare.

My boss is always making negative and derisive comments about the way I do my work. What should I do?

See if you can find a private moment when you can explain how this makes you feel and ask your boss to stop doing it. You could suggest that he or she gives you clear guidelines and constructive feedback that will help you to meet his or her expectations and develop your talents. Point out that constant nagging affects the way you work and that you would be much more effective if he or she took a positive interest in what you do. If the negativity continues, you may decide to lodge a complaint of discrimination against your boss. If you take this route, make sure you have a record of the incidents and a note of the witnesses present. You might also decide to seek further advice from your human resources department if you have one; ask that your conversation be kept confidential until you're absolutely sure you want to act in this way.

My boss has favourites and I am definitely not one of them. As a result, I'm not given essential information and I miss out on good opportunities. How can I change things?

Lack of communication often contributes to workplace misunderstandings and can certainly exacerbate a difficult situation. Try approaching your boss with information about what you're doing and talk about your methods and goals. If your boss persists in denying you the information you need, you may have a case of bullying against him or her.

I have a boss who is really moody and bad-tempered, making work almost intolerable. Is there anything I can do to change this? I'm happy where I work other than that.

Observe whether there is a pattern in this behaviour and try to work out how you could influence the situation for the better. Once you've made your observations, you could try giving constructive feedback, letting your boss know how his or her mood swings affect you. Use assertive language and ask if there is anything you can do to alleviate the cause of the problem. If the behaviour persists, consult your human resources department to see if there are any formal procedures in place to deal with such a situation.

MAKE IT HAPPEN

Consider the impact on your own health and happiness

Rather than deal with the problem directly, many people are tempted to live with the difficulties of having a troublesome boss. Instead of addressing the issue, they brush it under the carpet by looking for ways of minimising the impact he or she has on their working lives. However, employing avoidance tactics or finding ways to offset the emotional damage can be time-consuming and stressful. Focusing on your own well-being may encourage you to tackle the issue rationally and try to reach an accommodation that will prevent you from jeopardising your health or feeling that you have to leave your job.

Understand your boss

When you come to look more closely at your relationship with your boss, the first thing to do is to work out how much of it is due to the structure of the organisation—for example, your boss necessarily has to give you tasks, some of which you may not enjoy—and how much is due to truly unreasonable behaviour.

Looking at the wider issues in the organisation may provide the key to the problem. 'Difficult boss syndrome' is rarely caused simply by a personality clash: more often than not, there are broader organisational factors that can go some way to explaining seemingly unreasonable behaviour.

However uncomfortable it may feel, try putting yourself in your boss's shoes. Recognise the objectives that define his or her role and think through the pressures they are under. Make a mental list of your boss's strengths, preferred working style, idiosyncrasies, values, and beliefs. Observe his or her behaviour and reactions, and watch where he or she chooses to focus attention. This will help you deepen your understanding. Very often, when we feel disliked or when we dislike someone, we avoid building this understanding and instead look for ways of avoiding the issues.

Compare the way you both perceive your role

As part of the process of understanding your boss, compare the perceptions you both have of your role and the criteria used to judge your success. You may feel that you're performing well, but if you're putting your energy into tasks that your boss doesn't feel are relevant, you will be seen as performing poorly.

Take the initiative to explore your boss's expectations and agree on your objectives. This will clarify your role and give you a better idea of how to progress in the organisation.

Understand yourself

Having scrutinised your boss and developed a greater understanding of him or her, try doing the same exercise on yourself. Sometimes a lack of self-knowledge leads to us being surprised by our reactions and the feedback we get. Ask for input from your colleagues while you're doing this. Ask them what they observe when you interact with your boss, how you come across to them, and how you could manage your communication differently. Although their perceptions may not represent the absolute truth about you, it nonetheless reflects the image you create.

Think through some of the past encounters you've had with your boss and reflect upon them objectively, perhaps with a friend or colleague who knows you well. Maybe one situation happens over and over again, which suggests that you harbour a value or belief that is being repeatedly compromised. If you can understand what this is, you can learn to manage these situations more effectively. You may need to consider changing some of your behaviour and this may prompt a reciprocal behavioural change in your boss. If you don't change anything about the way you interact with your boss, the relationship will remain unaltered, so this is definitely worth a try.

For example, perhaps you value attention to detail, but your boss is a big-picture person. Every time you ask for more detailed information, you'll be drawing attention to one of your boss's vulnerabilities, and he or she is likely to become unco-operative or irritated by your request. Once you've observed your respective patterns, you can begin to work around them or accommodate them.

Remember that the relationship is mutual

In order to be effective, managers need a co-operative and productive team. But in order to be part of such a team, each member needs their manager to provide the resources and support they need to do their job properly. An unsupportive boss can be just as nightmarish as a vindictive one.

When managers neglect to give their employees the information and feedback they need, employees are forced to second-guess their boss's requirements. This inevitably leads to misunderstandings on both sides. The knock-on effects of this are an atmosphere of distrust and ill-will, and mutual recriminations—not to mention the negative impact on the organisation's productivity levels. Ask for the information and resources you require, or find other ways to get these, as this will put you in control of the situation and protect you from the need to improvise.

Nightmare situations can arise when employees' needs aren't met. Some people become angry and resentful of the manager's authority; some find ways of challenging decisions in order to assert their own power; and others develop agendas of their own that are neither helpful nor productive.

One-sided relationships are a recipe for revolution! It is rare in business to find relationships where there is absolutely *no* reciprocal power. Remember that if you're no longer willing to spend time managing your difficult boss, you still have the ultimate power: you can just walk away.

WHAT TO AVOID

You take your boss's behaviour personally

It is very tempting to take the behaviour of a difficult boss personally. However, it is very unlikely that *you* are the problem. It may be something you do, it may be the values you hold, or it may be that you remind your boss of someone he or she doesn't get on with. The only person who loses out if you take it personally is you.

You don't remain detached

Many difficult relationships deteriorate to the point where they are fraught with contempt and confrontation. This is never helpful in a work setting and only makes matters uncomfortable for everyone. If you find yourself being drawn into an angry exchange, try to remain emotionally detached and listen actively to what is being said to (or shouted at) you. It may provide you with clues about why the situation has developed and allow you to get straight to the point of concern. Ask for a private review afterwards to explore the incident. You may find that this brings to the surface issues that are relatively easy to deal with and that will prevent further outbursts from occurring.

You never confront the issue

Because facing up to difficult people is not an easy thing to do, many people avoid biting the bullet. However, this will only prolong a miserable situation. Acquiescence enables bullying to thrive and allows the aggressors to hold power. Break the cycle by taking responsibility for your share of the problem and examining what it is you're doing to provoke conflict between you and your boss. Doing nothing is not a viable option.

USEFUL LINKS

Bully OnLine: **www.bullyonline.org**
ImproveNow.com: **www.improvenow.com**
Monster.com:
http://midcareer.monster.com/articles/careerdevelopment/stresseffects
troubleatwork: **www.troubleatwork.org.uk**

Deal with Bullying or Harassment

Anyone who has ever been bullied will know how demoralising and difficult it can be. When it occurs in the workplace it can be a seemingly inescapable nightmare, the effects of which are sure to take their toll over time on the physical as well as mental well-being of the victim.
Bullying and physical abuse lie at the extreme end of the spectrum, with more subtle forms of harassment at the other end. What is tolerated in the workplace will depend very much upon the culture of the organisation and the attitudes of its leaders. Some businesses ignore all forms of harassment; others make a point of creating a culture where intimidation of any sort is cause for reprimand or dismissal. It is worth reflecting on your organisation's culture to see what exists, both on and under the surface. This actionlist provides advice both for victims of harassment and the colleagues or managers around them.

I've seen a colleague being bullied and no one intervened. What should I have done?

Technically, the choice to deal with the bullying you witnessed rests with the one being harassed, but this is easier said than done. This kind of behaviour often affects the whole team, and you therefore have grounds to get involved if you wish. You could start by asking your harassed colleague about the treatment he or she received. The person may indicate that they don't want to make a fuss about it and will leave it at that. Alternatively, you could speak to the bully, explaining the impact of his or her behaviour on the team as a whole. When doing this, use good feedback techniques. For example, begin all your statements with 'I . . .', and base them on things that you have personally observed.

How do I know when joking turns to bullying?
The difference between a good joke and bullying can be subtle. However, if the person being bullied is demeaned and disempowered in some way, or if the joke becomes personally critical and destructive, then the line has been crossed.

I feel I'm being bullied, but my boss disguises his actions with jest. How do I deal with this?
Bullies are skilled in undermining confidence, and victims begin to question whether they are doing something wrong, or perhaps imagining things. One way of dealing with this is to write down the incidents in a journal, including the context in which they took place. Ask for feedback from observers and include their comments. Over time, you will be able to see if there is a pattern to the treatment you have been receiving. Also, the record may be useful if you decide to take the matter further.

I've seen victims 'asking' to be bullied. How does this happen?
Once someone's confidence has been broken, they become 'easy pickings' and can inadvertently help to encourage bullying behaviour. If this is the case, you should still approach the victim and express your concern. If the problem persists, you would be wise to bring it up in a staff meeting, or to report it to the person's supervisor—or to another manager of equal or greater rank.

MAKE IT HAPPEN

Understand the forms bullying can take

The recipient of bullying is often in a weaker position, physically, emotionally, or hierarchically. Victims are usually unable or unwilling to stand up for themselves, due to what they feel will be the unacceptable consequences, such as an escalation of abusive behaviour or the threat of redundancy. This fear allows the behaviour to continue.

Any form of harassment can have a serious impact on the morale of staff in the business, and can affect the performance and health of individuals. Not only is it simply wrong, but it's unlawful, and should be treated seriously.

Examples of different forms of harassment

These include:

* all manner of physical contact from touching, pushing, and shoving, to serious assault
* intrusive or obsessive behaviour, such as constant pestering, baiting, or dogging a person's movements
* tricks being played that result in risk or danger to the individual

* group bullying, where the individual is overpowered by a number of aggressors

Less direct harassment may include:

* the spreading of rumours, jokes, or offensive personal remarks
* written statements, letters, or graffiti
* actions that isolate the individual and prevent them from doing their work effectively
* non-co-operation, or sabotage of professional objectives
* pressure for sexual favours
* obscene gestures and comments
* the orchestration of situations that compromise the individual
* manipulative 'political' behaviour, that may include bribery or blackmail

Determine when the line has been crossed

Often, people find it hard to know whether the line of harassment has been crossed. If they confront the perpetrators, they can be accused of 'being a poor sport', or worse. Such accusations are often levelled to mask what is going on, and can seriously undermine the victim's confidence.

If you are the one being bullied, seek feedback from those who may have observed any incidents. Their objectivity will help put perspective on the situation if you're worried that you may be over-reacting. It may be that their account gives you more ammunition to deal with the problem appropriately. Select your witness carefully though—ones you can trust to be allies throughout the ordeal, and who won't 'flip' on you under pressure.

If the harassment is infrequent and seems harmless, try not to take it too personally. Bullying says more about the character of the bully than it does about the person being bullied. However, if the bullying is persistent or escalates, you must confront it and report it. Even if you don't wish to face the bully head on, there are likely to be other ways of asserting your rights.

Check in the employees' handbook, if you have one. There are probably procedures in place to assist you in dealing with your situation. You may be advised to report the incident(s) to your manager but, should you feel uncomfortable about this—for example, if your manager is part of the problem—you may wish to go directly to the human resources department. If you decide to lodge a formal complaint, make sure you have a record of the incidents and a note of the witnesses present.

Work to maintain a non-bullying atmosphere

Left unchecked, bullying can destroy the morale of valued employees and put the surrounding people into a state of fear. If you're a manager, you have a responsibility to report bullying elsewhere in the organisation, even if it doesn't affect your staff. However, you don't want to create an atmosphere of persecution either. Try to strike a balance between vigilance and freedom of choice.

Bear in mind your legal obligations to your staff. Remember that turning a blind eye to the problem may at some point make you culpable as well. You need to reassure staff that their complaints will be taken seriously and dealt with fairly. Most people are reluctant to report harassment because of the potential impact on their position/job. Explain what steps have to be taken, and estimate the length of time involved in the process.

Remember to give any potential complainant a few days in which to reconsider making a formal complaint. Don't exert pressure to take the issue further if the recipient decides to let the matter go—it's his or her choice and this should be respected. However, make sure that the organisation's policy manual spells out how to proceed if the person does decide to pursue the charge. It will probably involve investigating the details to establish what happened, and in what context. This may involve interviews with the victim, alleged abuser, and witnesses. Notes—based on facts, not hearsay and opinions—should be taken and filed with the human resources department or representative.

Cases of serious assault are rare, but when they occur, they may go beyond the scope of the organisation to deal with them. It may be necessary to contact a security officer or the police, and you may also need medical intervention and/or counselling for the victim, perhaps the perpetrator, and even some affected colleagues.

The incident could also involve an external third party, such as a customer. It is important to have a plan in place for such events, and then react in as calm and professional a manner as possible. The more serious the problem, the more your employees will depend on you to bring the matter to a close as quickly and judiciously as you can. Minimising 'collateral damage' helps restore equilibrium more quickly.

WHAT TO AVOID

You act before you know all the facts

Wading in with accusations when you think you've witnessed an episode of bullying could make matters worse: you may have misjudged the situation. Unless it's a serious incident, it's best to observe and question before intervening. In this way, all parties are given a chance to explain their behaviour and resolve the situation calmly.

You mistake a genuine extrovert for a bully

Extroverts frequently speak their minds before really thinking about what they are saying—which can sound confrontational and be mistaken for harassment. Being extroverts, however, they are often receptive to questioning and keen to point out that they were just testing the boundaries, or joking. By sharing your perception and inviting theirs, it's possible to clarify and dispel the situation without further entanglement.

You don't consider that the bully may need help too

It is easy to assume that bullies are strong characters. Indeed, it's often to create this impression that they become bullies in the first place. In fact, most bullies are insecure and behave as they do to mask a lack of knowledge or skill. Or perhaps they are mirroring behaviour further up the organisation, thinking that this may help them advance. One way of handling such a person is to offer them coaching, so that they can be helped to understand the underlying cause, and succeed in changing their behaviour.

USEFUL LINKS

ACAS: **www.acas.org.uk/publications/al05.html**
Bully OnLine: **www.bullyonline.org/workbully/index.htm**
ImproveNow.com: **www.improvenow.com**
TroubleAtWork: **www.troubleatwork.org.uk/about.asp**

Helen Reed – Fighting back against workplace bullying

Helen Reed worked as a presenter and reporter for local radio and TV for seven years. Her contract with her employer was ended in 2001 after Helen had experienced workplace bullying from a manager for over two years and had engaged the help of her union to fight her corner. She was finally dismissed for refusing to agree a settlement with her employers as it had an attached 'gagging' clause. She went on alone to win the right to a tribunal hearing after being accused of making a vexatious claim, and finally won a tribunal for unfair dismissal. Helen believes that 'no amount of settlement is enough to be silenced', and that it is against our human rights to be forced into silence about abuse that continues in the workplace. She also believes that this enforced silence is another bullying technique which prevents the truth from being heard; if bullying is ever to be brought to an end at work, it must be brought to light and confronted. Here Helen explains how she is dealing with the aftermath of her experiences and how she is using what she's learnt to help others nationwide.

Learning painful but useful lessons

'Being bullied at work changed my life profoundly and taught me some powerful but painful lessons – that's why it's important to me to help others negotiate the minefield that goes with the territory. As time went on, it became clear to me that the organisation for whom I'd been proud to work, and who I once believed to have the utmost integrity, could not be relied upon to do the right thing or be trusted to protect staff from a difficult and abusive environment. What I discovered was a culture of institutionalised bullying, where management bullies were protected. I initially assumed that because what was happening to me was wrong, someone would be interested and would be able to help. In particular, I thought that because I was working for a large organisation, there would be employment rights and procedures to protect the employee. Instead, I found that while some anti-harassment and anti-bullying procedures were in place at least theoretically, with some helpful-sounding phrases (such as 'the perception of the individual must always be taken seriously'), no-one applied them to real situations or was in the least interested in taking responsibility for implementing them.

'I am a believer in unions and am now active in my own to help combat bullying in all organisations. Unions can be very helpful, but I'd advise others not to always assume that their union will be able to help them as effectively as they would like. The law is non-existent, effectiveness of union negotiation is patchy, and knowledge of bullying in the workplace is still limited. The first point of contact with the union is the union rep, and a good one will always be supportive and interested and try to help provide the necessary knowledge to deal with a situation or get more help where necessary. The problem is that this is still a field of abuse where lack of knowledge and understanding may hinder your case. Assertiveness and confidence on the part of the union rep are vital when dealing with the bully as he or she is usually in a position of power and may be very intimidating. Therefore workers 'standing together' and the activation of the union chapel as a support system is essential, so that the target does not have to suffer in isolation. Bullying thrives by isolating the victim.

'If you find yourself in a difficult position where you're not getting the support you feel is necessary, do contact the union head office directly to get the assistance of an official who covers your area of work. Again, even though I have seen some excellent representation, some officials may be more useful or able than others and some may even try to dissuade you from taking action at all. For example, too frequently people are put under pressure or encouraged by the union to take offers that have gagging orders attached. This practice should be outlawed, I feel, as the technique of silencing does nothing to prevent bullying behaviour for future potential targets and also provides only a short term cover-up for employers; a bully will always surface again to undermine the workplace. Unions are important, but they can be inconsistent, busy, and pressured; you need to be lucky with the individuals you deal with and also unafraid to demand the assistance you need.

'In my experience, the HR department also proved to be completely ineffective in helping me as a target of bullying and existed to support management rather than intercede on behalf of employees. I have also witnessed this in most other cases. The same went for the occupational health representative. When I went to report stress-related conditions, no notes were taken, so there was no record of any of the situations I'd been having to deal with. This attitude of denial was apparent throughout the organisation, even senior management and the then Director General were not prepared to acknowledge that there may be serious problems and a 'culture of cover-up' to be dealt with. Rather than create the safe and fair workplace that we're all entitled to, there was an attitude that management could not be wrong under any circumstances. I feel that they hid this lack of action behind the façade of a defunct and undemocratic grievance procedure that has no independent judgment or right of appeal. This can easily be confirmed by union figures which prove they hadn't won a grievance procedure against management in more than 20 years. The bullied have virtually nowhere to turn and find themselves having to cope with a wall of silence while senior members of staff who could and should help, choose to bury their heads in the sand rather than stand up for others and speak out.

'A workplace culture that protects even a small percentage of bullying managers creates a climate of fear. This has a subtle but profound effect on everyone. Colleagues or acquaintances won't, or feel they can't, help you. They worry that they may be labelled as trouble-makers, that they would also suffer at work, and that their careers may be blighted or abruptly ended. Then there is the guilt that ineffective management and colleagues may feel when they don't support you. It's a psychological fact that when we feel guilt we eventually project that onto the party we feel guilty about, after all it has to go somewhere. So it's probable for the already bullied target to become a sort of 'no-go zone' and be made to feel like a workplace leper. This only adds to feelings of isolation, as you're not only being bullied, but you're being ignored too. I experienced this myself and did find it extremely painful, but I had to remind myself that others are afraid and had mortgages to pay, and tried to be as understanding as I could. It's hard but important not to take it personally if supporters or friends drop away; instead give yourself a real pat on the back for having the courage to carry on with what you believe is right. Remember that you are doing what most people just aren't able to do. Gandhi once said, "even if you have to be in a minority of one to speak out, the truth is the truth". Bear in mind too that eventually, everyone in your workplace will benefit from the stand you're making.

'Sadly, many bullying targets will get very little help, so it's important to appreciate any support you *do* get. You also need to be ready to stand up for yourself and to take action as and when you can. Keep faith in yourself, act quickly, and don't take 'no' for an answer. People will try to fob you off, but counter this by being assertive, calm and as unemotional as possible in your communications and consistent in your message. Follow up any conversation with an email or a letter, and keep detailed notes and copies of any correspondence. This is vital, as later on you may have to prove a whole sequence of events.

'Bear in mind that for virtually all targets of bullying (as well as whistle-blowing, which is effectively what you become once you "blow the whistle" on the bully), life just won't be the same again. You have been subjected to an extended period of psychological abuse and may be very frayed at the edges, (many targets actually suffer Post Traumatic Stress syndrome with all the associated problems). You're in this situation for the long haul, and it can be very painful if you are branded a trouble-maker when you know you're just trying to stand up for yourself. The irony is, we know from research, that those who are bullied are in fact usually hardworking, considerate, and good at their jobs and this is precisely why they are being bullied. Bullies are the people with the real problem – they are troubled characters, insecure, inadequate, manipulative, jealous, devious, dysfunctional, sometimes even clinically ill – sad and damaging people who try to boost their own failings by attacking others. This not only affects the target directly but the whole atmosphere, creativity and productivity of the entire workplace. It's estimated that the issue of workplace bulling costs industry billions each year in sickness and associated costs.

'Making a stand against a bully is gruelling, but try as far as you can to maintain your self-esteem and remember that what has happened is not your fault; the responsibility always lies with the bully.'

Looking back

'I wish I'd acted sooner. Attempting to be an understanding, reasonable human being does not protect you from the bully. It can take months to realise that the weird, painful, and devastating behaviour you're being subjected to is, in fact, bullying and often you'll assume that you've done something wrong or by that time feel unconfident and undermined. But don't be too good-natured; remember that by fighting back you're not causing a fuss unnecessarily – you are being treated unfairly and you have every right to try and improve your own situation. Understandably, many people hope that things will blow over or clear themselves up, but this rarely happens. You owe it to yourself to think 'I'm not putting up with this', and to take action, keeping clear and detailed records of everything as you go. Remember what Goethe said: "Whatever you can do or think you can do, begin it. Boldness has genius, power and magic in it. Begin it now".

'It was a shock to find that currently there is no law against bullying. The legal system and the employment system aren't necessarily there to protect the vulnerable, as one might assume. They can be manipulated and often are, to the employers' benefit. Bullying is not yet illegal and the legal system can be a nightmare. Again one assumes that there must be a law to protect you, or at least that the solicitors or union lawyers will do everything in their power to help you. But in many cases you may discover that really it all comes down to money.

'In my own experience, the solicitors who represented the union were on a fixed yearly payment, and when on their advice (even though I had a very strong case) at the 11th hour, the union said that they would withdraw their support and I would be on my own unless I accepted a settlement with attached gagging clause, I was horrified. What happened to fairness and justice? After dozens of what I felt were intimidating calls from both union and lawyer I realised what was happening. Why would the solicitors want any cases to go to tribunal when they would have to engage an expensive barrister to represent someone? Perhaps they feel that it's better for them to pressurise the employee to accept any offer with a gagging clause, even though this may be immoral and detrimental to his or her long-term career prospects and well being. It also leaves workplace bullying conveniently swept under the carpet and never shames the employer into fulfilling their ethical obligations.

'What also doesn't help, I feel, is that the employment tribunal system itself is not currently equipped to deal with bullying cases. It has no legal framework to judge them within, so the cases have to be heard as unfair dismissal or constructive dismissal cases. You may or may not get effective representation, even employment law solicitors seem to have patchy knowledge of bullying issues. Tribunal judges/chairpersons may or may not understand or be sympathetic to bullying in the workplace issues and may be influenced by the reputation of a powerful organisation. Even on winning a case they virtually never demand that the employer re-instate the employee and settlements are usually paltry. It's a lottery that is undoubtedly weighted in the employer's favour.

'Looking back, I'd have borne in mind the overall effect on my health; the stress, depression, frustration, and isolation. It really is very gruelling emotionally. There can be also be serious knock-on effects of dealing with so much pressure—and loved ones, family, and friends are all affected. Some relationships may not even stand the test of this overwhelming stress and you have to give yourself a lot of respect for carrying on regardless. It's vital to look into strategies for dealing with stress early on so that you can cope with what's being thrown at you.

'On a bigger scale, knowing what I know now, I'd have had more faith in myself, demanded action be taken sooner, and been less fearful about upsetting anyone and the prospect of losing my job. After all, how can you continue working somewhere that compromises your sense of justice and integrity? After all you have to live with yourself. You might be out of a job anyway whatever happens, so don't compromise and speak out as quickly and clearly as possible. Stick it out as much as you can, but if things become very bad and you're finding it hard to cope day-by-day, it may be necessary for your health and well-being to leave and then pursue a case for constructive dismissal.'

Drawing out the positives

'Nothing would have ever changed or been transformed in this world unless the few had stood up for what's right. After all, it's the mightiest challenges and struggles in life that help us to grow and develop and become evolved in terms of wisdom or spirituality. Those who keep their heads in the sand while others suffer may well lose their own integrity or be selling their souls for the sake of a quiet life! As a result of what happened to me, I feel I've developed a much deeper understanding of human behaviour; the whole experience has been a profound life lesson for me. I've also learned an enormous amount about the legal system and employment rights (or lack of them). The system is often unfair and it can be hard at times to find sympathetic or interested legal representation. You may even find that in some cases, *you* know best – trust yourself, your intuition, and realise that you aren't as ignorant as you think (or as others would have you believe). It's easy to be intimidated by officials of all kinds, but don't be.

'I've gained a deeper understanding of inequality and prejudice, and I think I've become a more compassionate person. Many illusions have been shattered and reality gained. I'm certainly much more aware of how tough life can be and how you need personal resources of strength to deal with what life throws at you. Even if everyone else abandons you, you still have yourself. I think I'm a wiser person, but I hope that the experience hasn't made me a harder one. While being bullied and fighting my own corner in the face of so much indifference was an awful experience, I met a few marvellous people along the way who displayed real loyalty and courage. They've helped and inspired me enormously to value what really matters in life.

'Since my job ended, I've become heavily involved with my union in spite of (or maybe even because of) the fact that I felt they let myself and others down. I'm still the only member of the union who has been through a similar situation and yet who has not signed a gagging clause with my former employer. I felt very strongly that it was important to use my experience to make sure that the union worked more effectively for its members and that it had a proper anti-bullying campaign, useful information, and support for anyone else suffering as I and countless others have.

'Very few people want to know the real truth about bullying. It's probably the biggest tolerated abuse in our society today and people are often keen to silence those who try to fight against it, but we must try to look out for others in our workplaces and society. Wherever possible I've worked to highlight this issue and raise awareness of it. I have written about it for the media, given presentations, and been part of panel discussions. Within the union I've pioneered a national anti-bullying campaign of workshops and am working to raise the profile of this issue to make sure that anyone who is out of work as a result of bullying is no longer isolated and has a support network. We've used union funds to create the campaign and put together posters, leaflets, and a booklet for targets of bullying called *Stand Together Against Bullying*.

'I'm also working on further practical measures in the fight against bullying: I'm putting pressure on employers to renegotiate their grievance procedures which in many cases are unfair, undemocratic, and offer no independent judgment. I have encouraged my own MP to take the Dignity at Work Bill through parliament. I'm also communicating the issues to other MPs so they can add their support. If successful, it will finally make bullying in the workplace illegal.

'The way forward is not through anger, fighting, and resentment but through understanding, providing knowledge, and bringing people together with a shared purpose that can build a better workplace for all. Tolerating bullying in the workplace really does not serve anyone, but of course overcoming the fear and accepted bad practice that leads to collusion and lethargy is a slow process.

'Is there a happy ending? Who knows, but maybe there is a beginning. The writer Byron Katie has a favourite saying that springs to mind: "God save us from seeking love, approval, and appreciation – then we are free". If I had not stood up to tell the truth about bullying, something in me would have died – instead at least I feel alive. If you are a target of bullying, face the fear that is limiting you and preventing you from taking action; believe in yourself, stand up straight away and say "no". After all, what's the worst that can happen? You may lose your job, you may lose a few so-called friends, but if you don't you may lose your peace of mind and well-being. I guarantee you'll end the abuse sooner, gain your own unshakeable self-respect, and find the people who really matter.'

USEFUL LINKS

www.helenreed.co.uk
www.bullyonline.org

Cope with Discrimination

Discrimination against individuals on the basis of their race, age, gender, cultural background, or physical/mental impairment is unlawful. In the United Kingdom, legislation to prevent discrimination on the basis of age is due to be implemented in 2006; until then, a code of practice has been drawn up for employers to follow. However, not all employers obey the rules, and enforcing the law can be a nightmare in itself.

Everyone has an equal right to employment with fair remuneration in an environment that is free from discrimination. There are few experiences more depressing than being treated unfairly because of who you are. Fortunately, there are established ways in which you can tackle any type of discrimination and bring the nightmare to an end.

I believe that I have been discriminated against on the basis of my ethnic background. What should I do?

Firstly, don't wait too long; there are time limits for bringing a case under the Race Relations Act. Racial discrimination is not easy to prove, so you'll need to gather as much evidence as possible and create a good record of the incident(s) along with a list of any witnesses. Seek guidance from trusted friends and professional confidants at the earliest opportunity and explore the legal assistance that you may be eligible for. You can go to your union, the Citizen's Advice Bureau, or the Commission for Racial Equality.

My boss has always been respectful before, but he recently made a sexual advance while we were at an official function and I felt really threatened. Am I able to take action under the Sex Discrimination Act?

If your boss has made even a single sexual advance on you, you may have grounds for a complaint. You don't have to experience persistent sexual harassment before you ask for help—if it's sufficiently serious, one incident can amount to sex discrimination. However, before you start down this road, think about taking your complaint to the human resources department or to a trusted superior to see if there are any internal policies that can support or protect you and help to resolve the situation.

I have discovered that my colleague receives a much better package of benefits than I do, and was recently awarded a bonus that I knew nothing about. Do I have grounds for a claim?

Yes, equal pay law embraces benefits, bonuses, pensions, holiday, and sick pay as well as salary. If you can prove that your job is comparable with that of your colleague, involving the same level of skills and knowledge, then you are likely to have a case. However, you must be able to demonstrate this before you can proceed to a tribunal with your claim.

MAKE IT HAPPEN

Discrimination is a huge subject, and there are many resources you can turn to if you feel that you've been discriminated against. However, the following will provide a useful starting point. More detailed information can be found using the extensive links at the end of this actionlist.

It may be that you're being discriminated against in more than one way. Take a look at each of the following steps in turn, checking if they apply to you.

Racial discrimination

As mentioned on p.235, there are time limits for bringing a case under the Race Relations Act, so do act quickly. Gather as much evidence as possible and create a good record of the incident(s) along with a list of any witnesses. As discussed, racial discrimination isn't easy to prove, and the burden of proof will be on you. Talk to people you trust and seek legal help.

Sex discrimination

The Sex Discrimination Act 1975 makes it unlawful for employers in the United Kingdom to treat women or men less favourably in employment matters because of their sex or marital status.

If you were dismissed for poor performance while a poorly performing colleague of the opposite gender retained their job, you may have a claim for sex discrimination. This would also be the case if, for example, you were dismissed for being persistently late while a colleague of the opposite sex with the same timekeeping habits was not.

If you were selected for redundancy, you may have a claim if you can show that the selection criteria used affected one sex more than the other and that there was no rational justification for this.

Equal pay

The issue of pay within the area of sex discrimination is covered specifically by the Equal Pay Act 1970. The Equal Pay Act doesn't cover you for being treated differently to members of the same sex, only the opposite sex. However, because the majority of part-timers still tend to be women, there is also a clause relating to the rights of part-timers.

There are two ways of looking at equal pay. Sometimes a person is paid less than a colleague of the opposite sex for doing the same job. Other times, one individual is paid less than another of the opposite sex for doing work of equivalent value. Both these situations are discriminatory and may be unlawful. Equal pay rights apply to both sexes.

Equal pay legislation extends beyond just wages and salaries; it also covers bonuses, benefits, overtime, holiday pay, sick pay, performance-related pay, and occupational pensions.

Examples of pay discrimination
There are several ways in which pay discrimination can take place. Here are some examples:

* A woman is appointed on a lower salary than her male counterparts.
* A woman on maternity leave is denied a bonus received by other staff.
* The jobs that women occupy are given different job titles and grades to those of male
* colleagues doing virtually the same work.
* Part-time staff have no entitlement to sick pay or holiday pay.
* All staff are placed on individual contracts and not allowed to discuss their pay rates.

Your rights to equal pay are set out in the Equal Pay Act 1970. You can take your claim for equal pay to an employment tribunal at any time while you're in the job, or within six months of leaving employment.

Sexual harassment

The Sex Discrimination Act makes it unlawful for employers to treat a woman less favourably than a man (or a man less favourably than a woman) by subjecting her or him to any emotional or physical harm. The Act also applies to individuals undergoing gender reassignment.

You can only make a claim of sexual harassment if the incident(s) took place during 'the course of employment'—that is at work or at a work-related function.

Sexual harassment is defined as unwelcome physical, verbal, or non-verbal conduct of a sexual nature. Cases are most likely to be brought as civil claims in an employment tribunal.

Examples of sexual harassment at work
These include:

* requests or demands for sexual favours by either gender
* comments about your appearance which are derisory or demeaning
* remarks that are designed to cause offence
* intrusive questions or speculations about your sex life
* any behaviour related to gender that creates an intimidating, hostile, or humiliating
* working environment

Incidents involving touching or more extreme physical threats are criminal offences and should be reported to the police as well as your employer.

Disability discrimination

If you're disabled, or have had a disability, the Disability Discrimination Act (DDA) makes it unlawful for you to be discriminated against in the areas of:

* employment
* access to goods, facilities, and services
* the management, buying, or renting of land or property

The DDA was passed in 1995 to introduce new measures aimed at ending the discrimination which many disabled people face in these areas.

It uses the term 'disability' to describe 'anyone with a physical or mental impairment which has a substantial and long-term adverse effect upon their ability to carry out normal day-to-day activities' according to the DDA. This includes:

* **Physical impairment**—the weakening or adverse change of a part of the body caused through illness, by accident, or from birth
* **Mental impairment**—learning disabilities and all recognised mental illnesses

Ageism

In October 2000, the UK government supported the European Directive on Equal Treatment and committed to implementing age-related legislation by 2006. A six-year implementation period was agreed to allow time for the formulation of clear, beneficial age legislation in close consultation with individuals, employers and expert groups.

In the meantime, the Government launched the 'Code of Practice on Age Diversity in Employment' in June 1999. This voluntary code for employers sets 'good practice' standards for non-ageist approaches to:

* recruitment and selection
* training and development
* promotion and succession
* redundancy and retirement

It's worth checking out the Code of Practice using the links at the end of this chapter. It can be a valuable yardstick for judging your organisation's policies.

Victimisation

Your employer shouldn't discriminate against you because you've taken a case of discrimination to a tribunal. People who have helped you by giving evidence or providing information are also protected from such victimisation.

WHAT TO AVOID

You rush into legislation

Rushing to make a claim, or threatening to do so, because you believe that you've been discriminated against at work is a mistake. The process of taking action is lengthy and evidence needs to be produced to back up your claim. Even when this is available, the procedures are stressful and time consuming. It's always best to see if you can find another way around the problem. Start by broaching the subject with the 'perpetrator' or having a discussion with the human resources department or an external source of advice.

You're not sure of your ground

Misunderstanding a situation or someone's behaviour can lead to false claims of discrimination. It is important to be sure of your facts and do all the research necessary to ensure that you have the grounds for a claim. Although you'll have to talk with colleagues and perhaps consult with others in the organisation, do this confidentially to avoid drawing attention to a situation that may not develop into a claim.

You think that office parties don't count

It's a mistake to think that being 'off duty' or away from the work premises with your colleagues protects you from being accused of harassment. Under the Sex Discrimination Act, sex discrimination is outlawed in a wide variety of contexts that are related to your employment. In certain circumstances, action can be taken if it can be shown that the (social) event at which the incident occurred was linked to your employment.

USEFUL LINKS

Age Positive: **www.agepositive.gov.uk**
Commission for Racial Equality: **www.cre.gov.uk**
Disability Discrimination Act 1995:
www.hmso.gov.uk/acts/acts1995/1995050.htm
Disability.gov.uk: **www.disability.gov.uk**
Disability Rights Commission: **www.drc-gb.org**
Employment Rights Act 1996: **www.hmso.gov.uk/acts/acts1996/1996018.htm**
Equal Opportunities Commission: **www.eoc.org.uk**
Global Action on Ageing: **www.globalaging.org/elderrights/world/uklabor.htm**

Transform Poor Performance

Poor performance can result from many causes, such as:

* **inability to manage perception or pressure**
* **failure to prioritise**
* **lack of skill, knowledge, or motivation**
* **conflict of personalities or styles**
* **over-promotion (often termed 'the Peter Principle'), where the person is actually out of his or her depth**
* **lack of resources, support, or co-operation from others**
* **change in performance management systems or processes**

Given the cost of recruitment, it's always worth trying to help an individual to move from poor to acceptable performance. So effective management of performance—particularly poor performance—is crucial. This actionlist explores some of the ways in which performance issues can be addressed.

We've recently restructured our business, and my assistant seems unable to cope. What do I do?

People often take time to adjust to new situations, and some cope with change better than others. Talk to your assistant and explore exactly what differences the restructuring has made to his or her working life. This kind of problem often emerges when communication channels are unclear, which can make it difficult for someone to prioritise or understand what needs to be done—it can also make them feel they have no support. You may need to help your assistant build the necessary new relationships, provide more support, and be clear on priorities.

Several members of the sales team I manage consistently fail to meet their targets, which is very demotivating for the rest of the team. What do I do?

Some theories about running sales teams suggest that you constantly churn the bottom group of poor performers, separating the wheat from the chaff. Managing poor performance can be highly time-consuming, particularly when you want to be spending time supporting stronger performers. You need to ensure that you understand why this group consistently fails to meet targets, and actively manage around clear goals and parameters. Ensure that you're able to manage the consequences.

I feel unhappy and unappreciated in my job, which is affecting my performance. What's your advice?

Where performance is being affected, it's important that you discuss your feelings with your manager. We can often outgrow roles, or find we need different challenges to feel rewarded. Work with your manager to understand what may have happened. What type of recognition or appreciation would help? Explore whether the pressures in the role have changed, or whether you have different life goals. Sometimes when our circumstances change, the expectation we have of ourselves also changes. Remember it's more cost-effective for organisations to re-motivate an existing employee than to recruit, train, and develop a new one.

MAKE IT HAPPEN

Understand the importance of performance management systems

Frequently, by the time the poor performance has been identified, damage has already been done. Prevention is better than cure, so establishing performance management systems—structured methods of identifying and improving poor performance—is ideal. These require that each individual has clear objectives, understands how these affect others, is aware of what's needed to deliver the objectives, and is confident of having the necessary skills and experience.

Putting these systems in place *before* problems ever arise will save considerable management time and worry.

Define poor performance

Poor performance is defined by a range of factors, some organisation-specific, some role-specific. It's important that the manager can decipher which are conduct issues and which are capability/competence issues, as each may require a different course of action. For example:

Conduct	Capability/Competence
Lateness, absenteeism	Failure to carry out tasks reasonably
Attitude	Failure to perform duties to an adequate standard
Bad language	Failure to provide high standards of customer care
Sex/racial discrimination	Unsatisfactory references
Negligence or abuse of company property	Infringement of regulations
Abusive behaviour to colleagues, managers, or customers	Failure to observe company policies and procedures

Take steps as an organisation

The organisation must act with consistency and fairness and, where possible, be able to show that it has provided guidelines and coaching to achieve the desired actions and behaviour. If the problem fails to be resolved, a disciplinary procedure may need to be followed. Here are some guidelines.

* Ensure that a full investigation is carried out.
* Hold a formal hearing. Make sure the employee is given written notice of it. The employee is entitled to representation.
* Review all evidence. Formally outline the disciplinary action to be taken.
* Consider separating out conduct and capability issues, as many organisations do when undertaking disciplinary actions. In the case of capability, the employee is given two chances to improve. However, if the problem is one of conduct, the process is less lenient. It's important to build in time to improve as part of the disciplinary process.

Take steps as a manager

In any situation, prevention is the preferred option. However where this is not possible the manager needs to:

* be fair and unbiased at all times
* behave consistently
* pay personal attention to the matter
* understand whether it's a conduct or capability issue
* work within the guidelines and procedures if it reaches the stage of disciplinary action
* recognise the importance of training and guidance

Take steps as a 'poor performer'

Where you feel that you don't have the skills, experience, or knowledge to achieve the objectives set you, it's better to ask for help before it becomes a performance management issue.

Try to understand why you haven't met your objectives. What support would help you improve your performance? If the goals aren't clear, ask for them to be redefined so that you can work towards them and manage the expectation of others.

Where your poor performance might be related to your attitude, try to understand how others react to your behaviour. Remember that what works in one culture doesn't always move easily to others. *How* you say something is as important as *what* you say. Try to identify friction points before they become serious performance issues.

Preventative measures for the business

The best way to deal with poor performance is actually to take steps to avoid it. For example:

* Communication is critical: leaders need to make explicit the goals of the business; managers need to break these down so that individuals understand how their targets relate to the overall business, and therefore how important their contribution is.
* Don't over-promote people. Just because someone does a great job at one level doesn't necessarily mean that person can tackle the next level.
* Ensure that managers are spending time with individuals to identify risk areas before they become performance issues.
* Don't over-engineer goals and objectives. Try to stay realistic about what can be done.
* Be aware of the culture of the business and ensure goals are set appropriately.

WHAT TO AVOID

You over-react and ignore factors that may have contributed to poor performance

If you are a manager, make sure that when you deal with poor performance, you remain unbiased, fair, and consistent. Always explore why it has occurred and what could have contributed to it. Is it part of a pattern, or is it a one-off situation which is likely to be easily resolved? Over-reacting to situations is not good for the employee, for you, or for the organisation.

You set the bar too high and objectives aren't explicit enough

When setting goals, it's important to ensure that they're clearly defined and that they're achievable. Remember that different people have different capabilities. Check that your expectations fit with the culture of the business (some businesses have cultures where expectations are set higher than reality—so failing to meet explicit goals is forgiven). Set clear, short process milestones, so that you can quickly recognise where performance may slip. Most important of all, communicate regularly. Performance targets discussed at the beginning of the year and then measured at the end may not be fair.

You fail to address poor performance issues early enough

Performance needs to be measurable. The easier it is to measure, the easier it is to manage. Checks need to be made at regular intervals to understand how close an individual is to achieving, or not achieving, targets. Schedule regular reviews and encourage employees to monitor their own performance. Ask them for feedback on their progress. Managers often set objectives and leave people to it—but if the goals aren't met, it can be critical for the business. Good performance management ensures that possible failure is identified early on and the risk managed appropriately.

You don't give poor performers the time and coaching they need to turn themselves around

If someone is performing poorly, it's not usually appropriate simply to prescribe coaching and hope for the best. Coaching isn't a tool for turning poor performers to good performers—it's better used as a proactive tool to develop a potentially good performer. So confirm first that the individual has the capability to fulfil their role, then identify what needs to be done to help them succeed. Coaching in this context is then positive and motivational. Often it's a good idea to give new role holders increasingly demanding performance measures until they've settled in. Always make sure you build in a fair amount of time for the employee to make the necessary improvements.

You fail to understand the difference between poor performance and personality clashes

Personality clashes are difficult to deal with and, if coupled with poor performance, they can become highly charged. Where issues may be personality-driven, bring in an impartial third party to 'referee'. Separate out the issues and look at different ways of dealing with them. Resolving one may well have knock-on effects on the others.

In some cases poor performance may be a perceived rather than a real problem. This can happen when there is a difference in understanding between a manager and his or her subordinate: they may, for example, each go about tasks very differently, but no less effectively.

USEFUL LINKS

Business Know-how: **www.businessknowhow.com/manage/poorperf1.htm**
HRM: **www.hrmanagementdevelopment.co.uk/contact.htm**

Succeed As a New Manager

Congratulations, you've been appointed as a manager—either for the first time, or for the first time at this level. You're likely to be responsible for managing a team of up to 15 people, either in a company you already work for, or in a new organisation. This is obviously very exciting for you, though you may feel somewhat daunted at the prospect, especially if you were previously a member of the team you will now be managing.
However, provided you follow a few basic rules, there is no reason why such fears shouldn't be easily overcome, and your new role will give you excellent scope to stretch your wings and fulfil your potential. This actionlist is intended to give you these basic rules and help smooth the path forward into this new phase of your working life.

I'm afraid I might not be up to the job. How can I overcome this fear?
It's only natural to have some feelings along these lines, and most people do when faced with a new challenge. However it's important to get such worries under control, as a crisis of confidence may affect your chance of success. Try some positive self-talk, reminding yourself of your skills and competence to do the job—after all, the company has recognised them, otherwise you wouldn't have been offered the role! It's also important to look after your health: make sure you get plenty of sleep and exercise, so you feel fighting fit and ready to take on anything.

Is it likely that my new job will affect my home life?
Almost certainly, yes. Moving into any new job can be stressful, and even more so when new or extra levels of responsibility are involved. The trick is to make sure you're prepared for it, and face the fact that your life may be more demanding than ever before. Talk this over with your family and friends at an early stage; it will be a huge help if they are ready to lend their support while you get to grips with your new role, and also keep 'home' distractions to a minimum to let you focus.

Will I need to change my persona at work?
No, not essentially, but you may need to adjust your attitude and the way you think about your job. A lot of management is about standing back from the detail and seeing the 'big picture' of what is happening, so that you can make strategic decisions about how to act. Rather than getting involved in the nitty-gritty of individual tasks (as you may have done as a team member), try to cultivate an objective overview. If you can learn to see the wood for the trees, this will naturally lead to you behaving in a way that suits the circumstances.

MAKE IT HAPPEN

Research and plan your new job

First things first: if you're moving to a new employer, find out everything possible about the company you'll be working for, the department or section you'll be in, the job itself, and anything else you can think of. Don't prejudge what you're going to find, and don't be bound by what you've done before or how any of your previous employers operated. It's also a good idea to find out a bit about your predecessor: why he or she left, what style they preferred, how people responded to that, what may need to be changed, and so on. (If you're staying in the same company, you may know this already, but it's worth doing some extra research.)

From all this information, try to form at least a tentative plan in advance—it's much harder to do this once you're in the post. What do you want to achieve? How might you need to develop yourself to match the new demands? Reflect as honestly as you can on your strengths and weaknesses: how might you deploy your qualities and experience to advantage, and compensate for your limitations?

Engage with your team

Once you start your new job, make this your first priority. What is the purpose of your department, team, or unit? What work is being done, what's the current state of play, what customer expectations need to be met? Get all your team members together as soon as possible to introduce yourself, and then arrange meetings with each of them individually. While keeping these meetings as friendly and informal as you can, allow a generous amount of time and plan some kind of framework for the discussion. Listen carefully to what people have to say, and get information about them as individuals. Most importantly, ask each person the question: what should I do or not do to help you perform your job effectively?

Plan some 'quick wins'

Now is the time to plan a few targets that you can hit quickly and easily, that help you to feel more at home and on top of things. Achieving these also eases the pressure you feel to perform and create a positive first impression, and begins the relationship-building process. Quick wins might include things like familiarising yourself with systems or ways of working if you're new to the company (for example, the internal e-mail system); setting up an early discussion with your line manager, arranging introductory meetings with suppliers or customers (external and internal), or even taking your team to the pub one lunchtime.

Clarify what expectations others have of you

You may be lucky enough to have been given a detailed job description, but the chances are there are still large gaps in your understanding about the task and priorities, what is or isn't acceptable in the new environment, and on what criteria you will be judged by your boss, peers, customers, and others. Don't be afraid to ask a lot of questions to clarify these issues, and then be very honest with yourself. Can you meet these standards? If not, what might you need to do? Who could help, and what might the price be?

Beware of 'new broom' syndrome

While you will evidently be keen to get going and to make your mark, it is important that you tread delicately—at least to start with. Don't assume that your new team will welcome your style or your ideas with open arms, even if your predecessor was unpopular. They need to feel they can trust you and that you respect what they've been doing previously, before you can count on their support and co-operation. Above all, don't depart too dramatically and quickly from established practice.

Show your commitment to individual development

From your initial meetings with your team, you will know what their individual aspirations and hopes are for their jobs going forward. Follow up by setting a code of management practice that you tell all team members about, and then follow it rigorously. This code might include commitments to assess training needs, to hold regular team meetings and one-to-one sessions, to set specific goals, and to evaluate performance against these goals.

Support this code by the way you yourself behave towards team members. Make a point of appreciating extra time and effort that people put in, listening properly to what they say, and being generous in your praise of their good qualities or achievements. The point is, by demonstrating to your team that you as their manager are on their side and will do everything in your power to support them, you will gain their trust and acceptance, and the performance of the whole team will be greatly enhanced.

Lead by example

An effective manager needs to be a role model, so it almost goes without saying that you must be set an example for how you want your team members to behave. Lead by involving people in establishing group objectives, setting standards, and achieving deadlines, and demonstrate your own strong personal commitment to achieving the team's goals. Set an example too by maintaining high standards in your appearance and general behaviour, and by establishing warm, friendly relationships.

Take stock regularly

At end of your first week, identify issues that need attention and make a plan for following week. Get into the habit each week of setting aside time for review and planning. Don't let your mistakes lead to self doubt: everyone makes them, and good managers learn from them, while bad ones repeat them. The pattern of behaviour you set in your first three months will be extremely hard to change later.

WHAT TO AVOID

You make promises that may be difficult or impossible to keep

It is tempting, during the phase of settling in and relationship building, to make all kinds of promises to your team, boss, or customers in the interests of creating a good impression. However you will be judged on whether or not those promises are fulfilled, so make sure you exercise caution in what you undertake to deliver. Under-promising and over-delivering are infinitely preferable to the other way round.

You form alliances based on first impressions

Common myth has it that first impressions usually turn out to be accurate, but this is often not true. Your understanding of people and circumstances may change substantially as you learn more about them, and it's important that you don't cement yourself into new relationships that later turn out to be inappropriate or which might alienate other, potentially more useful, allies.

You maintain too close a friendship with former team mates

Although it's important to create cordial relationships with your team members, it's also important to distance yourself a little from those who report to you, so that you can remain objective and unbiased in your actions. This can be difficult when you have previously been a member of the team yourself, but if you don't, you run the danger of being seen as a manager who has 'favourites' and of allowing your personal feelings to affect your judgment. This will not be good for the morale of the team, and you will lose much of your authority. Explain your position to particular friends, be seen to maintain a professional relationship at work, and keep purely social interaction for outside the office.

You allow yourself to be trapped into accepting the status quo

Whatever anyone says about 'the way things are done round here', the old ways are not always the best. Reserve your right to postpone judgment until you are thoroughly familiar with your team and your role and then, if things need changing, change them, remembering, of course, to be sensitive in the way you do it.

USEFUL LINKS

HR Guide: **www.hr-guide.com**
HR Next: **www.hrnext.com**
HR Village: **www.hrvillage.com**

Susannah Briggs — Learning the ropes as a new manager

Susannah Briggs graduated in 2001 and, after gaining an MSc in Voluntary Sector Organisation and working for a couple of charities, started working for the civil service. She was promoted after a year and began her new management role six months ago. Susannah is responsible for a small team and here she describes how she's adapted to the change in her role.

Finding the best training for you

'My previous job was in a different department to the one I currently work in and the person I now manage was already in the post before I joined my current department on promotion. I'm currently a policy advisor and I manage a policy assistant. Luckily I've experience of the scope of that role as it was the one I was promoted from.

'When I was thinking of moving on from my last position, a management role was something I specifically looked out for. I felt that if I wanted to move up the ladder, it would be good to have some management experience early on, as it always looks impressive on a CV. My training has consisted of a week's residential training course, which is part of the civil service general training; it is compulsory for everyone once they reach this grade, but I didn't really find it that helpful and in fact it was much more useful to talk to more senior people in the department and to find out what they thought about things. Speaking to them about their experiences of managing within the department, as well as asking for general advice, was a far more personalised kind of training which gave me much more insight into what would be expected of me once I started in my new role.

'More recently I've been on a staff appraisal and feedback course, where we had training on how to appraise staff performance and how to give feedback (positive and negative). There were a series of role plays and opportunities to practise different techniques of approaching personnel problems. The feedback from these role plays was really helpful and made me feel more confident when I came back to the office and had to do staff appraisals.'

Learning from the challenges

'I enjoy the challenges I face in this new position – it's completely different from anything I had done before. I like the way I'm acquiring new skills every day; from day one in this new job my responsibilities were very much increased and it all seemed pretty daunting. It has been – and still is – a steep learning curve, and really does feel like a big responsibility. Having said that, it's also an exciting challenge.

'Coping with this challenge has been made easier by the support I've had from more senior staff. They've given me advice on different aspects of the job throughout the reporting year, from carrying out monthly reviews to handling issues of sick leave and conflict within the team. They've also stressed to me the importance of 360-degree feedback, that is, where feedback on a person's role comes from more than one source. I've taken care to make sure that the person I manage has had the chance to tell me how she feels our relationship is developing.

'At the same time, I do still find some things difficult. It can be tricky managing someone who is older than me, and who has been in the job longer than me. Initially I lacked confidence about the situation – but the longer you do it the surer you feel about your own abilities in your new role.'

Boosting your skills

'I have had to focus on developing several of my personal qualities in order to match the new demands on me. The main area of development has been, I think, my negotiating skills. There have been some difficulties between the person I manage and the rest of the team and in these disputes there hasn't necessarily been one person obviously in the right and the other in the wrong. As a result. I've had to learn to negotiate between the person I am responsible for and people with more experience than me.

'I've also had to build up my confidence about speaking to more senior people regarding problems I've have encountered, and at the same time learnt to appear confident to the person I manage, so she can have confidence in me. We had a rather shaky start, as I should have put less emphasis on being friendly and more emphasis on building a professional relationship. When I started, I was very aware of being a first-time manager and very nervous. I made a joke of it and told the person I manage that I didn't know what I was doing and that she'd have to tell me what I was doing wrong. If I were to start my job over again, I'd try to appear confident from the outset and not advertise any of my insecurities or concerns. Once you let someone know you're nervous, they'll pick up on your hesitancy, which opens the way for them to challenge you and question your authority. If you start off with an air of confidence they'll have more respect for you. Inspiring confidence in others is the key, and to do that you need to feel confident about your abilities rather than worried about them. Talk to your own manager or other people you trust rather than mention any of your problems or uncertainties to the person you manage.

'One thing I would recommend would be not to take things for granted. If you go away for a period of time, leave detailed instructions about what needs to be done in your absence. While *you* may see that a particular job follows naturally from another and expect someone to do something from their own initiative, he or she may not have a detailed enough understanding of the situation, or may have misunderstood what you meant. When you brief someone, be very clear about what you want done and also give them the autonomy they need to carry out the tasks. When you are out of the office, it should be very clear what you expect from them and what they expect from you. If there is any ambiguity, that can lead to misunderstandings and embarrassment. However, don't patronise the other person as that will do nothing to help your relationship!

'If you're about to take up a new position as a manager, I really recommend planning ahead. Ask other people you trust for their advice and think about your own experiences of having great and dreadful managers. You can then put all you've learnt or observed into practice from day one. My experience of management so far has been rewarding and, in spite of a few difficulties at the beginning, overall I think it has been, and remains, an enjoyable and positive experience.'

Build Great Teams

The problem about the word 'teamwork' is that it has become too popular and has therefore lost its meaning. A person thought to be good at teamwork is all too often someone who fits into a group and keeps out of trouble. Complying with majority decisions and being willing to do anything that's required is seen as being ideal behaviour, but if everyone behaved like that, a team just wouldn't

work effectively—a flock of sheep may hang together well, but their only accomplishment is to eat grass.

Teams and team-based working have developed into the normal way of structuring organisations and undertaking tasks, yet managing teams is a difficult aspect of leadership and is usually developed through experience. Every leader has his or her own style, and when developing a high performing team this needs to combine with an understanding of:

- **the benefits of team-building—what it can achieve and what the leader should be striving for**
- **team roles and dynamics—how teams work and achieve their greatest success**
- **the key stages of team development—what they are and how to support the team in each stage**
- **the features of a successful team and team leader**
- **how to avoid potential problems and pitfalls**

What makes a good team leader?

Leadership, in broad strokes, is the capacity to establish direction and motivate others towards working for a common aim. Successful teamwork depends on the team leader's ability to make sure all team members know their common aim and what they each need to do to achieve it.

Naturally, all teams are different and have their own dynamic, and all leaders develop their own style for forming, developing, and leading them, but there are some general characteristics of a good team leader. For a team to work, it's essential that all members are committed, so leaders must be supportive, enthusiastic, and motivating people to work with. They must organise and communicate well in order to co-ordinate team efforts both *within* the team and with others *outside* the team. During difficult or stressful times, team leaders need to be approachable, good listeners who can offer feedback and advice.

What are the features of a good team?

It goes without saying that successful teams are ones in which people don't waste time trying to achieve success at the expense of others. Instead, they work at understanding each other, and communicate honestly and openly. They're committed to the team's success and are respectful and supportive of each other, sharing information and experience.

Conflict is unavoidable in most work situations, but a good team will work through it and reach an understanding by generating new ideas. A good team also acknowledges the role of the leader and understands when he or she needs to act and make a decision (in an emergency, for example, or if there is a major problem or disagreement).

MAKE IT HAPPEN

Focus on the work

For anyone interested in productive teamwork, it's often better to start with the work rather than the team. First of all, think about whether the job in hand really does need a team to tackle it. Some types of work, such as repetitive or unskilled tasks and, at the other extreme, specialist activities, are best performed by loners. Rounding up such people and making them members of a team risks producing a double disadvantage: their personal productivity falls and their privacy is invaded. While it's currently popular to strive for such an 'all inclusive' approach in the workplace and some people argue that isolated workers need a social dimension to their work, there are often few benefits to forcing this set-up on someone. Introverts need work suitable for introverts, while extroverts need work appropriate to extroverts.

Enable the team to succeed

The team approach for organising work depends on empowerment, that is, making sure that each person is allowed to perform to the best of his or her abilities. This relies on trust, the confidence that a manager places on the qualities and calibre of the employees. It also depends on how well members of a group have developed an understanding of each other's strengths and weaknesses. That's why, if your budget allows, training in teamwork is so important and why it helps to understand the language of team roles.

Reward teams at the right time

All teams need to be assessed, but how should it be done so that it's positive and constructive? One way is to set objectives for teams and judge how well these have been met. This view is popular in the 'top-down' school of management, where, as the name would suggest, senior managers make all the decisions and these are then passed down through the ranks to employees. In larger organisations, this approach is given added impetus by performance-related bonuses.

The argument put forward is that teams need fixed incentives to perform well, an assumption linked with the converse view that without such an incentive the team will not perform satisfactorily. However, it's possible for this approach is likely to backfire. Success in meeting given criteria depends partly on circumstances and contingencies, and may not be commensurate with effort or skill. Objectives may be too easy to reach or too difficult. In the end, people may focus more on the shortcomings of the incentive than on the sense and purpose of their work. Retrospective awards for good team performance (that is, given once the project is complete) are better received than prospective rewards for teams given set targets.

Stick to the essentials of effective teamworking

Again, start with the work and think about whether it really calls for a team at all. If you do decide that a team is the best way to tackle a task, work out who will be doing what; also, decide which remaining responsibilities can be assigned to individuals, and make them subject to personal accountability.

If possible, train your team so that it plays to the best strengths of its individual players. Make sure each person is allowed to develop ownership, pride, and maximum commitment to the team's responsibilities. One way you can do this as team leader is by delegating effectively. Finally, understand what motivates the team—what gives it its momentum?

WHAT TO AVOID

You misunderstand people

While it's obviously crucial that you understand the nature of the work being undertaken, you also need to be aware of the skills, experience and approach of those doing the work. Taking account of people's strengths and motivations can certainly help to build or break teams.

You fail to understand teams and what they need to succeed

Don't become too glib about the terminology—'team' and 'teamwork' too easily become meaningless words, so check their significance. Remember to spend time on evaluating whether you really need a team to complete a given task before you embark on a team exercise, and if you do go ahead bear in mind that not everyone flourishes in a team—some people will need more support than others.

If you're the team leader, remember that you have to allow team members the freedom to do what their role entails—empower them. Give them all the information they need and set boundaries to make sure that things happen.

USEFUL LINKS

Belbin: **www.belbin.com**
businessballs.com **www.businessballs.com/teambuilding.htm**

Learn How to Appraise Others

As you advance in your career and become responsible for managing other people, it's likely that you will need to conduct performance appraisals. These face-to-face discussions (ideally undertaken annually) are an opportunity for an employee's work to be discussed and reviewed, and should aim to improve motivation and performance during the coming year. Unfortunately, many managers dislike conducting appraisals and worse, many employees rate their appraisals as worthless—or something even less flattering. In reality, appraisals are a major opportunity for both managers and staff. This actionlist will review:

* **why appraisals are necessary and what the benefits are to managers and staff. Primarily, they ensure and improve future performance.**

* **how effective appraisals should be planned and undertaken to maximise their positive impact while avoiding negative pitfalls.**
* **the impact of appraisals on the long-term success of an organisation. Appraisals provide considerable opportunity for improving on-going operations, effective management, and catalysing change.**

What are the reasons for performance appraisals?

There are many positive reasons why appraisals are necessary. They give managers an opportunity to review individuals' past performance, plan their future work and role, and set and agree specific individual goals for the future. Making time to hold a meeting with the person to be appraised also allows for on-the-spot coaching which in turn can identify development needs and set up development activity.

In addition, appraisals can:

* allow the exchange of feedback
* reinforce or extend the reporting relationship
* act as a catalyst for delegating work
* focus on longer-term career progression
* underpin or increase motivation

It's also worth bearing in mind that there is a close relationship between appraisals and employment legislation (for example, lack of appraisal may make it impossible to terminate someone's employment).

Overall the underlying intention is to improve future performance. The good appraisal presupposes that even the best performance can be improved, and seeks to increase the likelihood of future plans being brought to fruition.

How should the appraisal be organised?

For a well-organised appraisal, you need to:

* allow enough time. Few appraisals will be accomplished properly in less than an hour; some may last two or three hours or more—and will still be time usefully spent.
* allow no disturbances. Pausing to take even one telephone call sends out the wrong signals.
* create a suitable environment. Appraisals should be held somewhere private, comfortable, perhaps less formal than across a desk, yet suitably business-like.
* put the individual at ease. Remember that, even with good communication beforehand, appraisals may be viewed as somewhat traumatic. Anything that can be done to counter this is useful.

MAKE IT HAPPEN

Prepare throughout the year

Unsurprisingly, the key to effective appraisals is preparation by both parties. The manager must:

* spend sufficient time with staff during the year.
* communicate clearly and thoroughly the purpose and form of the appraisal so that people know what to expect. Employees should understand the need for appraisal, its importance, the specific objectives it addresses, and how both parties can get the best from it.
* prepare throughout the year, keeping clear records. Keeping an appraisal collection file means you don't have to rely on memory. In this, you should note matters that can usefully be raised at appraisals, making notes and filing copies of documents that will assist the process.

The person being appraised should keep running records and should plan in detail the kind of meeting he or she intends to have.

Successful appraisal is the culmination of a year's worth of thinking. Recalling every detail of an employee's working year is difficult, but you can only appraise properly by being informed.

Relevant background information needs checking: for example, the appraisee's job description (which may need amendment after the appraisal), specific past objectives, possible changes to the job, its responsibilities, or circumstances, and the records of any previous appraisals.

Prepare and plan carefully

* Prepare written notification. As well as confirming mutually convenient timing, this should recap the purpose of the appraisal and highlight background information. Distribute copies of any documents or forms you intend to use or refer to during the meeting.
* Study the person's file, making sure that you have all the information you need about what was supposed to happen during the year and what actually did happen. Make notes of points needing discussion and ensure that you can navigate the documents easily as the meeting progresses.
* Review agreed standards and identify any that are no longer relevant or that need to be changed.
* Draft a provisional assessment. Brief notes can provide a starting point, prompt the agenda, and link to the system. Don't prejudge the discussion or make decisions prematurely.
* Assess your initial thoughts. Check your rationale, asking yourself the question 'why?' as you note each thing down. If no clear answer comes, more research may be necessary.
* Consider specific areas of the appraisal. It may be clear that some training is necessary, for example. Again without prejudging, it may be useful to

check out what might be suitable so that you have ready suggestions at the meeting.

* Think ahead. Remember that the most important part of the discussion will be about the future. You may need to plan particular projects and tasks, taking both development and operational considerations into account.
* Consult with others. Speak to those who work or deal with the person to get a complete picture.
* Be clear about the link with a pay review. Many managers feel this should be kept for a separate occasion, as otherwise it can be difficult to stop people from thinking all that matters is the potential increase.

Handle the appraisal effectively

Before you go any further, make completely sure that everybody being appraised understands the need for appraisal, its importance, its objectives, and its mutual benefits. When the appraisal starts:

* explain the agenda and how things will be handled. Remember to ask what the employee's priorities are.
* act to direct the proceedings. Do not, however, ride roughshod over the other person.
* ask questions. Open questions prompt and focus discussion.
* listen. The meeting is primarily an opportunity for the person being appraised to communicate. In a well-conducted appraisal, he or she should do most of the talking; the manager's job is to make that happen.
* keep primarily to agreed performance factors. Don't indulge in amateur psychology or attempt to measure personality factors—it's how someone actually does their job that's important here.
* use the system. Stick to an agenda or follow an appraisal form to guide the meeting; working through the form systematically will ensure most of what needs to happen does.
* encourage discussion. Consider the employee's personal strengths and weaknesses, successes and failures, and their implications for the future. Concentrate the appraisal process on future performance, and don't confuse it with discussion of remuneration.
* set out action plans. Agree those that can be decided there and then (who will do what, when); note those needing more deliberation in terms of when and how action will be taken. Deal with each factor separately, for example, by devoting time to development action.
* conclude on a positive note. Always thank the person for the role he or she has played and for the past year's work. Link this to any subsequent documentation.
* follow up appraisals promptly, sending all necessary written material to the person and flagging any opportunity for further discussion.

WHAT TO AVOID

You treat appraisals as an end, rather than a means to an end

Appraisals achieve most when placed in a long-term context and linked to ongoing operations. Bear in mind:

* the ongoing management relationship: an effective appraisal should make all management processes through the year easier.
* the link with training and development: consultation, counselling, mentoring, and informal discussions are all just as important extensions of appraisal as formal training.
* motivation: appraisals must themselves be motivational, and what stems from them must help someone remain motivated going forward.

You dwell too much on the past

This shouldn't really account for more than 60% of the discussion at most; you also need to discuss future activities, priorities, development needs, and objectives.

You're too directive or too critical

Successful appraisals are dynamic, positive discussions, not a witch-hunt or a chance to heap blame and ignominy on someone. (If you do need to tackle a problem, do it when the problem arises, and don't just store it up for the appraisal!)

Your comments and feedback aren't clear enough

You must be clear, honest, and open in your comments. The more you hedge, the more chance there is that misunderstandings will creep in.

You fail to follow up after the meeting

There is one key action here: to complete all documentation and confirmations that are necessary promptly after the meeting. Send copies to the person appraised, flagging any opportunity for further discussion. If your business is big enough to have a personnel department, send a copy there too.

USEFUL LINKS

AllBusiness: **www.allbusiness.com/articles/content/15085.asp**
Businessballs.com: **www.businessballs.com/performanceappraisals.htm**
performance-appraisals.org: **http://performance-appraisals.org**

Give and Receive Feedback Well

When the thought of having to give or receive feedback arises, most people assume that the experience will be a negative and uncomfortable one. This isn't necessarily the case, though, and in fact it's good practice to highlight positive achievements or traits in any type of feedback situation.

Feedback is, in fact, a gift. If you're giving feedback, your main motivation is usually to see someone change their behaviour for the better. Feedback is rarely given with ill-intent, and so it can help people understand how they're perceived and how they may make positive changes to influence those perceptions. Perceptions are, of course, not always reality, but they're very real in their consequences, so being aware of these will help you choose whether or not to perpetuate them.

I recently experienced some feedback in my performance appraisal that I felt was unreasonable and misrepresented my motivations. What's the best way of dealing with such a situation?

If you're receiving feedback from someone who doesn't understand the process well or who has not had a lot of practice, you may need to coach or guide them by asking them specific questions that will encourage them to express themselves more clearly and suggest ways forward for you. For instance, if they told you that your recent presentation wasn't good, ask them what it was that you did to create that impression and what they think you could do differently another time.

You could also share any political dilemmas that you had in deciding your approach and ask what further ideas they had that you could have considered. For example, you may have had to contend with different interests or agendas amongst those in your audience, such as those between sales and marketing, or the opposing forces of cost-cutting and achieving quality standards.

Finally, if you feel it's appropriate, tell the other person how their feedback has made you feel so that he or she has an opportunity to change his or her style.

I find it difficult to speak to my manager and it's hard to make her see me in a better light. What can I do?

If you have a difficult relationship with the person who is giving you feedback, there may be occasions when you feel unable to respond, unfairly judged, or put on the spot. If this is the case, thank them for their comments and say that you'd like to consider them for a short while (during which you can seek advice from friends or colleagues) and ask for the meeting to be reconvened at a (not too distant) later date.

I'm the manager in a team where one of the team members isn't pulling his weight. This is beginning to cause bad feeling among everyone else. What's the most effective way of dealing with this?

Talk to the person involved as soon as you can, giving feedback from your own perspective, not on behalf of the rest of the team. (For example, use 'I . . .' statements not 'We . . .') Start with a question like 'How do you think the team is working?' This will help you to uncover his feelings and give you a useful inroad to the situation. If that approach doesn't help, though, continue with something like: 'You really are an important member of the team and you bring a great deal of expertise to it but lately, you've seemed rather unhappy. Is there anything you need or would like to discuss?'

This acknowledges a positive achievement first, and should protect the recipient from feeling criticised. You can then have a discussion about what's going on, what you'd like to see happen to resolve it, and how you might help to make that happen.

I've just received some 360 degree feedback which concerns me. How can I learn more about why I'm getting certain feedback if I can't confront the respondents?

360 degree feedback is a one-way process and is usually based on a promise of confidentiality. It's a process whereby key colleagues or 'stakeholders' in a company comment on someone's performance so that he or she can get a picture of how others perceive them.

Confrontation is not a desired outcome of 360 degree feedback, or indeed of any other form of feedback. As the process is confidential, it allows people to speak freely, but the downside for feedback recipients is that, obviously, they don't know who said what, and this may make them feel frustrated. The positive side of the process is that it may tune you in to common perceptions people have about you and raise your awareness to potential behavioural issues that you may wish to deal with. There is nothing to stop you asking for further feedback from a different audience if you need more input on the perceptions that have been highlighted to you. Try not to preface any requests for additional help with a moan or complaint, though, even if your ego is feeling a bit bruised.

I've recently been given a managerial position which involves conducting performance reviews, and I know that one in particular will be challenging. How do I give feedback in this setting?

Unfortunately, annual performance appraisals tend to be the only time that people receive feedback on how they're doing. It's much better to give and receive feedback more regularly than this so that problems can be ironed out as and when they arise. If a review is looming, however, make sure that you're familiar with the reviewee's objectives and that you can back up your feedback (whether positive or negative) with evidence. Do not use hearsay or rumour to inform your feedback and don't get locked into giving your opinion or advice unless your offer of it is accepted or it's asked for by the reviewee. This is a trap that can give rise to defensive behaviour and may lead to the review being ended early.

MAKE IT HAPPEN

Giving and receiving feedback is one of many forms of communication that goes on every day at work. However, rather than being abstract, theoretical, or debatable, feedback is essentially extremely personal and thus highly relevant to the recipient. Unfortunately, many people feel that the most common type of feedback they receive is critical. Sadly we rarely receive as much praise as we do criticism, even though we know that someone receiving lots of positive encouragement performs much more effectively than those who are constantly put down.

Feedback is a mechanism for conveying to people how they're experienced and perceived by others. It provides the recipient with an opportunity to take decisions about whether or not they wish to change their behaviour and the consequences of doing that. There are two parties associated with feedback: the giver and the receiver. Both may benefit from understanding and learning how to manage the dynamics of feedback.

Giving feedback

Giving feedback is not easy. The very thought of it may conjure up bad memories if you've been on the receiving end of badly thought out or tactless feedback yourself, and if it's an area with which you're unfamiliar or uncomfortable, a feedback session can easily spiral into a critical and defensive exchange rather than be a positive and illuminating experience.

Here are some important steps in making sure that the delivery of your feedback is constructive and well received:

* **Find an appropriate venue**: Make sure that the feedback session is held in a private place and that you can speak to the recipient without being distracted or interrupted. If you have an office, turn your phone on to voicemail or ask someone to field your calls, and remember to turn off your mobile phone.
* **Make sure the reviewee is prepared**: If you're conducting a performance review, brief the reviewee so he or she has clear expectations on what will be taking place. This is usually built into the process through timed activities and deadlines but it's as well to make a mental check that each party is clear about the purpose and boundaries of the meeting beforehand. You may ask the reviewee to prepare in a particular way for the meeting by describing the objectives they've met and how they've met them, reflecting on how they think they've been perceived and what development or additional resources they need to help them perform in their roles more effectively.
* **Set the scene and create a conducive context for the feedback**: This would include preparing or copying any relevant documents, setting aside sufficient time, a private room, and some water or refreshments. Frame your intervention carefully so that the recipient understands where you're coming from and what you're commenting upon. Be sure that he or she is willing to receive your feedback before you attempt to give it. If you think you feel defensiveness at the outset, address it directly. 'I sense that you're uncomfortable with this process. Is there anything I can do to make it easier for you?' You might want to add some reassurances also such as 'Any comments we make today will stay within the confines of this room'.
* **Be positive**: Lead with a positive piece of feedback to demonstrate that you've noticed and valued particular behaviour. Deliver the feedback, taking care to be sensitive to the recipient's likely reactions and responding with your full attention and consideration. The feedback should be descriptive rather than evaluative and focus on behaviour that can be changed rather than on personality. For example: 'When you were under pressure, I felt that you become quite

dismissive of me and didn't welcome my suggestions', rather than 'You were aggressive!' Remember to speak for yourself only, this means using 'I' statements rather than hiding behind the views of a colleague or group.

* **Ask for feedback on the way you handled the feedback session**: Even if the session was difficult, it's an opportunity to build bridges and show your willingness to learn.
* **Honour any agreements made during the meeting**: If you've promised some additional resources, greater involvement in a project, or some training, confirm this afterwards in writing and follow it through.
* **Demonstrate the behaviour you wish to see**: It's no good asking for something from others that you're not prepared to do yourself. You may want to introduce a culture of ongoing feedback so that issues aren't left for the performance review.

Receiving feedback

The way we act reflects who we are to the world and when this is criticised or questioned, it can feel like an assault on our personalities. If you receive feedback that you find challenging or hard to deal with, try to see it as information that allows you to make informed choices about how you're perceived by others. In some circumstances, of course, the feedback (or the manner of it) may say more about the person communicating it to you than it does about you, but whether this is the case or not the best thing to do is to thank the person for their feedback and assure them that you'll think about it further. You're not compelled to accept feedback and you may choose to maintain the behaviour that feels right for you.

Remember the following when you're receiving feedback:

* **Listen carefully**: Even if you feel under attack, try not to leap to your own defence until you've had a chance to think about and understand the feedback thoroughly. Be genuinely open to hearing what the other person is saying and try not to interrupt or jump to conclusions. Active listening techniques may be helpful for you here.
* **Ask questions to clarify what's being said and why**: You are completely entitled to ask for specific examples and instances of the types of behaviour that are at the root of the feedback. If the atmosphere is becoming tense, introduce a more positive approach by asking for examples of the behaviour they'd like to see more of.
* **Keep calm**: Even if you feel upset, try not to enter into an argument there and then; just accept what's being said and deal with your emotions another time and in another place. Stay calm and focus on the rest of the feedback.

Remember that giving feedback can be an uncomfortable experience too and people generally don't do it unless they feel that you can benefit from their observations. Try and remain engaged throughout and don't start a 'tit for tat' exchange.

Receiving feedback doesn't mean that you can't talk to the other person about your behaviour. For example, you may want to ask if the giver has any suggestions about what you could do differently. You don't have to accept them, but at least it demonstrates a willingness on your part to take the feedback seriously.

Thank the person giving you feedback for taking the time and trouble to share their perceptions with you.

Honest and well-presented feedback allows people to enjoy good, open relationships. If feedback is a common feature of the way people communicate, issues aren't left to fester and grow out of all proportion. Some organisations have been known to benefit from instigating a culture of 'instant constructive feedback' which encourages employees to address issues as they arise rather than leave them to fester or develop into crises. This approach not only diffuses the more destructive or passive–aggressive styles of relating to others, but it can have a genuine impact on profitability as ideas may be freely exchanged and innovative approaches discussed.

WHAT TO AVOID

The feedback session falters because of a personality clash

Giving feedback can very quickly turn into a personality clash when the means of achieving an objective is debated hotly and defensively. This happens when either or both parties believe they are right and are heavily invested in their own approach. In such a situation, people can become entrenched and dogmatic when a suggestion to do things differently is made. Try to maintain good rapport throughout, which includes the free expression of views, a genuine desire to understand each other's perspectives, and the absence of premature judgment or closure. If a feedback session veers off track, it can be brought back by calling a 'time out' and then clarifying once more what the session is supposed to achieve. Reassessing what you're doing gives you an opportunity to talk through your values and assumptions and also provides a clear framework for the remainder of the session.

You make assumptions

Making assumptions about others' values, motivations, or intentions can quickly lead to the deterioration of rapport. Avoid this by making sure that each person has an opportunity to make these explicit. Don't assume you know the motivation behind someone's behaviour but instead give them the chance to explain this early in the feedback session, perhaps as you set the context for your discussion. For example, ask open questions such as, 'What were you hoping to convey when you gave your presentation?' From their answers, you can get very useful insights into that person's way of thinking and acting.

You don't admit there's a problem

If things start getting out of hand, acknowledge that things are going wrong. By showing your vulnerability and humility, you'll be able to create a mood of trust and rebuild rapport.

USEFUL LINKS

The ACTIVE REVIEWING guide: **http://reviewing.co.uk/archives/art/3_9.htm**
Career Management Skills: **www.netwise.ac.uk/cms/teach/feedback.html**
Giving and Receiving Feedback:
www.mapnp.org/library/commskls/feedback/feedback.htm
Personal-development.com:
www.personal-development.com/chuck/index.html
SelfhelpMagazine.com:
www.selfhelpmagazine.com/articles/growth/feedback.html

Understand Non-verbal Behaviour

It's widely recognised that the majority of information about human behaviour is conveyed through non-verbal signals. Being able to understand and use this powerful but subtle form of communication will help you shape the kinds of relationships you have with people, and this in turn will enable you to steer your way through delicate, political situations and deal with difficult people.

Non-verbal communication involves many different 'channels' that convey meaning beyond what's being said. These include gestures, body movements, facial expressions, and even vocal tone and pitch. Much of the non-verbal information we get from people comes from the eyes. This explains why it's often hard to convey subtle meanings over the telephone or through the written word. It's not an exact science, although we sometimes make judgments as if it were.

Since non-verbal behaviour, or body language, is such a natural part of our communication toolkit, its interpretation offers a key to greater human understanding and relationship building. However, this art should be treated with a degree of caution. Misinterpretation, especially when dealing in a highly politicised organisation, can have damaging consequences.

How do I know when someone is bluffing?

Usually, when people are communicating in a straightforward way, their non-verbals are consistent with their words. They say, 'Look over there!', and reinforce the message by pointing simultaneously towards the intended focus of attention. Or they might admit, 'I'm unhappy about that', and their face and body droop too. When people are bluffing, their gestures are usually inconsistent with their speech. Someone may say, 'The deal is almost in the bag!' . . . but you notice a nervous body pattern, like the shifting of feet or the tapping of fingers. Unusual averting of eye contact or blinking of the eyes can also indicate an inconsistency, which communication experts call *leakage*.

How do I build rapport in a meeting where there are many different people?

One way of establishing rapport is by working the room. Suppose that you're addressing a group of professionals from a podium. Make sure you seek information from everyone, acknowledge every contribution, give anyone who hesitates plenty of space, and support anyone who finds it difficult to speak in front of a group. If there are too many people in the room to pay attention to each one, invite contributions from those who are most extrovert and build rapport with them. This will give others confidence in your ability to connect with people.

How do I know from someone's body language when the person is getting angry, and what should I do?

Tone of voice, subtle changes in facial expression, and gestures head the list of clues. For example, maybe someone will start pacing up and down or banging the table while still smiling pleasantly to hide true but socially unacceptable feelings. Your reaction to increased anger depends on the situation and your personality. You can choose to try to calm things down by demonstrating that you're actively listening to the other person's frustrations and asking him or her open questions to encourage dialogue. You may prefer to back off until the heat dies down. If you decide to pull back, analyse what happened and how you reacted. If you think you might have contributed to the person's anger, consider how you might do things differently next time. You may like to revisit the incident with the person later and try to work together on a way to communicate more effectively in the future.

How do I know when someone is not telling the truth?

There are a number of gestures that betray lying, most having to do with hiding the mouth with a hand. Other forms include touching one's nose or running a finger along the inside of a collar. Eye contact is another sign, if a previously 'normal' eye-contact pattern shifts suddenly to a darting or averted gaze. Likewise, if the pace of blinking picks up appreciably, there may be more than a speck of dust involved!

MAKE IT HAPPEN

Understand gestures

The six most universal human emotions—happiness, anger, sadness, envy, fear, and love—can be seen on the face of anyone in the world, for example, in the form of smiles and scowls. Other common universal gestures include the 'I don't know' shrug, a 'yes' nod, and a side-to-side head shake, meaning 'no'. Gestures that you may think are universal but actually convey different messages in difficult cultures include the thumbs up, the forefinger/thumb ring, and the 'V' sign. Although well established in the United Kingdom as signs for OK and victory respectively, they have offensive alternative meanings in other cultures!

Many gestures come in 'clusters'. If you look at people during a meeting, you're likely to see gestures involving hands (they may be signalling that they're evaluating what's being said by balancing their chin on their thumb with their middle finger running along their bottom lip and their index finger pointing up their cheek), their limbs (one arm may be clamped against the body by the other elbow), and their entire bodies (if someone's torso is leaning back from the vertical, that person is signalling distance from what's being said). This cluster of non-verbal gestures indicates that the listener is reserving judgment on what's being said. If you feel that a cluster of gestures is conveying something about what the person really thinks, ask them to share their thoughts.

Match and mirror

If you watch two people talking in a relaxed and unselfconscious manner, you may notice that their bodies have taken on a similar demeanour. Both may have crossed their legs, or settled into their chairs in similar postures. If they're eating or drinking, they may do so at the same rate. This is called *matching* or *mirroring*, and it occurs naturally between two people who feel that they're on the same wavelength. Matching and mirroring can be used consciously as a technique to achieve rapport with someone, but you need to be subtle. Exaggerated mirroring looks like mimicry, and the other person is likely to feel embarrassed or angry.

Watch what your counterparts do in their body language. Then follow the pattern of their non-verbal communication and reflect it back. When this feels natural, see if you can take the lead by changing your body position and watch to see if they follow. Very often they do. Once you begin to get a feel for this process, see if you can use it in a situation that is problematic.

Understand facial expressions

Most non-verbal signals conveyed by the face are done so by the eyes. Good eye contact is an effective way of building rapport. Not only can you 'read' the other's disposition, you can also convey, very subtly, messages that will reinforce what you're saying.

However, too much eye contact can be intrusive or too intimate. Those who do not want to be exposed on the 'soul level' may use techniques to break or block eye contact. This includes eye movements such as the 'over the shoulder stare', or the long, fluttery, blink that effectively draws the shutters down. In a business setting, it's important to confine your gaze to the eyes and forehead, and forego the more intimate glance to the lips or upper body. If you hold your stare for too long, it may be considered hostile, so try to limit the time to around two thirds of the conversation. If you reduce the timing to below one third, you may appear timid or 'shifty'.

Speak the same language

While the language we use is clearly not one of the components of non-verbal behaviour, it's an important part of that same unconscious and instinctive toolkit we use to communicate with others. According to neurolinguistic programming (NLP)—the science of tapping into the unconscious mind to reveal what's going on beneath the surface—language can indicate a great deal about how an individual views the world. Depending on which of the five senses they subconsciously favour, people may fall into one of five noticeable types:

* visual (sight)
* auditory (hearing)
* kinaesthetic (touch)

* olfactory (smell)
* gustatory (taste)

You can establish rapport with people more effectively by paying attention to their individual preferences for 'sensual' cues.

When talking to someone you don't know well, listen to the kinds of words he or she selects. Once you've identified which of the five categories they belong to, you can respond by using the same kind of language.

In other words, when you're building rapport with someone, using the same kind of language significantly enhances the level of understanding between you.

Listen actively

Active listening is a rare skill, but it's very effective in helping you build rapport with people and avoid the kind of misunderstandings that land you in awkward situations. It can also yield valuable information, enabling us to do our jobs more efficiently.

Demonstrate that you've understood and are interested in what's being said in conversation. This kind of active listening requires good eye contact, lots of head nods, and responses such as 'Ah ha', 'Mmmm', and 'I understand what you mean'. You could also summarise what has been said to demonstrate your understanding, and ask open questions such as, 'Can you tell me more about . . .?' and 'What do you think . . .?'.

Different types of vocabulary

visual language	includes terms like *appear, show, focused, well defined, in light of, dim view, get a perspective on*. For example, a person might say something like, 'I have a *vision* of what this organisation will *look* like in five year's time. I can *see* that it will take lots of energy to create what's in my *mind's eye*'. You can respond similarly: 'You build a very *clear picture* for me. I can *see* that this will be a challenge, but your *farsightedness* will surely enable you to reach your *dream*'.
auditory language	includes terms like *listen, tune in/out, rumour, clear as a bell, unheard of, word for word*, and *be all ears*. An auditory person might say, 'I *hear* that you've been promoted. You must have done a *resoundingly* good job!' You could respond, 'Yes, I have been *called* upon to *sound* out the market and *ring* some changes in the way we sell our products'.
kinaesthetic language	includes terms like *sense, feel, move towards, grasp, get hold of, solid, make contact, touch, concrete, pull some strings*, and *sensitive*.

olfactory language	includes terms like *smell, odour, rotten, aromatic*, and *fragrance*.
gustatory language	includes terms like *bitter, sweet, sour, salty* and other taste-related words.

Understand props

Many people use props to reinforce their messages, the most common being extensions of the hand such as fingers, pen, pointer, or even a cigarette. Using a prop extends the space taken up by the body, and the person is perceived as more confident and powerful.

Adjusting a tie, fussing with the hair, or tugging at a cuff is representative of 'preening'. People often use this behaviour to endear themselves to others, although these gestures can instead be perceived as nervousness. Clenching coffee cups or wine glasses close to the body allows them to be used as defence mechanisms. They effectively close off the more vulnerable parts of the body.

The way people in a group sit can convey powerful messages about the pecking order. Taking the chair at the head of the table automatically puts someone in the controlling position. Leaning back with arms behind the head and one leg crossed horizontally across the other conveys feelings of superiority. A closed or crunched body position can mean disapproval, defensiveness, or a lack of interest.

Understand territory

People travel through the world with a conceptual egg-shaped zone of personal space around their bodies, and feel invaded if others trespass into it. They often protect their territory by placing a desk between them and others, standing behind a chair or counter, or clasping an object like a handbag or briefcase to them as if it were a shield.

It's interesting to watch people in groups. If you see two or three men talking, you might notice them shifting their weight from one foot to the other. This is part of a ritual of creating territorial boundaries. They might also make themselves appear taller by rocking forward onto the balls of their feet to indicate power and confidence. When women are grouped, they're much more likely to mirror each other's non-verbal behaviour in an attempt to build lateral bridges.

It is, therefore, essential to place any 'bodywatching' observations *in context*, as most non-verbal communication is part of a broader dialogue.

Interpret in context

Much has been written about non-verbal communication, especially about how to read body language. This may give you insight into what's going on, but always remember to place your interpretation in context. For example, someone sitting in a meeting with his or her arms crossed is possibly being aggressive, reluctant, or disapproving. But, perhaps the person is shy, cold, or ill. Be cautious of jumping to conclusions about how someone is feeling without further information.

If you move to a new environment with a different political mentality, there could be a risk of misunderstandings at a non-verbal level. Perhaps your new boss is more emotional than your previous manager and expects a more energetic display of your enthusiasm for the job. Make sure you take time to observe what's going on around you and note how the different context makes you feel. Perhaps ask advice from someone in the new culture who shares something of your own experience—they may be able to provide a useful communications bridge.

Understand congruence

In order for non-verbal behaviour to work for you, all the non-verbal channels of communication must reinforce the message you're trying to convey. If you notice side-to-side head-shaking while someone is saying, 'I agree wholeheartedly with this decision', you're seeing an example of incongruence; the person's words and body language are contradictory. People come across as inauthentic when one or more of their channels of communication are 'saying' opposite things.

WHAT TO AVOID

You're unsubtle

People new to the techniques of non-verbal communication can be over-enthusiastic practitioners. Observe yourself objectively to make sure you aren't offending others by broadly mimicking their speech or behaviour. Remember that most people instinctively send and interpret non-verbal signals all the time: don't assume you're the only one who's aware of non-verbal undercurrents. Finally, stay true to yourself. Be aware of your own natural style, and don't adopt behaviour that is incompatible with it.

You over-interpret

When people become aware of the power of body language, they can go overboard and think they've revealed a whole world of silent messages. However, false interpretations can cause damaging misunderstandings. Remember to take account of the context and do not jump to conclusions.

You try to bluff

Thinking you can bluff by deliberately altering your body language can do more harm than good. Unless you're a practised actor, it will be hard to overcome the body's inability to lie. There will always be mixed messages, signs that your channels of communication are not congruent. This is called *leakage* and it will be seen in one way or another.

You ignore context

Putting too much store by someone's non-verbal signals can lead to misinterpretation and misunderstandings. It's important to understand the context in which the signals are being transmitted and think through the possible scenarios before jumping in.

You rush in with an accusation based on someone's body language

Accusing someone of something that they aren't guilty of, based on erroneous observations, can be embarrassing and damaging. Always verify your interpretation through another channel before rushing in. You could say something like, 'I get the feeling you're uncomfortable with this course of action. Would you like to add something to the discussion?' This will draw out the real message and force the individual to come clean, or adjust his or her body language.

USEFUL LINKS

Mastery Insight Institute: **www.altfeld.com/mastery/seminars/desc-sb1.html**
The Non-verbal Dictionary of Gestures, Signs, and Body Language:
http://members.aol.com/nonverbal2/diction1.htm

Develop Your Creativity

Everyone has creative talent, but many people lack confidence in their own creativity. It's common to hear people say 'I'm not very creative', yet they manage their careers well and are extremely successful in bringing value to the businesses where they work. In fact, developing a more efficient approach to your own workload or introducing a time-saving project management system requires considerable creativity. Be reassured, then, that the term *creativity* can have a much broader meaning than simply being possessed of artistic talent.

Is creativity, born not made?

Creativity is certainly born—in all of us. Developing this talent depends on finding a channel for its expression. Find something that you enjoy doing, an interest that you've held for some time but not explored enough. Even if it's been in the back of your mind as a vague idea, if you focus on it and keep at it, your creative talent will begin to blossom. Many people start to draw or paint in this way. It starts as a whim, continues with lots of practice, and ends with some wonderfully inspiring works. Most importantly, regardless of the outcome, newly-discovered creativity has a knack of bringing you personal joy and a greater belief in your own creative powers and your developing confidence.

I know people who are incredibly creative but they just don't seem to be able to make it work for them. How can you 'ground' creative expression in the real world?

Some people love to explore ideas but don't have the interest or patience to turn ideas into action. But ideas, in themselves, are valuable—in fact most research and development begins with ideas. Instead of dismissing these people as dreamers, see if there's a place in your organisation where their skill can be encouraged and nurtured. People with these talents can be very valuable members of a product or service innovation group.

Organisations can't afford to waste time on 'fluffy', self-indulgent thinking. What's the business case for letting creativity loose?

Even the most logically derived thinking is born of the creative impulse, and in today's business environment, where good ideas are the only way of differentiating yourself from the competition, this creative impulse is essential. Some physicists believe that the smallest particle of matter is a thought, that we literally create our own reality. Surely organisations can use this force to create a successful reality that enables them to excel in their industry or market.

MAKE IT HAPPEN

Look at the world around you

Developing creativity requires the same amount of thought and attention as developing any other skill. Although some people seem to be more innately creative than others, it's wrong to think that some individuals have it and others don't. Creativity is a natural form of human expression.

Take a look at the world you've created around yourself. Your home and working space are a creative expression of who you are and so are the social networks you've created for yourself. What about the gifts you give to the special people in your life, or the hobbies and activities you like? Think about your work; what have you done differently from others who have held your job? What kind of relationships have you developed with your colleagues? What positive impacts have these had? All these things are evidence of your creativity. All we need to do is to recognise that creativity takes many forms, become aware of the process, and be rewarded by making it a conscious activity.

Useful techniques

There are many useful techniques that allow creativity to flow more consciously.

* **Brainstorming.** Brainstorming generates a free flow of ideas, associations, and concepts, however 'foolish' they may seem at the outset. Energy generated by a brainstorming group is contagious, fostering creative leaps and jumps. The speed of the process bypasses the logical circuitry of the left side of the brain, allowing imaginative ideas from the right side—the creative side—to emerge uncensored—perhaps offering possibilities for innovative product or service ideas.
* **Getting in the 'zone'.** Artists, athletes, and craftspeople often experience the phenomenon of being in the creative zone, a state in which it's almost as if they are running on automatic pilot. This usually happens when people are so totally absorbed in what they're doing that their creative energy takes over and generates its own momentum. The total concentration seems to switch something in the brain that enables completely unfettered expression. Science confirms that there are chemical and biological changes accompanying this state.
* **Stimulating the creative side of the brain.** The right side of the brain is where

intuitive and creative abilities reside, whereas the left side is where logical thinking takes place. A number of techniques exist that allow you to transfer at will from left side to right, thereby enabling you to tap into your reserves of inspiration and innovation. One activity that can trigger this is to write or draw with your non-dominant hand, just allowing your instinct to control your hand. The result is a product of the creative side of the brain. Visualisation is also very helpful. Close your eyes and draw what's in your mind's eye. Your imagination is also part of your right-brain activity.

Writing down a few pages of your thoughts on a daily basis—whatever comes into your mind—will also open up your channels of creativity. It's important that you don't get in your own way during this activity, so just let ideas flow without judging or filtering them. After doing this for a while, you'll find that your mind is much freer and your expression more fluid. Your ability to formulate ideas, think abstractly, and make decisions is likely to improve, while counterproductive tendencies like having tunnel vision or being judgmental will diminish.

* **Relaxation/meditation.** Logical thinking generates beta waves in the brain. Meditation and relaxation techniques produce alpha waves, which have myriad positive effects, including creative thought. With practice, you can meditate even in the midst of chaos—a busy park or a train station. Breathing techniques can also help clear your mind and achieve the change from beta to alpha waves. This 'state of mind' has been found to be an exceptionally good way to enhance learning, as it clears the path for new thoughts and inspiration.

Listening to soothing, uncomplicated music can also 'tune' the brain into a different wavelength.

* **Doing something out of context.** Being creative is about breaking habits and being open to new thoughts and experiences. Try doing something that you've never done before—something undemanding like going to an event that you wouldn't normally be interested in, or driving a different route to work. You may be amazed how this simple technique can open the creative floodgates.

If you're struggling to come up with an idea to solve a particularly difficult problem, try asking a child or elderly relative. Without the clutter of knowledge (or, conversely, with the wisdom of experience), someone coming fresh to the problem can often trigger insights that, with a little application, can be surprisingly effective.

WHAT TO AVOID

You don't keep an open mind

People who don't have time for, or don't value, creative talent often miss out on a flow of ideas that could be the next big thing. Allow creative energy the freedom to express itself without censure.

You don't do a 'reality check'
Just because an idea is exciting it doesn't mean it will be useful! Organisations looking for a unique product may be tempted to pick up on ideas that really have very little mileage in them. It's important to have some sort of reality check, to ensure that only those ideas that are viable actually end up on the market. If the timing or context is wrong, there is a danger that big, often expensive, mistakes will be made.

You're not receptive enough to new ideas
Sometimes the most obvious ideas are dismissed because they threaten the status quo or challenge long-held, never-questioned values. Bottled water is a good example. It was launched at a time when drinking water was considered to be a commodity that should be freely available to all. What originally seemed like a commercial non-starter has turned into a major sector of the beverage market. Always ask yourself, on what basis am I rejecting this idea? It might be the next 'bottled water initiative'.

You give up too soon
Don't expect too much of yourself too soon. Our pragmatic, do-it-now, bottom-line society doesn't always value the creative process. Taking steps to develop your own creativity may feel awkward to you and seem odd to others. Be patient and give yourself exploring time—free from censorship—before abandoning the effort. Rewards are often immediate, but if you need support, seek a teacher or mentor who can help you unleash the latent power of your right brain.

USEFUL LINKS

Brainstorming.co.uk: **www.brainstorming.co.uk/contents.html**
Creativity at Work: **www.creativityatwork.com**
CreativityPortal: **http://creativityportal.searchking.com**
Creativity Web:
http://members.optusnet.com.au/~charles57/Creative/index2.html
Mind Tools: **www.mindtools.com/pages/main/newMN_CT.htm**

Manage Others' Creativity

Everyone has a creative spark, but our beliefs often inhibit its ignition. Part of what managers do is to see the spark in their people, encourage its ignition, and then champion its success. In many cases, however, it's a manager's own dampened spirit that makes it impossible to recognise creativity in colleagues. Paradoxically, looking inwards is a good place to start for those seeking creativity in others.

In the modern world, ideas are the only means by which an organisation can differentiate itself in the market and attain competitive advantage.

Regurgitating what used to work is not enough; knowledge boundaries have to be pushed forward if success is to be attained, and as a result the concept of 'knowledge management' has never been more important.

A member of my team is always coming up with new ideas. However, rather than being helpful, this sometimes derails meetings and wastes time. How do I manage her creativity?

Some people are naturally creative and just can't help exploring new territory and concepts. Your team member is showing signs of needing an outlet through which her creativity may be channelled into innovative and practical solutions. If you create a context in which this can happen, she will then not have to seek every opportunity, appropriate or not.

I would like employees to have an outlet for their creativity, but our products don't lend themselves to innovation. How can I provide this?

The act of being creative doesn't mean that something transformational or earth-shattering should come from it. Creativity can be useful in many different ways. This includes thinking of new processes to improve quality and efficiency, structuring a business area differently to enhance the working environment, or finding different ways to store information for ease of accessibility.

You could bring the subject up at a management team meeting. If there is general interest, the team could arrange a review of each department or business unit. If the challenge were to develop creative thinking in each area of the business, many new ideas would come forward. In addition to helping the company think more creatively, such an activity would send a message to employees that management values (and maybe even rewards) creativity.

My job includes finding and facilitating creativity in my team. I find that this quality ebbs and flows naturally, and it's difficult to 'switch it on' when required. How can I sustain creativity at a high level?

You'll need to create an environment in which creativity is welcomed. This means providing opportunities and tools to bring creative thought to the surface, finding ways to break routines so that creativity can be refreshed and re-energised. It's important to focus and direct all creative activities towards desired outcomes. You may wish to provoke creative thought by introducing visitors to your brainstorming or product development meetings. When people get to know each other too well, they settle into a kind of comfort zone that can become stale. Introducing third parties can stir things up a bit!

MAKE IT HAPPEN

Identify the blockages

Creative thinking is divergent thinking—a non-linear process in which our brains build linkages between things never linked before. It allows us to speculate on future trends by expanding the realms of possibility. Managing creativity means sifting through these unrealised ideas and directing them towards new solutions.

As organisations grow, the pace of innovation and creativity tends to slow. In general that's a good thing, because managers need to focus on the business's core products and services. Nevertheless, organisations can go too far the other way and begin to construct institutionalised blocks to creativity.

Here are some of the blocks that you may see in your organisation:

* **a belief that creativity is only for some, not all.** To a certain degree, what you think is what you get. Depending on how we think about creativity, we can either block its expression or give it wings. New ideas are not necessarily based on a rare kind of brilliance. Rather, they often emerge simply from being able to think about the same old things from different perspectives, and place them in different contexts. This is a talent that we can all develop.
* **entrenched belief systems.** We seldom question our belief systems. They just exist in our subconscious mind, and we use them to make sense of the world, to filter and file sensory information according to fairly rigid parameters. We don't tend to examine their usefulness, unless forced to do so by extraordinary events. Learning to be open to possibilities that lie outside our belief system will open us up to creative thought.
* **fear of failure.** People fear making mistakes and being judged a fool, or worse. This fear can have paralysing effects, inhibiting innovative thought and nurturing mediocrity, just in order to fit in. In this world of fear, 'right' is rewarded and 'wrong' is punished. Yet these so-called rights and wrongs aren't absolute, but merely an accepted matter of opinion. Promoting a work culture that applauds creative exploration will help people to overcome their fear of failure.
* **ideas with no practical application.** All creative ideas have a life, not just the practical ones. It may take a hundred crazy ideas before one is 'grounded' in a product or service that adds value to the business. That one good idea validates the entire process, even the ninety-nine ideas that were discarded.
* **'knowing' what will work and what will not.** People make judgments based on what they know and what they believe. Judgments can give rise to prejudice, caution, spite, and many other bad reactions. Suspending judgment—on yourself and others—is a means of allowing new thoughts the opportunity to be born.
* **'Yes, but . . .' cynicism.** Sometimes people automatically cite reasons why something won't work. They're so attached to current reality—and perhaps so afraid of expanding their belief system—that they resist anything new. If this cynicism is given free rein (or if your management is infused with such naysayers), your organisation will have a scarcity of good ideas.

Overcoming blockages to stimulate creativity

Once identified, these blockages can be removed by building awareness, expanding communication channels, and encouraging people to reserve judgment until new ideas have had a proper airing. This is the skill of 'listening *for*' rather than 'listening *against*'.

Learn to listen

It's essential that active listening skills are encouraged throughout the organisation. This means truly attending to what's being said and being conscious of your perceptions. If you don't like someone's suggestion, ask yourself why. Examine the belief that you hold so closely that you protect it from being challenged.

Encourage 'creative tension'

Creative tension is a concept discussed in Peter Senge's book, *The Fifth Discipline*, and in Robert Fritz's *Creating*. It demands that opposing view holders challenge their entrenched beliefs and open themselves to the unthinkable or undoable. By allowing 'crazy' ideas room to develop, it's possible that extraordinary solutions may emerge.

Reward innovative thinking

To change the organisational culture to one where creativity has free rein, you need to reward innovative thinking—whether it leads anywhere or not. If rewards are contingent upon an idea being 'successful', people will be discouraged from contributing. Ideas can be gathered in a number of different ways—casual comments around the coffee machine, suggestion schemes, or structured brainstorming. However you do it, contributors need to be acknowledged for their efforts. Be sure to follow up, too, and let them see how the ideas are being progressed. There is nothing more disheartening than putting your creativity on the line, only to have it ignored.

Track ideas

Creating organisational structures and systems to capture, channel, and track creativity will ensure that fewer good ideas get lost. Having a system to develop and incorporate good ideas helps remove the dependency on a few individuals to be the creative thinkers for the whole lot.

Value diversity

It's often the case that creators aren't implementers. The beauty of a healthy organisation is that something rare and wonderful comes from variety. What emerges from such a mix of talents and thought patterns isn't always the shortest line between two points. But it's often new and invigorating—and sometimes extremely profitable!

WHAT TO AVOID

Creativity isn't harnessed properly

A great deal of time, energy, and money can be wasted in chasing ideas that have no practical value. Although in the broadest sense all ideas have merit, in a commercial setting it's important to ensure that they serve the aims of the business. This means having criteria that allow decisions to be made about which ideas will be further explored and which will not. A scattergun approach to ideas generation isn't always helpful.

You judge ideas too early

Jumping to judgment too early can extinguish good ideas. People have long-held institutional memories of ideas that did not work, often backed up by war stories that quash new initiatives. Authoritative pronouncements on the viability of an idea must be discouraged. Contexts change and what may not have worked at one time, may work at another. Try to create an accepting, open culture so that ideas can get off the ground. Once the ideas have been properly discussed, judgment can then be brought to bear as 'prioritisation', 'synthesis', and 'analysis'.

You over-analyse

Over-reliance upon analysis can paralyse creative thought. The gathering of knowledge or information does not—of itself—propel creative thought, so try to put limits on this for creativity's sake.

USEFUL LINKS

Creativity at Work: **www.creativityatwork.com**
creativityportal: **www.creativityportal.searchking.com**
Creativity Web:
http://members.optusnet.com.au/~charles57/Creative/index2.html
CREAX: **www.creax.com/creaxnet/creax_net.php**
omega23.com: **www.omega23.com/creativity.html**

Develop Your People

The case for developing your people is well established; it makes sense for the organisation, it makes sense for the team, and it makes sense for the individuals concerned.

From the *organisational* perspective, it's clearly beneficial to make the best of the talent held in your community of employees. This is because there are few competitive options other than the creativity and imagination of those contributing to the fortunes of the business. The possibilities of gaining competitive advantage through pricing, distribution and service levels have been largely exhausted so differentiation rests with innovations that change the 'experience' someone has of a product rather than the 'fact' of a product.

From the *team* perspective, harnessing its collective talent increases its effectiveness and motivates everyone involved to learn, develop, and contribute more to their roles.

From the *individual* perspective, development brings new possibilities for career progression as well as personal rewards and recognition for the value that is ploughed back into the business as a result. What can be more rewarding that seeing the fruits of your talent flourish within the business, or developing the skills that will enable you to progress within (or without) the business in the long run?

Instigating a culture that welcomes development will also reflect well on the manager who organises the processes that help people meet tough targets. There are no 'losers' if the art of developing people is performed properly, but there are pitfalls that must be negotiated along the route to the business's success.

I have been asked by members of my team to pay for some training which I don't believe has any immediate benefit for the business. I don't want to dampen their enthusiasm but I equally don't want to incur unnecessary costs that I can't justify to my line manager. What should I do?

It's good that your team are keen to be developed but you need to direct their enthusiasm towards serving the business's needs, not just their own. Ask them to explain why they've chosen these training options and encourage them to tell you what benefits these will bring to the business. If they can't justify their choice, try negotiating a way forward that takes in elements of their needs as well as yours.

I'm trying to encourage my high-potential team members to follow a distance learning programme that results in them gaining a valuable qualification, but one of them tends to miss tutorials and never submits work on time. How can I encourage more commitment?

Even though *you* think the qualification is valuable, your team member may not. The course may not match up with what he or she wants to do, or he or she may not be suited to a distance learning programme. People learn in different ways and you may find that a more hands-on approach works better for this person. Suggest a 'stretch' project or a period of secondment in a different part of the business. The gains may be achieved in a different way to the one you'd envisaged, but they'll be just as valuable.

I have been running a training programme for my team which I feel has been completely ineffective. The evaluation sheets would suggest that the programme is a great success, though. What's going on?

Some training programmes are enjoyable and get good ratings from participants, but they might not result in anybody learning anything. Other courses are more challenging and get poor ratings but ironically *do* result in behavioural changes. It's all a matter of perception. Are you sure you're measuring the right things? Evaluation sheets are sometimes called 'happy sheets', and as this nickname would suggest, they merely give you a measure of enjoyment. Try focusing on what are known as 'learning outcomes' instead; for example, you could ask people to list the learning points they've taken away from the experience rather than whether or not they enjoyed the session leader's style. You may find the results illuminating.

MAKE IT HAPPEN

Development should not be an indiscriminate activity that generates random skills, but rather a focused programme that connects the business's objectives with each employee's talents and skills. This focus is necessary if the planned development will help people achieve their goals. It's important, then, to start off the process with a 'diagnosis' that highlights the knowledge or skills gaps that are making the organisation ineffective or worse, making it vulnerable to failure or collapse. This diagnosis is based on the assumption that the organisation's mission is clear and that all employees buy in to it.

Diagnosing the need—an organisational perspective

The most obvious indications of a company's need to develop its employees are financial. Forecasts aren't met, the share price is falling, costs are spiralling, cash isn't flowing, and so on. In addition, competitors may be challenging your once prized position, your market share may be diminishing, or a new innovation may have totally eclipsed your product range. This, along with high absenteeism, loss of key staff, and poor motivation must surely wake up an organisation to the need to act decisively and fast. Once the problem has been recognised, an honest and precise appraisal must be undertaken to work out where the development effort needs to be focused for early results and then what longer-term initiatives need to be established to guarantee a constant stream of talent will entering the business. These initiatives could include a particular recruitment process, succession plan, or people policy that will allow continual development and the attainment of organisational objectives.

Training needs analysis—a team perspective

A training needs analysis can only be conducted meaningfully if the organisational objectives have been broken down and translated into functional, departmental, and team targets—all players must know their part in order to work out whether or not they're able to play it properly. The gaps in knowledge and skill that are identified create the development agenda and build a picture of what the team lacks as a whole. In matrix or flatter organisational structures (where, as you might guess, there isn't a hierarchy as such), teams tend to be mobile with members joining and leaving according to the particular project that is being undertaken. One person can also be a member of several teams.

Despite these structural constraints, each team member must be responsible for contributing to the collective success of the team; everyone also needs to be part of the analysis and development solution. It's important to agree team roles that use the individual members' strengths. A full complement of team roles must be allocated or resourced to ensure that all the bases are covered. Those who are particularly strong in one activity may also be useful coaches to new members or those who want to diversify their skills. Once a project has come to an end or a target has been achieved (or not), bring together the team members to analyse the team's performance, distil learning from the experience, and create a development agenda that prepares the team for future challenges.

Performance appraisals—and individual perspective

On a more personal basis, 360 degree surveys (in which all those with a vested interest in with a person's performance give him or her feedback) and performance appraisals highlight those areas that need to be addressed by the individual. These should be put alongside their career aspirations so that they feel passionate about their development plan and are committed to following it to its conclusion. If people aren't motivated to learn new skills or broaden their experience, they'll only create obstacles to the progress happening around them. All parties need to agree on the way forward and provide resources to support people in their development activities. Remember that feedback on development targets should not be reserved for the (probably annual) performance review—giving positive feedback frequently is a good way of helping someone learn and adapt as they go along. Praising good work will help 'ground' new behaviour in a person's repertoire.

Identify development opportunities

The days when the only solution to a lack of knowledge, skill, or experience was a training programme have gone. The mindset that 'one size fits all' is outmoded and there's a greater appreciation of the individual's unique talent profile and their personal development needs. Creating a development plan requires more imagination and a higher degree of tailoring if the breadth of talent needed is to be tapped. Not only are there the options of a company-specific or an open programme, but there are also opportunities for work shadowing, job sharing, 'stretch' assignments, special project allocation, sabbaticals, secondments, coaching, and mentoring. Distance learning and attendance of part-time release programmes are also options, as are e-learning initiatives that allow people to pick and choose the programmes that they feel will build their skills most effectively.

Evaluate effectiveness

Once an organisation has recognised the importance of development and invested in it, it needs to check that it's receiving something in return. This isn't always an easy task, as much of the benefit is 'soft'. For example, what value do you place on a motivated workforce, good relationships with colleagues and suppliers, and customer satisfaction? Some experts believe that it's possible to estimate the financial value of these results by looking at the cost of *not* having achieved them, while others advocate such a tight tailoring of training objectives to outcomes that it's merely a question of simple mathematics to estimate the return on investment after having accounted for all relevant costs. The bottom line (in all senses) is that development initiatives need to be effective at building a more successful organisation.

Review and follow-up

Once the initial trigger of the need for development has passed, it's easy to lose momentum and the initiatives can lose focus. To maintain this, review all development activities against performance targets and set new objectives to ensure ongoing benefits to the business. It's no good launching an initiative with a fanfare of trumpets only to see it peter out quietly until the next organisational panic forces new action. People get cynical about these patterns and soon they won't put in the effort necessary for successful development. Establishing a performance culture creates expectations and develops a language that can be used to maintain momentum. Development plans, taken seriously and discussed frequently, keep them active and alive.

We all collect experiences and learn new things throughout life. Development is a natural human trait that follows us wherever we go so we may as well make the most of this characteristic and manage it according to our personal aims and objectives. Developing people is easy when you tap into their values and natural enthusiasm or passions. It's also extremely rewarding to see people thrive and grow under your care. Challenge yourself, therefore, to talk to your team see if you can find a way to work with them in identifying their development needs and sparking off their interest in personal and professional growth.

WHAT TO AVOID

You impose your views on someone else

Thinking you know what someone else 'needs' and imposing this on them is a sure way of wasting time, money, and energy unless they agree with you. It's important for the person experiencing development to take part in the objective-setting and decision-making process if the rewards are to be felt at the team level.

You assume everyone will be motivated

Once a development culture is established somewhere, it's easy to assume that everyone is motivated to learn and is willing to put time and energy into their development plan. This isn't always the case, though, and there will be some who genuinely do not want to take on more responsibility or further their careers. If you find that you're managing someone who feels like this, spend some time trying to understand what rewards they *do* seek from their work and direct them towards those activities that require competent and consistent performance.

You expect too much of others

Development takes a great deal of time and inevitably, choices have to be made that may have an impact on an individual's personal life. The time needed for study may impact an individual's family life, for instance, or impose a level of commitment that results in other's, perhaps the individual's colleagues or team members, making choices or sacrifices of their own. Take care not to overload anyone's development plan and don't expect him or her to work all hours in order to meet role and development objectives. Try making some of a person's development targets part of his or her role specification so that one activity serves the other. For example, it's a good idea to teach someone how to create budgets or plan a project in an existent and relevant setting (that is, by giving them a real budget to work out or a live project to plan) than to leave it all in the realms of abstract theory. In this way, you can reduce the burden and also get some immediate value for the business.

USEFUL LINKS

Businessballs.com: **www.businessballs.com/traindev.htm**
Department for Trade and Industry:
www.dti.gov.uk/greatplacetowork/develop.htm
HRMGuide.co.uk: **www.hrmguide.co.uk**
Personal-development.com: **http://personal-development.com**

INDEX

Index